AF647603

FINANCIAL MARKETS AND INSTITUTIONS

By the Same Author

- Financial Services in India
- Portfolio Management

About the Author

Dr. G. Ramesh Babu, Lecturer in Commerce, S.S.R. Jyothi College, Khammam, has vast teaching experience of 18 years at U.G. and P.G. levels. Academically, he is Ph.D. in Industrial Finance. He has published many papers in various management and commerce journals of repute and has also presented papers in various conferences. He is an active member of the All India Management Association, New Delhi; Associate Member of Society for Capital Market and Research, New Delhi; and Associate Member of Indian Institute of Public Administration, New Delhi. His areas of interest include Financial Systems and Capital Market.

FINANCIAL MARKETS
AND
INSTITUTIONS

Useful for MBA (Finance), M.Com, MFA, MFC,
PGDBM, PGDBF, CFA, CA, ICWA, CS,
MS (Finance), and Civil Services

G.RAMESH BABU
Department of Commerce,
S.S.R. Jyothi College,
Khammam (AP)

CONCEPT PUBLISHING COMPANY, NEW DELHI-110059

Cataloging in Publication Data—DK
Courtesy: D.K. Agencies (P) Ltd. <docinfo@dkagencies.com>

Ramesh Babu, G. (Gunda), 1963-
Financial markets and institutions / G. Ramesh Babu.
p. cm.
In Indian context.
Includes index.
ISBN 8180692582
1. Stock exchanges—India. 2. Financial institutions—India. I. Title.

DDC 332.642 095 4 21

All rights reserved. No part of this work may be reproduced, stored in a retrieval system, or transmitted in any form or by any means electronic, mechanical, photocopying, micro-filming recording or otherwise, without the prior written permission of the copyright owner and the publisher.

ISBN 81-8069-258-2 (H.B.)

First Published 2006

© G. Ramesh Babu

Published and Printed by
Ashok Kumar Mittal
Concept Publishing Company
A/15-16, Commercial Block, Mohan Garden
New Delhi-110059 (INDIA)

Phones : 25351460, 25351794
Fax : 091-11-25357103
Email : publishing@conceptpub.com

Dedicated to
Lord Krishna

My Parents Laxminarayana and Kasturi

My kids	*Harish*	*Gowthami*
	Nitheesh	*Sowmya*
	Dinesh	*Ramya*
My wife	*Vani*	

FOREWORD

With the process of Globalisation, Liberalisation and Privatization throughout the world, the importance of corporate setup has occupied dominance. With the emergence of corporation, the need for mobilisation of funds from nook and corner of a country occupies significance. In the process of mobilisation of finances, several financial institutions and services of various other institutions occupies importance.

In India also globalisation process is gaining momentum on par with other countries. In the present days, it is difficult to see the formation of a company without the active support of various financial markets and institutions. In the content of their development, the effort of Dr. G. Ramesh is attempting to the present consolidated contribution of various institutions in India, is laudable.

This attempt will go a long way in solving the dearth of literature on the topics concerned. This book will be found useful by many professional bodies and individuals concerned.

I wish him all success

Prof. P. Madhusudan Rao
E-mail: professorpmadhusudanarao@yahoo.com

PREFACE

The functional area of finance is a subject of growing importance and interest. After liberalization, privatization and globalisation, the world is becoming a global market. The important development of global markets is the resurgence of market forces importing tremendous impact on all spheres technological, economic, political and cultural. The national boundaries have become less significant with the interlinked effect of technology, information flows and foreign investment mobility.

The entire globe is rotating on the movement of flow of funds in the digital era. The money can be used efficient to counter the poverty. Efficient utilisation of the fund is most important to build a strong economy. A well regulated modern financial sector is essential in digital economy.

A system is a set of interrelated parts working together to achieve something. The financial system is indispensable for the rapid economic growth of a country. The development of a nation depends upon the better financial architecture. A good financial system may stimulate the wealth of a nation. The financial system is complex and it is closely connected with various aspects i.e., Financial Market, Financial Institutions, Financial Services and Financial Instruments.

Financial Markets are the nerve centre of the economy. They provide better facilities for buying and selling of all the financial claims and services. They enhance the liquidity of the financial assets. The requirement of funds by the corporate sector is fulfilled by the dynamic financial markets.

In this book an attempt is made to give a comprehensive coverage of financial markets aspects. This book has been written as per the syllabus prescribed for the MBA (Finance), M.Com, MFA, MFC, PGDBA, PGDFM, CA, CS, ICWA and M.S. (Finance). I am confident that this book will help the students, faculty members, executives in finance area, non-banking finance companies, stock brokers, registrars and fund managers of mutual fund as well as to those individuals who desire to upgrade their knowledge and skill.

Since the book is synthesis, I am indebited to all the authors who have contributed to the world of finance area. I hope that I have interpreted their views correctly. I am also indebited to my seniors and professionals and impossible to list them all. Anyhow for evincing personal interest undertaking a project of this magnitude and making invaluable suggestions from time to time. I would like to thank all those who had directly and indirectly encouraged in completion of this book. I received invaluable suggestions from many luminaries. Though it is difficult to thank all of them individually, it is my pleasure to express greatful thanks to Sri K. Ram Mohan, president, Jyothi Education Society, Dr. D. Ramachandra Bose, Principal, SSR Jyothi College; Sri P. Raghurama Rao, Treasurer, JES, Khammam and Sri K.V. Kameswar Rao, former principal, SSRJ College, Khammam. I am also thankful to my professors Prof. P. Madhusudan Rao, Prof. Narasimha Murthy, Prof. A. Shankaraiah, Prof. V. Gangadhar, Prof. S. Raviprakash, Prof. Sudarshan, Prof. Rajeswar Rao, Prof. Krishna Reddy whose elderly advice has been of immense use to me. I am also place on record my sincere thanks to my teachers Sri P.V. Anjameyulu, Sri G. Satyanarayana, Sri Kamaraju Panthulu and Dr. K. Srinivas Rao.

I owe my gratitude to Sri S.P. Sinha, and Sri Ashok Kumar Mittal of Concept Publications giving their personal attention in expediting publishing of this book.

Dr. G. Ramesh Babu
E-mail: rameshbabu-6317@rediffmail.com

CONTENTS

Foreward by **Prof. P. Madhusudan Rao** vii

Preface ix

PART I

Indian Financial System 3

Introduction – Finance Ratio – Relation Ratio – New Issue Ratio – Initial Issues – Further Issues – New Money Issues – No New Money Issues – Bonus Issues – Exchange Issue – Intermediation Ratio – Evaluation of Financial System – The Financial System upto 1951 – Financial System from 1951-1990 (Phase II-III) – Public Sector Participation – Institutional Structure – Investor's Protection – Companies Act – Prospectus – Allotment – Commissions and Discounts – Kinds of Share Capital – Controller of Capital Issues – Securities Contract Regulation Act, 1956 – Monopolies Restrictive Trade Practice – FERA – Participation in the Corporate Management by the PFI – Privatisation – Reorganisation – Commercial Banks – The Emergence of New Private Banks – The History of Banking – The Future of Banking – Non-banking Financial Companies – Mutual Funds – Public Financial Institutions – Capital Market – Investor's Protection

Part II

Financial Markets 45

Introduction – Money Market – Characteristics of the Money Market – The Need for a Money Market – The Goals of the Money Market Investor – Recent Developments in the Money Market – Average Daily Turnover in Call Money Market – Daily Call Money Rates – Capital Market – Introduction – Definition – Nature and Constituents – The

Growth of the Capital Market – Components of the Capital Market – Public Issues – Recent Developments in NIM – Mega Issues – Functions of NIM/Public Issues – Origination – Underwriting – Distribution – Mechanics of Floating New Issue – Public Issue – Offer for Sale – Private Placement – Features – Public Issue Process – Pre-issue activities – Post-issue Activities – List of Annexures – New Issue Market – Copy of the Due Diligence – Public Issue: 3-Day Monitoring Report – Secondary Market – Introduction – Functions of the Stock Exchange – Origin and Growth – Organisation – Listing of Securities – Advantages of Listing – Procedure for Dealing at the Stock Exchange – Liquidation in Full – Liquidation by the Payment of Differences – Carry Over – Types of Speculators – Bull – Bear – Stag – Lame Duck – Bull Deal – Bear Deal – Advantages – Disadvantages – Types of Speculative Deals – Membership – Types of Operators – Types of Orders – Stock Exchange in India – Brokers – Indian Brokers – General Obligations – Suspension – Cancellation – Capital Adequacy Norms – Minimum Capital – Additional Capital – Client and Broker – Sub-brokers – Registration of Sub-brokers – General obligations – Foreign Brokers – Registration – Transactions – Market Operations – Bombay Stock Exchange (BSE) – Introduction – Securities and Exchange Board of India (SEBI) – Introduction – Organisation of the SEBI – Objectives of the SEBI – Powers of the SEBI – SEBI Act, 1992 – Constitution of the SEBI – Registration – Financial Support from the Government – Penalties – Appellate Tribunal – Government Control – Step taken by the SEBI to reform the Capital market – Buy Back Securities – Tender offer – Escrow Account – Payment of the Consideration – Destruction of the share certificates – Buy Back from the Open Market – Book Building Process – Stock Exchange – From Odd Lot Buy back – General Obligations – Obligations of the Merchant Banker – Penalty Procedure – Takeover SEBI Regulations – Amalgamations and Mergers Process – Exemptions – Minimum Offer Price – Bailout Takeover – SEBI and Insider Trading – Prohibition of Fraudulent and Unfair Trade Practices – Procedure for Action in case of default – SEBI Guidelines to Stock broker/ Sub-Brokers – Registration of Stock-Broker – Registration of Sub-brokers – Code of conduct of the Stock Broker – Relations with General Public – Relations with the Investors – Relations with other brokers – General Obligations and Responsibilities – The Procedure for Inspection – Procedure in Case of Default – SEBI Investors' Protection – Investor Protection – Provisions of the Companies Act – Provisions of the Securities Contract Regulation Act, 1956 – Listing Guidelines on Investors Protection – Investor's Guidance Series – Investors Guidance – Investors Guidance – Investor Guidance – Issuing banks – Investors – Registrars – Computerised Process of Redressal of Investors Grievances – Company Law Amendment – Companies Act Anomalies

Part III

Financial Institutions **195**

Introduction – Reverse Bank of India – Introduction – Definition – Functions – Authorities – Currency issuing authority – Monitoring Authority – Banker to the Union Government – Foreign Exchange Regulation Authority – Promoting Authority – Monetary Policy of the RBI – Techniques of the Monetary Control – Open Market Operations – Refinance and Bank Rate – Cash Reserve Ratio (CRR) – Statutory Liquidity Ratio – Credit Planning – Regulation of Interest Rates – Credit Norms – Credit Authorisation Scheme – Selective Credit Control – Banking Institutions – Introduction – Characteristics – Functions – Basic Functions – Accepting of Deposits – Fixed Deposits – Current Account – Savings Bank Account – Money Multiplier Account – Other Accounts – Advancing of Loans – Loans – Cash Credit – Overdraft – Discounting of Bills – Other Functions – The Role of Banks in Financial System – Agents Functions – Kinds of Banks – Commercial Banks – Industrial Banks – Agricultural Banks – Exchange Banks – Central Banks – Savings Banks – Miscellaneous Banks – Types of Commercial Bank – Branch banking – Disadvantages – Unit banking – Group Banking – Chain Banking – Deposit Banking – Commercial Banking in India – Structure of the System – Credibiity – Banking Policies – Credit – Diversification – Priorities Sector – Small Scale

Industries – Exports – Agricultural Finance – Institutional Credit – Regulation of Bank Credit – Structural Changes – National Credit Council – Agriculture Finance Corporation Ltd. – Nationalisation – Industrial Finance Corporation of India – Introduction – Share Capital – Management – Functions – Financial Assistance – Promotional Assistance – Industrial Development Bank of India – Objectives – Capital and Financial Resources – Management – Functions – Features – Term loans – Specified Sector Loans – Refinance of Loans – Technical Development Fund Scheme – Bills Re-Discounting Scheme – Seed Capital Assistance Scheme – Development Assistance Fund – Industrial Credit and Investment Corporation of India (ICICI) – Objectives and Functions – Capital and Sources of Funds – Management – Types of Financial Assistance – Importance of Financial Institutions – Specialised Financial Institutions – Investment Institutions – Export and Import Bank of India (EXIM) Bank – National Bank for Agriculture and Rural Development (NABARD) – Shipping Credit and Investment Corporation of India (SCICI) – Tourism Finance Corporation of India – Introduction – Risk Capital and Technology Finance Corporation (RCTFC) – Industrial Reconstruction Bank of India (IRBI) – Functions – Insurance Regulation Authority – Introduction – Functions – Salient Features – The Stock Holding Corporation of India – Introduction – The Discount and Finance House of India (DFHI) – Functions – Technology Development and Information Company of India Ltd. (TDICI) – Introduction – Custodians – Registration – Obligations – Uniform Norms – Depository System – Introduction – Problems – Depositories Act 1996 – Bye-laws – SEBI and Regulations – Registration – Certificate of Commencement of Business – Depository Participant – Rights of the Depository – Rights of the Depository Participants – Inspection – Default – State Financial Corporations (SFCs) – Functions – Resources – mall Industries and Development Bank of India (SIDBI) – Resources – Merchant Banking – Introduction – Origin of the Merchant Bankers – Definition of the Merchant Banking – Main Objectives of the Merchant Banking Company – Obligations and Responsibilities – Code of Conduct –

Merchant Banking in India – Activities/Services Rendered by the Merchant Banks – Guidelines of the SEBI – First Issue of New Companies – First Issue by the Existing Private/ Closely held Companies – Public Issue by the Existing Limited Companies – Underwriting – Issue of FCD/PCD/ NCD – New Financial Instruments – Reservation in Issues – Deployment of the Issue Proceeds – Employee Stock Option Scheme – Promoter's Contribution – Bonus Issue – Protection of the Debenture Holders – Servicing of the Debentures – Protection of the Debenture Holders Interest – General – Guidelines of the Ministry of Finance – Companies Act, 1956 – Securities Contract (Regulation) Act, 1956 – Listing Guidelines of the Stock Exchange – Companies Act, 2000 – Registration of Merchant Bankers and Regulation – Authorised Activities – Terms of Authorisation – Penalty System – General Defaults – Minor Defaults – Major Defaults – Serious Defaults – Defaults in the Prospectus – Project Preparation and Appraisal – Project Identification – Project Selection – Feasibility Study – Appraisal of the Project – Financial Analysis – Social Cost Benefit Analysis – Pre-Issue Management – Issue of Shares – Public Issue through Prospectus – Offer for Sale – Private Placement – Marketing Coordination and Underwriting of Issue – Coordination – Marketing – Underwriting – Post Issue Management – Financial Institutions

Index 331

PART - I

❖ Indian Financial System

1

INDIAN FINANCIAL SYSTEM

Introduction

A well regulated modern financial sector is essential in a globalised digital economy. Financial innovation has contributed to the development. The market based economies have in general done better because of the constant identification and improved satisfaction of the consumer needs including the need for the financial products. Finance has a tendency towards the boom bust cycles. Markets can discover prices and reveal the information about the future trends. But the information is suspected because of the bandwagon effects; market participants follow each other and are uncertain about fundamentals. **Monetary** policy should encourage the finance through stimulating the real sector and minimising the shocks to finance. The ultimate justification of finance lies in improving the real sector productivity.

India's experience in the financial reforms illustrate some of the principles. Reforms offered a real opportunity for India to catch up to leap from being extremely backward to state of the art than many countries, which are locked into the older and a less efficient technology. Good progress has been made in the market microstructure. The Financial Institutions are looking for the well established firms to lend to the banks only want to lend to the government or the consumer. The **initial public offering** market has collapsed. **Financial reforms** in most of the countries led to over expansion of credit regulators and were not able to keep up since regulatory skills were often lacking and major crisis followed.

A system is a set of interrelated parts working together to achieve something. The financial system may be said to be made up of all those channels through which the savings become available for the investment. The financial system is indispensable for the rapid economic growth of a country. The process of economic development mainly depends upon the parallel growth of the financial organisations. The financial system may influence the level of national income standard of living, employment opportunities and welfare of the society. The development of a nation depends upon the proper **financial system**. A strong financial system may facilitate the growth of the national economy. A financial system helps to increase the output of a nation and leads to productivity. The productivity of a nation depends upon the efficiency. Productivity creates the wealth of a nation. The enhanced value of the wealth of a nation may make it a prosperous country. The wealth creation is not only carried out by a productivity element but also depends upon the savings of the nation.

Finance is the provision of money. It is exclusively concerned with the procurement of funds and cash. It is concerned with cash and every thing that takes place for the smooth functioning of a business concern. Finance is not only involved in the procurement of funds but also in their effective utilisation in business. **Capital formation** depends on the finance which is made available. Modern economies are influenced by expansion, diversification, attitudes of the savers and risk aversion of the investors. The level of economic activities is the barometre of a nation's development. The supply and volume of money and credit enhances the worth of a nation. The process of capital formation in an economy is called financial system. The financial system can create wonders in the economic development of a nation. It is a weapon to counter the poverty. It is a tool to construct a good and strong economy. It can make investments dreams into realities. The wealth of a nation can only be constructed through a better financial system. It directly helps increase the savings by offering better returns to the savers. The system will convert the savers into investors successfully. It not only encourages the investment but also makes efficient allocation of the resources in different investment channels. The system enhances the efficiency of the business concern which reflects in the economic development. The relationship between economic development and financial development is mutually reinforcing. The financial development is a part of the economic development. The development creates and nourishes the economy. The financial system is complex and it is closely connected with various aspects *i.e.* financial instruments, financial institutions, financial markets and financial services. It occupies a crucial role in the functioning of the economy. It includes all those activities dealing in finance and are organised into a system. The growth of the Indian Financial System is accompanied by the diversification and financial innovation. India has witnessed all types of financial innovations. Financial innovation can be defined as "the introduction of financial instrument or services or practice or introducing new uses of funds or finding out new sources of funds or introducing new process or techniques to handle the day-to-day operations or carrying out a new organisations".[1] At present the Indian economy has a highly diversified structure of financial institutions. In the year **1700**, India was actually the world's second largest economy, accounting for **22.6** per cent of world income, second only to **China**[2]. Three hundred year ago, it was among the handful at the bottom and just chips in with around 5 per cent of the world income. The Indian economy is at a threshold now; it has to decide whether it wants to revert to the introverted policies of the past or take on the challenge of globalisation. The digital economic position is presented below for a thorough understanding of the Indian Financial System.[3]

Particulars	*1950-51*	*1960-61*	*1970-71*	*1980-81*	*1990-91*	*2000-01*
1. Per Capita Income (Rs.)	3687.4	4429.8	5002.3	5352.7	7322.8	10204.12
2. Food production (million tonnes)	48.1	7.2	94.9	113.4	154.3	180.2
3. Wholesale price index	6.5	4.1	5.3	17.7	10.2	7.1
4. GD capital formation	8.7	14.4	15.4	20.3	26.3	23.3
5. Of which public sector	2.8	6.9	6.4	7.4	9.3	7.1
6. Private sector	7.7	7.8	9.4	10.3	14.7	16.2
7. Gross domestic savings	8.9	11.6	14.6	18.9	23.1	22.3
8. Of which household sector	6.2	7.3	10.1	13.8	19.3	19.8
9. Private sector	0.9	1.6	1.5	1.6	2.7	3.7
10. Public sector	1.8	2.6	2.9	3.4	1.1	**–1.2**
11. Current A/c deficit	0.3	**–2.2**	**–0.9**	**–1.5**	**–4.8**	**–1.3**
12. Forex Reserves ($)	2161	637	975	6823	5834	35058
13. Government expenditure	0.35	0.9	1.9	5.6	15.1	30.7

Economics move from being agriculture led to industry led to being services led. India has transited straight from agriculture to services.

Till the late 1960s the government's focus was on the public sector at one end of the manufacturing scale and on the small scale sector at the other, pampering both with subsidies. The private sector was ignored. The period between 1969 and 1972 saw the emergence of several industry killing legislations—for instance, the Industrial Licensing Act, 1969, The MRTP Act, 1970 and the string of nationalisations – all belong to this period.

The shift from Agriculture[4]

Year	*Percentage to GDP*	*Sector*
1951-52	54.6	Agriculture
1961-62	45.0	Forestry, Fishing
1971-72	43.4	
1981-82	37.2	
1991-92	31.5	
1999-2000	27.1	

Statement showing the role of financial services in economy

Year	*Percentage to GDP*	*Sector*
1951-52	10.2	Financial Services
1961-62	11.5	Banking
1971-72	10.3	Insurances
1981-82	9.2	Real estate and Business services
1991-92	11.3	
1999-2000	11.7	

Statement showing the role of manufacturing sector in the economy (1951-2000)

Year	*Percentage to GDP*	*Sector*
1951-52	16.1	(Manufacturing, Construction,
1961-62	21.4	Electricity, Gas and water supply,
1971-72	22.7	Mining and Quarrying)
1981-82	25.8	
1991-92	26.4	
1999-2000	26.1	

A large number of new financial assets are to be introduced to fulfil the needs of the dynamic corporate sector. The innovative instruments can leverage the corporate financial muscle. The wealth creation of a nation can be measured through the following powerful devices.

1. Finance Ratio
2. Relation Ratio
3. New Issue Ratio

Finance Ratio

Finance Ratio is a macro analysis of an economy. It measures the total analysis of primary and secondary claims of the national income. National income is an important component of an economy. The national income is a source, primarily to the government and population of a nation. It is the income and wealth of the people. This income is of the productive activities which are carried out by both public and private sector.

Relation Ratio

The Relation Ratio is known as Financial Interrelation ratio. It reveals the relationship between the financial assets and physical assets. It is a ratio between financial structure and real assets structure of the economy. It shows the financial capability of a nation. The financial strength of a nation is the indicator of the economic growth.

New Issue Ratio

New Issue Ratio means the equity shares which are offered by the newly promoted enterprises to the general public for the first time. It is also known as the **"IPO"**—initial public offering. The new issues are also called as the public issues. This public issues are known as the "primary issues". The primary issues consists of the following methods:

- (a) Initial issues
- (b) Further issues
- (c) New money issues
- (d) No new money issues
- (e) Bonus issue
- (f) Exchange issue
- (g) Intermediation ratio

(a) Initial Issues

It is the first issue of shares to the public by a newly promoted company. It is popularly known as the **"IPOs"**. A new company defined as one which has not completed 12 months of commercial operation and its audited operative results are not available. It is set up by the entrepreneurs without a track record. These new companies will be permitted to issue the capital to the public only at **par**. This promoter contribution is subjected to the lock in period of **five years**.

(b) Further Issues

The shares are issued by the existing companies. The existed companies will be allowed to raise the fresh capital by freely pricing their issues. The issue price will be determined in consultation with the lead managers to the issue. These companies must disclose the draft prospectus to the SEBI and should ensure adequacy. The prospectus should contain the full details of the company and justification for the price of the issue.

(c) New Money Issues

The newly created securities are issued by the companies.

(d) No New Money Issues

The shares are sold in the market by the underwriters. The issue of shares at the first moment are allotted by the company to the underwriters for an agreed price. In turn the underwriters will sell the equity to the public at a higher price.

(e) **Bonus Issue**

The shares which are offered to the existing shareholders freely are called bonus issues. They are made by the companies when the financial environment is quite encouraging to the issuing company. The strong fundamentals of the company influences the factors for the issue of bonus shares.

(f) **Exchange Issue**

The process of the securities among the companies is known as exchange issue.

The contribution of the new issues reflect the industrial growth of a country. The new issues facilitate the transfer of funds from the savers to the entrepreneurs. The new ratio indicates the relationship between the primary issues and capital formation in the country. The number of IPOs made recently have rarely crossed **20**[5]. The public issues of these companies were made at huge discounts as per the guidelines laid down by the **SEBI**. The craze for the IPOs is presented below.[6]

Year	*No. of issues*	*Amount raised (Rs. in crores)*
1989-90	160	673
1990-91	109	706
1991-92	158	736
1992-93	468	3883
1993-94	695	8340
1994-95	1231	9919
1995-96	1351	5560
1996-97	716	4646
1997-98	52	908
1998-99	18	379
1999-2000	52	2644
2000-2001	114	2474

(g) Intermediation Ratio

It is the relationship between the primary and secondary issues of the securities. It is the ratio of the secondary to the primary issues. It indicates the importance of the mediator as mobilise of the funds relative to the real sectors. The financial intermediaries are very important persons in the mobilisation of the savings. They mobilise the funds of savings made by the households towards the development of a country. The financial system has become much more integrated than even before.

The financial system can be classified as organised and unorganised sectors. The financial capability of the country is highly influenced by:

(*a*) The entry of the government in trading of commodities.
(*b*) The evaluation of the financial institutions.
(*c*) The expansion of the network of the rural banks.
(*d*) Increasing the activities of the financial intermediaries.
(*e*) The transformation of the financial institutions.
(*f*) The introduction of the innovative financial instruments.
(*g*) The introduction of the Industrial Policy, 1991 did away with licensing for all about 18 industries. The policy may also help the economy and be creator of wealth. The following factors may boost the economy:

1. The policy 1991 allowed the foreign investment upto 51 per cent in high priority industries.
2. The policy reduced the number of sectors reserved for the public sector from 12 to 08.

3. The two reform packages allowed the tradable import benefits against exports. Pruned the canalised imports list and scrapped the actual users norms of several categories.
4. The policy gave permission to the companies that they can expand their activities without the approval of the MRTP reference.

The automobile policy opened up the auto sector to the foreign manufactures.

The New Power Policy, 1991 allowed the private participation in power generation.

The speedy disposal of disinvestment in PSUs, the amendment of the SEBI Act and new issue pricing made the market determined.

The Indian financial system may be classified as organised and unorganised sector.

The organised sector of the financial system is controlled by the RBI and the government. The components of the organised financial system are:

(a) Money Market,
(b) Government Security Market, and
(c) Capital Market.

All these components will be discussed in forthcoming pages. The unorganised sector of the financial system comprises the following parties:

(a) Moneylenders,
(b) Indigenous bankers,
(c) Lending pawn brokers,
(d) Landlords, and
(e) Traders.

The unorganised financial system is relatively less controllable. It cannot be directly amended by the RBI. In addition to the above parties, there are a host of financial companies, investment companies, chit funds etc. which cannot be regulated by the RBI. The RBI is the lender and the SEBI is the regulator in the organised system.

The financial systems help to develop the economic growth through the savings investment process. The financial systems are the main elements in the capital formation of a nation. The capital formation is indispensable to speedy economic development. The process of capital formation in any economy involves three aspects **Savings, Finance and Investments**. The savings are the ability by which claims to resources are set aside. The savings are the money put a side for the future use. Finance is the provision of money. It is the life blood of a business enterprise. It comes from domestic savings, bank deposits, abroad and from the hands of the investors. **Investment** is the activity by which resources are actively committed to production. The development of a nation depends upon the level of economic activity. The volume of capital formation depends upon the domestic savings, efficiency of the financial organisations. The process of development is invariably accompanied by a parallel growth of financial organisations. The planned economic development had greatly influenced the course of financial development. The liberalisation, globalisation and privatisation has had important implications for the future of course of development of the financial system. The evaluation of the financial system requires a lot of skill.

Evaluation of Financial System

The evaluation of financial system has the three distinct phrases.

(a) The financial system upto 1951 (Phase I)
(b) The financial system from 1951, mid-Eighties (Phase II)
(c) The financial system from 1990 onwards (Phase III)

(a) ***The Financial System Prior 1951 (Phase I)***—The financial system prior to 1951 was popularly known as the "traditional economy". It has been defined by R.L. Bennet "as traditional economy is one in which the per capita output is low and constant[7]." The traditional economy reflects the low per capita income and slow development in the economy. During this period there will be no growth in the industrial financing. There will be no capital formation and savings. The industrial securities market is very narrow and undeveloped. The financial intermediatary system has not been developed during the period. The capital market is not perfect. There is no availability of long-term finance. The character of industrial entrepreneurship is very less. The industry has very restricted access to the outside savings. The financial system will not be responsive to the opportunities for the industrial investment during this period. The traditional system is incapable of substaining high rate of industrial growth. There are no clear industrial policies during this period. The industrial sector was neglected by the governments. The growth of the percapita income, savings, national income, purchasing capacity is very low.

(b) ***Financial System from 1951-1990 (Phase II-III)***—The traditional economy has failed to deliver the goods. The financial system is required for strengthening the economy. The system has provided the supply of finance and credit to varied business enterprises in diverse forms. The objectives of the financial system are to secure economic growth with social justice. The Constitution of India permits the scheme of planned economic development under the directive principles of state policy. The introduction of planning has had important implications for the financial system. The mixed economy system had been adopted during this period as the pattern of industrial development. The mixed economy is a combination of socialism and capitalism. The coordination between the two systems is a highly skilled and talented assignment. The socialism and capitalism are quite opposite. The socialism represents the public sector and the capitalism reflects the private sector. There is a strong need for an alignment of the financial mechanism with the priorities laid down by the government's economic policy. The planning system made the distribution of financial resources for the development of the country. There is a strong need to disburse the resources throughout the nation without any partiality. The development of a nation depends upon the politics. The politics made the country with regional imbalances among the states. The allocation of funds is the important task of the central government. The important elements of the financial organisation in a planned economic development may be categorised into four categories.

(i) Public Sector Participation.
(ii) Institutional Structure.
(iii) Investors Protection.
(iv) Participation in Corporate Management by the PFIs.

(i) Public Sector Participation

The evaluation of the financial system during this second phase is the progressive transfer from private ownership to public. The major important segment of the financial mechanism is to control the affairs of the private sector through nationalisation. Nationalisation is the powerful weapon to control the private sector. It leads the creation of entirely new institutions in the public sector. The nationalisation process was started in **1948** with the RBI. The RBI was nationalised in 1948 and it was the starting point to the transfer of powers from financial intermediaries to the government control. After the nationalisation of the RBI, it was followed by the setting up of the SBI in 1956 by taking over the Imperial Bank of India. Afterwards in the year 1956, **245** Life Insurance Companies were nationalised and merged with the **LIC**. In 1969, 14 major commercial banks were brought under the control of the central government. Indira Gandhi government nationalised the private sector banks, prior to that many banks like Central Bank (owned by the Tatas) United Commercial Banks (Birlas) and Syndicate Bank (Pais) were owned and managed by the businessmen. The businessmen who owned these banks channelised deposits into their own companies often ignoring the priority sector. The negligence was one of the reasons for the nationalisation of banks. Another reason was the government's desire to spread the banking habit in rural and semi-urban areas. The nationalisation is a device to the central government during this period. A chronological occurrence of series of events was presented below:

1949 : Enactment of Banking Regulation Act.
1955 : Nationalisation of SBI and its subsidiaries.
1961 : Insurance cover extends to deposits.
1969 : Nationalisation of 14 major banks.
1971 : Creation of Credit Guarantee Corporation.
1975 : Creation of Regional Rural Banks.
1980 : Nationalisation of 6 banks with deposit over Rs. 200 crore.

The history of banking is presented below for a thorough understanding of the banking sector:

Date	*Particulars*
1-4-1949	The RBI is nationalised by an act of Parliament.
4-9-1951	The government announces its plans to seek the developmental loans from the World Bank.
1-7-1955	The SBI comes into existence taking over the Imperial Bank operations.
1956	LICs are nationalised and brought under the government management.
3-7-1964	The IDBI is set up.
6-6-1966	Rupee is devalued by 36.5% to 7.50 from Rs. 4.26 to dollar.
19-6-1969	Fourteen banks are nationalised.
1973	The FERA comes into effect.
11-1-1978	Currency notes in denominations of Rs. 1000, Rs. 5,000 and Rs. 10,000 are withdrawn from circulation.
15-4-1980	Nationalisation of six banks.
19-11-86	The government of India launches Indira Vikas Patra.
1987	To mobilise resources for meeting drought related expenditure, the GOI introduces 9% Relief Bonds.
April 1988	To mobilise untapped rural savings a new instrument Kisan Vikas Patra is launched.

According to the first five year plan "The state has a special responsibility for developing the key industries like iron and steel, heavy chemicals, manufacturing of electrical equipments etc." The industrial policy resolution 1956 and later the second five year plan also stresses this point. The state will progressively assume predominance and direct responsibility for setting up new industrial undertakings and for developing the transport facilities. The two main objectives of the public sector were envisaged as occupying the commanding heights of the economy to help in industrial growth, creating necessary infrastructure to earn return on investment, and generate resources for development. There were other objectives such as redistribution of income and wealth, employment generation and balanced regional development.

In addition to nationalisation, the flow of credit and finance created a new type of institutions in the public sector. As the initial step, a special purpose institutions have been established as Developmental banks. The wide range of such institutions came into being same at national level and others at regional level. Another set of considerable significance was the creation of an investment trust organisation, UTI in the public sector. Therefore the public sector occupied a commanding position in the industrial financing system in India. The financial performance of the public sector enterprises was presented below:

(Rupees in Crores)

Year	*Capital employed*	*Gross profit*	*Net profit*
1968-69	3168	85	28
1999-2000	303411	62,532	14,555

(ii) Institutional Structure

The capital formation is the ingredient for the development of an economy. The emerge of a fairly well developed financial system during the second phase strengthened the institutional structure. The structure of the financial system in partly the result of modification and policies of the existing financial institution. The institutional structure contains the following contents:[8]

1. **Development Institutions**
2. **LIC**
3. **UTI**
4. **Commercial Banks**

All the above topics will be covered in depth in the preceding pages.

(iii) Investor's Protection

Savings are the most powerful weapons for the capital formation in the economy. The capital formation leads to the investment activity in the country. The investment activities will enhance the growth of the economy. The growth in the economy create the confidence among the investors. The inflow of capital depends upon the safeguards and protection available to the investors. The institutional structure requires extensive legal reforms to be carried out to provide protection to the investors. The industrial securities as a savings tool is not popular in India before 1951. The corporate laws and industrial securities market do not afford adequate protection to the investors, against the malpractices of market operators and company promoters. Therefore, the corporate frauds lead to lose all its faith in the corporate securities. The investors have lost their confidence because of the mismanagement of the companies. The government has taken drastic reforms to restore the investor's confidence, such as remodelling of the legal, administrative apparatus of companies and stock exchange. The government has taken measures for tightening the listing requirements of the stock exchanges, the control of capital issues and industrial licensing, MRTP and the ban on forward trading, abolition of oligopoly etc. The government also has taken initiative steps for the active participation of the public financial institutions in the management of the private sector. All these developments have toned up the quality of the corporate management in the interest of the shareholders. The important elements of the legislative measures adopted by the government are briefly presented below:

1. **Companies Act**
2. **Controller of Capital Issues (CCI)**
3. **Securities Contract Regulation Act (SCRA)**
4. **Monopoly Restrictive Trade Practice (MRTP)**
5. **Foreign Exchange Regulation Act (FERA)**

1. Companies Act

The Companies Act, 1956 occupies an important role in the development of corporate sector in India. It creates a healthy relationship among promoters, investors and management. The Act made drastic changes in the contents of prospectus, allotment of shares, terms and conditions and capital structure of the company. The Companies Act, 2000 contains a remarkable change in the disclosure norms. The Companies Act, 1956 had framed the following rules and regulations in the content of issue of shares:

(a) Prospectus (Sections 55 to 68A)

1. Drafting of prospectus. *Section 55*
2. Contents of prospectus. *Section 56*
3. Experts to be unconnected with the formation or management of a Company. *Section 57*

4. Experts content to issue the prospectus. *Section 58*
5. Advertisement of prospectus. *Section 58A*
6. Provisions relating to prospectus to apply to advt. *Section 58B*
7. Penalty and intepretation. *Section 59*
8. Registration of prospectus. *Section 60*
9. Terms of Contract mentioned in the prospectus. *Section 61*
10. Civil liabilities for mis-statements in the prospectus. *Section 62*
11. Criminal liability for mis-statements in the prospectus. *Section 63*
12. Documents containing the offer of shares. *Section 64*
13. Interpretation of the provisions relating to prospectus. *Section 65*
14. Newspaper advertisements of prospectus. *Section 66*
15. Construction of references to offer shares to the Public. *Section 67*
16. Penalty for fradulently inducing persons to invest money. *Section 68*
17. Personations for acquisition of shares. *Section 68A*

(b) Allotment (Sections 69 to 75)

1. Prohibition of allotment until receiving minimum subscription. *Section 69*
2. Prohibition of allotment in certain cases. *Section. 70*
3. Effect of irregular allotment. *Section 71*
4. Application for and allotment of shares and debentures. *Section 72*
5. Allotment of shares and debentures to be dealt in the stock exchange. *Section 73*
6. Manner of reckoning fifth, eight and tenth days in Sections 72 and 73
7. Returns as to allotments. *Section 75*

(c) Commissions and Discounts

1. Power to pay certain commissions and prohibition of payment of all other commissions, discounts. *Section 76*
2. Restrictions on purchase by the company or loans by the

company for purchasing of its own or its holding company's share. *Section 77*

3. Issue of shares at premium and discount application of premiums received on issue of shares. *Section 78*
4. Powers to issue shares at discount. *Section 79*
5. Power to issue redeemable preference shares. *Section 80*
6. Redemption of irredeemable preference shares. *Section 80A*
7. Further issue of capital. *Section 81*
8. Nature of shares. *Section 82*
9. Numbering of shares. *Section 83*
10. Certificates of shares. *Section 84*

(d) Kinds of Share Capital

1. Two kinds of share capital. *Section 85*
2. New issue of share capital to be of only two kinds. *Section 86*
3. Prohibition of issuė of shares with disproportionate rights. *Section 88*
4. Calls on shares of same class to be made on uniform basis. *Section 91*
5. Powers of company to accept unpaid shares though not called up. *Section 92*
6. Payment of dividend in proportion to the amount paid up. *Section 93*
7. Power of limited company to alter its share capital. *Section 94*
8. Share capital to stand increased where an order is made under Section 81(4), Section 94A
9. Notice to the Registrar of companies for consolidation of share capital for conversion of shares into stock. *Section 95*
10. Effect of conversion of shares into stock. *Section 96*
11. Notice of increase of share capital or of members. *Section 97*
12. Powers of unlimited company to provide for reserve share capital on registration. *Section 98*
13. Reserve liability of limited company. *Section 99*
14. Issues the certificate of shares, limitation of time for the issue of certificates. *Section 113.*

2. Controller of Capital Issues (CCI)

The investors protection has been made by the government through the Capital Issues Control Act, 1947. The control led to the creation of a healthy environment for the corporate sector. The government has taken the precautions about the wasteful expenditure made by the companies. The government has also taken into consideration of the Capital structure of the issuing company in the interest of the public. The act is powerful in the hands of the government. The act regulates the capital structure of the companies with a view to discourage the undesirable practices. The act also aims at protecting the investors of new enterprises. The government also examines the terms of new issues of capital. The act scrutinises the various implications of the merger and amalgamations in the interest of the shareholders and creditors of the companies. The act also regulates the foreign investment, including the terms and conditions of the capital. The Capital Control Act is administered through the Controller of Capital Issues in the Ministry of Finance, Government of India. It has been now functioning as Securities Exchange Board of India.

3. Securities Contract Regulation Act (SCRA), 1956

The Securities Contract Regulation Act came into force in 1956. The act was enforced through the directorate of stock exchanges under the Ministry of Finance. It provide reforms in trading methods and practices. The objective of the act is to restore the confidence of the investors towards a perfect capital market. It also takes initiatives towards the capital formation of the corporate sector. The act has the powerful provisions relating to any specific matter. The act has the power to withdraw the recognition of a stock exchange in the interest of the public. It also regulates about the listing of securities with the stock exchanges. It confers the Parliament to prevent undesirable transactions in securities by regulating the business of dealing. The act extends to the whole of India. The following provisions indicate the regulation of the act:

Sec. 3	Application for the recognition of the stock exchanges.
Sec. 4	Grant of recognition to the stock exchanges.
Sec. 5	Withdrawal of recognition.

Sec. 6	Powers of the Central Government to call for periodical returns.
Sec. 7	Annual reports to be furnished to the Central Government by the stock exchanges.
Sec. 7A	Power of recognised stock exchange to make rules restricting the voting rights.
Sec. 8	Powers of the Central Government to direct the rules to be made or to make rules.
Sec. 9	Powers of recognised stock exchanges to make bye laws.
Sec. 10	Powers to make or amend the bye laws of the recognised stock exchanges.
Sec. 11	Powers of the Central Government to supersede the governing body of a recognised stock exchange.
Sec. 12	Power to suspend the business of the recognised stock exchanges.
Sec. 13	Contracts—Contracts in the notified areas illegal in certain circumstances.
Sec. 14	Contracts in notified areas to be void in certain circumstances.
Sec. 15	Members may not act as principals in certain circumstances.
Sec. 16	Powers to prohibit the contracts in certain cases.
Sec. 17	Licensing of the dealers in securities in certain areas.
Sec. 18	Exclusion of the spot delivery contracts from Sections 13, 14, 15 and 17.
Sec. 19	Stock exchanges other than recognised stock exchanges are prohibited.
Sec. 20	Prohibition of options in the securities.
Sec. 21	Listing of securities—power to compel the listing of securities by the Public Companies.
Sec. 22	Right to appeal against the refusal of the stock exchanges to list of security of Public Companies.
Sec. 22A	Free transferability and registration of transfer of listed securities of the companies.
Sec. 23	Penalities and procedures
Sec. 24	Offences by Companies
Sec. 25	Certain offences to be cognizable.
Sec. 26	Jurisdiction to try the offences under this act.
Sec. 27	Miscellaneous Title to dividends.
Sec. 28	Act does not apply in certain cases.

Sec. 29	Protection of action takes in good faith.
Sec. 29A	Power to delegate.
Sec. 30	Powers to make rules.
Sec. 31	Repealed by the Repealing and Amending Act, 1960.

4. Monopoly Restrictive Trade Practice

The MRTP Act came into force in 1-6-1970. The main aim of the Act is to curb the monopoly by reducing the inequality and concentration of economic power. The monopoly is injurious to the public welfare. The Act can contribute to restore the public confidence in the corporate sector. It has been abolished recently.

5. FERA

The FERA came into force in 1973 with a view to regulate the foreign investment. It also created a public confidence in the industrial securities market. The Act deals with the foreign exchange in the export and import business of the corporate sector. It has been now modified as Foreign Exchange Management Act (FEMA).

(iv) Participation in the Corporate Management by the PFI

The radical changes in the Indian financial system was the participation of the financial institutions in the management of concerned companies. The institutional finance has reduced the shortage of finance and encouraged the various industries. During the second phase, the size of the institutional shareholding created the supply of finance. The public sector financial institutions dominated the private sector through their share holding. This situation had created that the private sector depended upon the assistance of the public sector. The management's tenure in office became dependent on their direct and indirect support. The UTI and LIC were able to exercise considerable pressure on the management through their voting powers. The Private Companies had to secure the board representation for decision-making. The public financial institutions may render the financial assistance in the form of direct term loans, by under writing the public issues, and subscribing the share capital. All these financial assistance can influence the managerial decisions of the private sector enterprises. These changes had arose because of the government policy towards the corporate sector. The policy decisions had been taken by the government, based on the recommendations of the Dutt Committee Report 1969. The Committee had also suggested that the term loans should be converted into the equity by the PFIs. The fundamental principle of the financial institution was not to stick to the control and management of the concerned enterprises. This radical change had took place in 1970-71. The traditional attitude reveals that if a financial institution did not satisfied with the performance of a invested company, the institution can switch over its share holding to others. But this situation creates a lot of practical problems. In some situations it is highly impossible to unload the share capital of that company. Therefore the option to sell the holding is not possible at all times to the institutional shareholders. Hence it requires to exercise the effective control over the performance of these companies to protect their holding.

Therefore the **Second phase** of the Indian Financial System is immature. The problem of industrial financing is due to the lack of a broad based efficient and responsive distributive mechanism. There is no clear industrial policy. There is too much control on the functioning of the corporate sector.

The Indian Financial System in post 1990 (Phase III): The Industrial Policy 1991 was announced by the Government of India. It was a step in the direction of streamlining the setting up of new units and simplying the procedures for the expansion of existing enterprises. The Industrial Policy 1991 aimed at the following objectives:

(a) Freedom from unnecessary bureaucratic controls.
(b) To abolish restrictions on direct foreign investment.
(c) To reduce the burden of the public sector enterprises.
(d) To maintain a high productivity levels.
(e) To liberalise the domestic industry.
(f) To abolish the MRTP Act.

The main features of the new industrial policy are presented below:

1. **Abolition of industrial licensing.**
2. **Reducing the role of PSUs.**
3. **Reducing the control of MRTP Act.**
4. **Foreign Technology.**
5. **Location Facility.**
6. **Convertibility clause removed.**

The new Industrial Policy 1991 has abolished the system of industrial licensing except for 18 industries. The industries under licensing are coal, petroleum, cigars, asbestos, its based products, plywood, and decorative veneers. Other wood based products, raw hides and skins, leather, motorcar, paper and newsprint, electronic, aerospace, defence equipment, industrial explosives, hazardous chemicals, drugs and pharmaceuticals, entertainment electronics, white goods, distillation and breewing of alcoholic drinks, manufactured tobacco substitutes. There is no need of licensing provision for the above industries which belong to the small scale industries.

The new Industrial Policy indicates to restructure the public sector and make it competitive with private sector. It also reduced the list of reserved industries from **18 to 8** for the public sector. The industries reserved for the public sector are atomic energy, coal and lignite, mineral oil, defence equipment, mining of copper, lead, zinc, rail transport. The industries which are reserved for the public sector will be gradually be opened to the private sector. It leads to privatisation.

The new policy states that the companies investment decision will be out of purview of the MRTP Act. They need not follow the MRTP Act. They need not obtain the approval for expansion, incorporation of new companies, mergers, take over and amalgamations. The MRTP is empowered to initiate investigations by the *suo motto* on complaints received from the individual consumers in regard to the monopolistic restrictive and unfair practices.

The new policy facilitates to invest upto 51 per cent foreign equity in the corporate sector. It prepared a list of 34 specified industries for automatic permission for the direct investment. The industries included in this list are electrical equipment, telecommunication equipment, tourism industry, chemicals, food processing, transportation, boilers and steam generating equipment trading companies which are engaged in export business. Automatic clearance will be given for the foreign technology agreements. There are no restrictions on the foreign technicians for testing of developed technology.

Another salient feature of the industrial policy is the "Location" of the industries. It facilitates no industrial approval from the centre if the location of the population is less than 10 lakhs for the specified industries. If the location is with more than 10 lakhs of population, industries other than non-polluting in nature will be located outside 25 km. of its periphery.

The new industrial policy removes the convertibility clause for converting the loans into equity shares by the financial institutions.

The main objective of the new policy is to abolish the licensing system and reduce the bureaucratic hardles. The license quota may be over but the Inspector Raj still reigns supreme.[9] Industries may have delicensed, but still highly regulated. Each industrial unit is visited by 40 to 60 inspectors within a month. The following is an illustrative but not an exhaustive:

Ministry	*No. of Inspectors*	*Work*
1. Industry	05	Check registration, inventories, tax payment, quality control, safety equipment.
2. Home	02	Check fire protection facilities and compliance with Explosives Act.
3. Planning and statistics	01	Collect data on production, manpower, manhours utilised and lost.
4. Finance	12	Five for income tax, seven from excise department.
5. Revenue	05	Enforcement, verification and recovery of sales tax, involvement professional tax, weights and measures.
6. State Government & Revenue Department	01	Registration of Professional
7. Labour	08	Checking compliance with different labour laws, checking the same records.
8. Municipal Corporation	02	Municipal bye-laws
Power and Energy	01	Electricity connections
Health and Family Welfare	02	Hygiene and Occupational Health
9. Urban Affairs and Employment	01	Sanitation
10. Environment and Forests	02	Pollution Control
11. Communications	01	Telecom facilities
12. Local Self Government	02	Octroi and mass raids
13. Food and Drug Administration	01	Safety standards

Major economic policy changes such as macro economic stabilisation, delicensing of industries, trade liberalisation, currency reforms, reduction in subsidies, financial sector reforms, privatisation, disinvestment, tax reforms and company law reforms simplifications and debureaucratisation are gradually implemented.

Indian financial system during the IIIrd phase is briefly outlined as follows.

(a) **Privatisation (Financial institution)**
(b) **Reorganisation**
(c) **Investor Protection**

(a) Privatisation

The financial system was under the control of the Central Government. Gradually the GOI wanted to privatise the PSUs in a phased manner. The privatisation is a part of the strategy. The government wants to reduce its liability from the public sector because of the mismanagement. Privatisation of the financial institution is a part of the New Industrial Policy. Therefore the GOI has taken the steps to practice the important financial institutions. The GOI converted the development financial institution **IFCI** into a public company. The development institutions IFCI and IDBI have offered their equity to the investors. The SEBI has permitted the private mutual funds under its guidelines. A number of private mutual funds came into existence under the control of the RBI. The R.N. Malhotra Committee recommended the scheme of reorganistion of the structure of the insurance industry. The enactment of Insurance Regulatory and Development Authority Act, 1999 leads to the rapid development in the insurance business. According to the Act, the private companies can enter into the insurance sector for the benefit of the public. Thus the monopoly of GIC has been dismantled in a phased manner. The public financial institutions are also permitted to sell the equity bonds and debentures to the public on par with the public limited companies. Therefore the government should not interfere in the routine life of the public sector enterprises. Hence radical changes have been arosed in the Indian economy due to introduction of privatisation.

(b) Reorganisation

The Indian Financial System is undergoing an outstanding transformation and it can create wonders in the capital market if it sticks on to strong policy. Every enterprise should be in a competent manner, highly skill and talented people with a proper strategy. All these factors can boost the profitability of the commercial enterprise.

Drastic changes have occurred in the financial sector with reference to the competitive markets. The sponsorship of the development finance institutions made the reorganisation of the institutional structure. The development banks, lending institutions, commercial banks, mutual funds, have entered into the capital market in an innovative way. The reorganisation of the institutional structure are made in the following areas:

1. **Commercial Banks**
2. **Non Banking Financial Companies**
3. **Mutual Funds**
4. **Public Financial Institutions**
5. **Capital Market**

1. Commercial Banks

The Commercial banks has undergone a major transformation with the introduction of the **LPG** (Liberalisation, Privatisation and Globalisation). The radical changes have been rising in the structure, operating, polices and accounting norms. The present environment has created the banking sector in the expansion process and in the development of the branch banking system. The branches are also opened in rural and semi-urban areas and the share of the priority sector increased in the total bank credit. But the branch banking has an adverse effect on the profitability and efficiency of the business. The RBI controls the banks through **SLR and CRR**. The prudential banking is required to run the business very smoothly. The branch banking policy made recommendations for the better functioning of the commercial banks. The prudential norms relating to the income, asset and capital adequacy are applicable to the public sector banks. The banks also expedite the recovery of over dues through the Debt Recovery Tribunals. The RBI has also published the names of the defaulters who failed in the country for the recovery of loans. The commercial banks are also facing the problems of **NPAs**. The non-performing assets of the PSB shot upto **Rs. 56,608 crores** in September 2001. This staggering number not only reduces the yield on advances but also has an adverse impact on the profitability of banks. The huge NPAs of the banks are mostly because of the debtor friendly forclosure and bankruptcy laws which allows the customers to default with impurity. The particulars of the NPAs are presented below:[10]

Year	Gross NPA (Rs. in crore)	Gross NPA as % of Gross advance	Net NPA	Net NPA as % of Net advance
1993	39253	23.2%	NA	NA
1994	41041	24.8%	NA	NA
1995	38385	19.5%	17567	10.7%
1996	41661	18%	18297	8.9%
1997	47300	15.7%	22340	8.1%
1998	50815	14.4%	23761	7.3%
1999	58722	14.7%	28020	7.6%
2000	53066	13%	26596	7%
2001*	56608	13%	27856	7%

* Figures upto September 1, 2001.

Statement showing the combined assets of the public sector banks (27 banks) (Rs. in crores)

Year	Assets
1996-97	5,05,698.40
1997-98	5,56,296.00
1998-99	6,49,503.94
1999-2000	7,70,144.92
2000-2001	8,90,951.73

Statement showing the profitability of the Banks

Year	P.S.U. Banks	New Private Sector Banks	Foreign Banks
1995-96	–0.07%	1.85%	1.58%
1996-97	0.57%	1.73%	1.19%
1997-98	0.77%	1.55%	0.97%
1998-99	0.42%	1.03%	0.69%
1999-2000	0.57%	0.97%	1.17%

(Net profit as a percentage of total assets).

Statement showing the Market Share in deposited by the PSB

	1995	1996	1997	1998	1999	2000
Deposits						
a. 27 PSBs	82.12%	82.85%	81.49%	80.51%	78.23%	77.34%
b. 19 Nationalised Banks	55.44%	55.26%	54.94%	53.73%	52.94%	52.02%
Advances						
a. 27 PSBs	76.56%	75.16%	73.70%	73.90%	75.26%	73.55%
b. 19 Nationalised Banks	48.26%	45.91%	44.93%	45.65%	47.39%	46.44%

The Emergence of New Private Banks

The eight new private banks that emerged on the Indian financial topography in 1994 cleared out the performers in the troubled section. Within seven years, these banks have grown to account 6% of the total assets and 10% of the total profits of the banking industry (2000-2001). It was the Narasimhan Committee (1991) that envisaged a large role for the private sector banks. The RBI agreed to make the sector more efficient and competitive. It issued, in January 1993, the guidelines governing the entry of the new private banks—a minimum paid up capital of **Rs. 100 crores** among others. This was the first time after the nationalisation of banks. The RBI issued the fresh banking licences to the private sector.

The NPBs have grown not only originally, but also through the mergers and acquisitions. The HDFC Bank merged with the Times Bank in the all stock deal valued at Rs. 200 crores in November 1999. The ICICI bank acquired the Bank of Baroda in a stock swap deal in December 2000 to become the largest among the new private banks.

The History of Banking

July 1 and 3, 1991—The RBI has devalued the rupee in a two step downward adjustment of 17.38 per cent.

July 3, 1991—The bank rate is hiked from 10 per cent to 11 per cent and further to 12 per cent on October 8, 1991.

November 1991—The Narasimhan Committee on reforming the financial system presented its report. Among other things, it suggested for the phase reduction of the SLR to 25 per cent in three years and the CRR to 10 per cent in four years.

April 1982—The RBI introduces the Risk Asset ratio system for the banks as a capital adequacy measure.

March 1, 1992—The dual exchange rate system is instituted under the liberalised exchange rate management enabling an orderly transition from a managed floating regime to a market determined one.

January 8, 1993—The FERA is amended and subsequently repealed. It was replaced by the FERA Amendment Act 1993.

January 1993—Issued guidelines for setting up the private sector banks.

March 1993—Rupee is made convertible on the trade account for starting the process of convertibility.

September 1993—New Bank of India merged with the PNB.

March 1994—With the receipt of the licence, the UTI Bank becomes the first private sector bank to operate.

June 13, 1994—The RBI issues guidelines on the prudential norms banks to achieve the minimum capital adequacy ratio of 6 per cent in their risk weighted assets and off balance sheet exposures by March 31, 95 and 8 per cent by March 96.

July 15, 1994—With an amendment to the Banking Companies Act, 1970, the nationalised banks are allowed to strengthen their capital base by tapping the capital market to public contribution of their capital upto 49 per cent.

August 1994—The second step towards the full convertibility is taken by making the rupee convertible on the current account.

October 1994—Oriental Bank of Commerce is the first nationalised bank to access the capital market to raise 387.24 crores.

October 1, 1995—Banks are allowed to fix their own interest rate on domestic term deposits for a period of two (2) years.

July 1996—The IRDA is set up to privatise the insurance sector.

May 9, 1997—The RBI issues the new norms for the NBFCs to improve their financial health and viability. They are required to apply for the registration with the RBI July 8, 1997.

December 7, 1997—The RBI constitutes a working group under the chairmanship of S.H. Khan to examine the harmonisation of the role and operations of the development finance institutions and banks.

April 24, 1998—The Khan Committee on the harmonisation of the role and operations of the development finance institutions and banks submits the recommendations suggesting a gradual move towards the Universal Banking.

August 9, 2000—Banks which have a minimum net worth of Rs. 500 crores and which satisfies the other criteria in regard to the capital adequacy are allowed to enter into the insurance business through a joint venture.

November 10, 2000—The guidelines for bank financing of equities and investments are issued. Banks are allowed to invest upto 5 per cent of its total outstanding domestic credit in the capital market.

January 3, 2001—Revised guidelines for licensing the new banks in the private sector are issued. These stipulate a minimum initial paid-up capital of Rs. 200 crores (to be raised to Rs. 300 crores within 3 years of commencement of business) with a minimum of 40 per cent as a contribution from the promoter.

March 15, 2001—The GOI reduces the interest rate payable on the relief bonds issued under the 1999 scheme from 9 per cent to 8.5 per cent.

April 19, 2001—Bank permitted to formulate the Fixed Deposit Schemes specially for senior citizens by offering higher and fixed rate of interest.

April 28, 2001—The RBI clarifies to approach the Universal Banking Term Lending and Refinancing Institutions.

The Future of Banking

The global environment has been changing. The size matters today and will matter even more tomorrow.

The increase in the competition will squeeze the profitability across the sector. Mostly they will hit the small banks. The larger banks will be able to mobilise sufficient capital to the bank asset expansion and fund investments in technology. Mergers and acquisitions are not new to the Indian Banking Sector. The government has used them in the past to bail out the weaker banks, through their mergers with other public sector banks. The new private banks has created a new environment in the history of market driven M&As in India. The amalgamation of the HDFC Bank with the Times Bank held a trend driven by the commercial considerations.

Mergers in the Banking Sector 1984-2001

Bank	*Year*	*Merged with*
Lakshmi Commercial Bank	1984	Canara Bank
Bank of Cochin	1984	SBI
Miraj State Bank	1984	UBI
Hindustan Commercial Bank	1985	PNB
Traders Bank	1987	Bank of Baroda
United Industrial Bank	88-89	Allahabad Bank
Bank of Tamilnadu	88-89	IOB
Bank of Thanjavur	88-89	Indian Bank
Parur Central Bank	88-89	Bank of India
Purbachal Bank	1990	CBI
New Bank of India	1993	PNB
BCCI	1993	SBI
Bank of Karad	1994	Bank of India
Kashinath Seth Bank	1995	SBI
Bari Doab Bank and Punjab Cooperative Bank	1997	OBC
Barilly Corporation Bank	1999	Bank of Baroda
Sikkim Bank	1999	UBI
Times Bank	1999	HDFC
Bank of Madura	2000	ICICI Bank

At present, Mobile banking became very popular. Mobile baking will always add on to the traditional banking channels. The number of consumers using it will increase with the corresponding rise in the number of cellular subscribers in the country. Today, we can make a balance enquiry, request for a cheque book, get a mini-statement of transactions or pay utility bills through the mobile. Still Indian banks have much to learn from Europe and Japan. For instance, in France, many phones come with a built in credit card slot, something that addresses several theory payment issues. In Japan, the users of the mobile service i-mode can carryout banking transactions online. I-mode has partnership with and several securities brokers. In Mumbai, it carries 19000 transactions a day and BPL 25,000.

The following policy matters have been taken to improve the efficiency and profitability of the banks:

1. **Closing of the unprofitable branches.**
2. **Mergers of Banks.**
3. **Deregulation of the interest rates on lending.**
4. **The reduction in SLR and CRR.**
5. **Greater operational flexibility.**
6. **The permission to the banks to directly undertake Leasing, Factoring and Hire Purchase Business (upto a maximum 10 per cent of total advances).**

2. Non-Banking Financial Companies (NBFC)

The Non-banking financial companies play an important role in the Indian Financial System. Recently the NBFCs has recorded a markable growth in terms of deposits. The NBFCs expanded their services in the financial sector. They involve in both fee-based and fund-based services. They actively involve in equipment leasing, hire purchase finance, factoring, discounting, venture capital, housing finance etc. All these activities are fund-based. They also involve in fee-based or advisory services which are presented below:

1. **Mergers and Acquisitions.**
2. **Loan Syndication.**
3. **Corporate Counselling.**
4. **Portfolio Management.**
5. **Issue Management.**

The regulatory frame work has been done on the basis of recommendations of the Khanna Committee and Vasudev Committee. The RBI has set up a separate department of Non-banking to supervise and monitor the activities of the NBFCs. The elements of the regulations are presented below:

1. **Prudential norms RBI Directions, 1998.**
2. **RBI Act—Chapter III-B, 1998.**
3. **RBI Acceptance of Deposits Regulations, 1998.**
4. **RBI Directions Audit Report, 1998.**

3. Mutual Funds

The Mutual Funds have been very popular in the Indian Financial System. The funds have been playing an important role in the stock market. They have been emerging as the back-bone of the Indian Capital Market. It is a vehicle for the institutionalisation of the security investments. The following factors influence the investment decisions of the small investors:

1. **Tax exemptions to the Unit holders.**
2. **Firm allotment to the Mutual Funds.**
3. **Proportionate allotment in case of over subscription.**
4. **The adjustment for capital gains tax.**
5. **The minimum limit in the Primary Market is raised from Rs. 1000 to Rs. 5000.**
6. **Full monitoring activities of the Mutual Funds by the SEBI.**

Mutual Funds in India began in 1964. The Unit Trust of India was launched in 1964. The scheme US-64 was also established in that year. It was only in 1987 that the banks and insurance companies got into the act with the SBI's initiative. Nearly 40 per cent of the funds were promoted by the banks and insurance companies. They were launched in between 1987 and 1993.[11] The first private mutual fund the **Kothari Pioneer** (Now known as ITI Pioneer) was launched in 1993. Large number of funds joined the party and the total assets under the management grew upto **Rs. 61,301 crores** in March 1994. With the fall of the Sensex, the investors preference shifted to the fixed income instruments in 1996. Most of the new entrants found it difficult to compete with the **UTI** which had assured the return debt products. The period 1996-98 was the worst period in the history of the Mutual Funds. But several Assets Management Companies used the opportunity to restructure their portfolios and got ready for the 1999 boom in equities. In 1999-2000, the value of assets under the management swelled to Rs. 1,07,946 crores. Then the great equity melt down happened. Today, there are 34 Mutual Fund Houses managing 614 schemes and Rs. 94,571 crores in assets. Not all of them will survive, but performance and transparency tell in the long run.

Statement Showing the Mutual Funds Boom

Year	*Corpus Fund in crores*
1964-69	65
1969-74	172
1974-79	402
1979-84	1261
1986-87	4563.68
1987-88	6738.81
1988-89	13455.65
1989-90	19110.92
1990-91	23060.45
1991-92	37480.20
1992-93	46988.02
1993-94	61301.21
1994-95	75050.21
1995-96	81026.52
1996-97	80539.00
1997-98	68984.00
1998-99	68472.00
1999-2000	107946.10
2000-2001	90587.00
2001	94571.00

4. Public Financial Institutions

The Public Financial Institutions occupy an important role in the financial system. They act as a substitute for the capital market and caters the needs of the growing industrial sector. But, recently they are gearing up to play the traditional role to supplement the capital market. They constitute the backbone of the financial system. They still play a dominant role. But the shift to the corporate financing declined its role. The Corporate Sector depends upon the non-institutional sources of finance. The greater access to the capital markets are provided by term loans, project financial undertaking, direct subscription, financing and also working capital to the industry. They also provide financial services such as Merchant Banking, Project Counselling. Portfolio management services, credit syndication, new issue management, mergers and acquisitions, Corporate advisory services, Registrar, STA, debenture trusteeship and sponsoring mutual funds.

The public financial institutions assumed the character of financial super market in addition to the term lending. The PFI changes in tune with the capital market. The focus is on the development finance and its major objective is to promote the entrepreneurship. Three credit rating agencies have been founded by them. The other institutions sponsored by them are Stock Holding Corporation, Investor Services of India and IFCI Custodial Services Ltd. They also established two stock exchanges namely the NSE and the O.T.C.

5. Capital Market

The Capital market is an important segment of the Indian Financial System. The Capital market emerged as a mechanism for allocating the resources in the economy. The structure of the capital market has witnessed significant changes. It can be categorised into Primary Market and Secondary Market. Another classification also can be made as Money Market and Securities Market. The Capital Market is regulated by the SEBI.

The Capital Market deals with long-term funds. It deals with shares, stocks, debentures and bonds. The funds which flow into the capital market comes from the savers. It diverts the resources from wasteful and unproductive channels to productive investments. The growth of the capital market indicates the growth of Joint Stock Companies and Corporate Sector.

In 1951, There were 28,500 companies with a paid-up capital of nearly Rs. 775 crores and as on 31-03-98, there were more than 2,00,000 companies with a paid-up capital of nearly Rs. 1,37,959 crores. The growth of investments has been quite phenomenal in recent years in accordance with the accelerated tempo of development in the Indian economy. The capital market consists of the gilt-edged market and the industrial securities market. The growth of the capital market is determined by the following factors:

1. **Rapid Industrialisation**
2. **Economic Development**
3. **Technology advances**
4. **Corporate performance**
5. **Regulatory framework**
6. **Participation of the FIIs in the Capital Market**
7. **Financial innovation**
8. **Economic and Financial Sector Reforms**
9. **Globalisation**
10. **Political Stability**
11. **NRI investment**
12. **International developments**
13. **Liquidity Factors**
14. **Agency Costs**
15. **Financial Intermediaries**
16. **Information and access**

Money Market is a market for the short-term funds. It provides the funds for less than a period of one year. It is dominated by the Central Bank. The RBI is the watch-dog of the monetary system. Money Market includes money, capital, bills and markets. In Money Market, the fund is being sold and purchased at a certain price. It is like the commodity market. It refers to lending and borrowing activities of banking, financial institutions and individuals. A number of instruments are introduced in the money market.

(a) **14 days treasury bills**
(b) **28 days treasury bills**
(c) **182 days treasury bills**
(d) **364 days treasury bills**
(e) **Commercial papers**
(f) **Certificate of deposits**
(g) **Money Market Mutual Fund (MMMF)**

(c) Investor's Protection

Today, the investors face several problems in the capital market. The corporate sector has come to rely on the securities market increasingly to finance its long-term requirements of funds. The Companies indulge in the malpractices. The innocent investors are exploited. The Companies indulge in malpractices in the following methods:

(a) **Wrong disclosure of material in prospectus.**
(b) **Manipulated Financial Information.**
(c) **Financial Window Dressing.**
(d) **Price rigging**
(e) **Insider trading.**
(f) **Private placement.**
(g) **Promoters quota**

The financial intermediaries indulge in irregularity like non-disclosure to the client, regarding the sale and purchase of shares and debentures, non-delivery of share certificates against payments, bad deliveries, excess commission charged, excess brokerage of Badla transactions.

In earlier phase, a fairly comprehensive legislative measures are taken. The regulatory framework are formed by the government departments. The capital issues had been controlled by the Ministry of Finance. According to the rules, every company should get the prior consent for the issue of capital to the public. The pricing and debt equity ratio were controlled by the government. The government also controls through the **Securities Contract Regulation Act.** It is administered by the Directorate of the Stock Exchange and the Ministry of Finance. The aim of the Act is to prevent the undesirable transactions in the market.

There is a strong need for the growing security market. It focusses the regulatory and its development depends on an autonomous body. It is to be achieved with the establishment of the Securities and Exchange Board of India. The SEBI was set up in 1988 and it commenced its operation in April 1992. The SEBI has become a statutory autonomous body. It is established for the purpose of protecting the investors' rights. It registers, regulates and monitors various intermediaries in the Capital Market. The SEBI issued the following guidelines with reference to the investors' protection.

1. **Publishing data regarding the price.**
2. **Inspecting the books of the brokers.**
3. **Receiving and redressing the investor's grievances promptly.**

4. **Enforcing the capital adequacy norms.**
5. **Amendment to the bye-laws of the stock exchanges**
6. **Redressal of the investors' grievances.**
7. **Enforcing the margin requirement strictly.**

The SEBI has introduced the prudential norms of capital adequacy for the brokers and also the norms for the broker-client relationship. It has undertaken the inspection of the stock exchanges.

The SEBI has been making the attempts to develop a strong cash market for the benefit of the investors. It encourages the transparency and fairness in the transactions. It handles the individual investor complaints. The organisational structure of all the components of Financial Markets, Financial Institutions and Financial Assets will be discussed in detail in the preceding chapters of this book.

The role of the Financial System is to accelerate the growth rate of the economic development. The standard of living and social welfare of the public depends upon the state of economy. This objective can be achieved through the mobilisation of savings. The savings may be diverted towards the productive way. The Present Indian Financial System is discussed in the next pages.

Summary

A well regulated modern financial sector is essential in a globalised digital economy. Financial innovation has contributed to the development. Finance has a tendency towards the boom bust cycles. The reforms offered a real opportunity for India to catch up to leap from being extremely backward state of the art than many countries which are locked into older less efficient and less technology. A system is a set of interrelated parts working together to achieve goal. A financial system helps to increase the output of a nation. Finance is the provision of money. It is exclusively concerned with the procurement of funds. The capital formation depends upon the finance which is available. Modern economies are highly influenced by expansion, diversification, attitudes of the savers and risk aversion of the investors. The Indian financial system is accompanied by the diversification and financial innovation. At present the Indian economy has a highly diversified structure of financial institutions. The economies move from being agriculture led to industry led to being services led. India has transited straight from agriculture to services. A large number of new

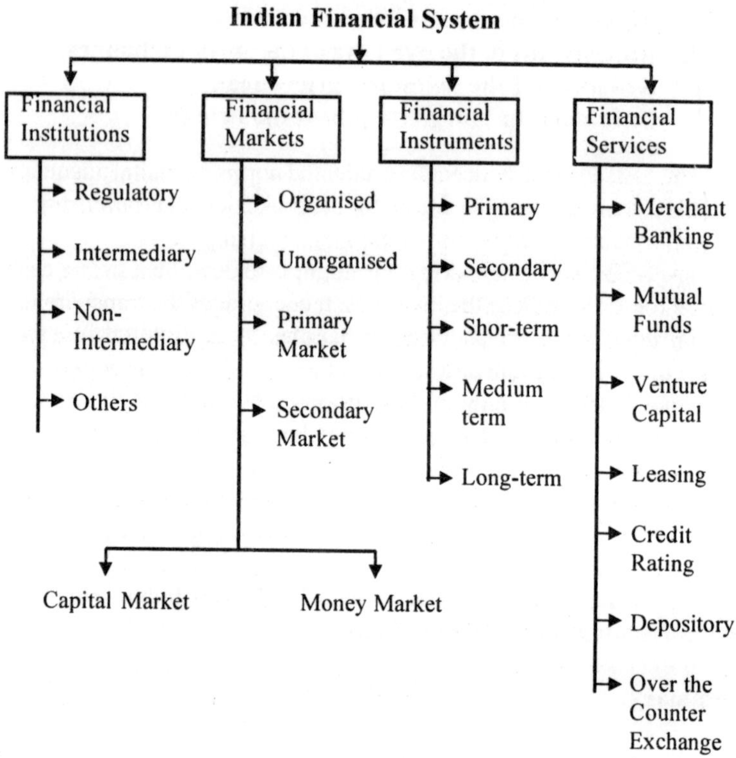

Source: L.M. Bhole, *Financial Institutions and Markets*, p. 4, 1998, Tata McGraw, Delhi.

financial assets are to be introduced to fulfill the needs of the dynamic corporate sector. The wealth creation of a nation can be measured through the ratios such as: Finance ratio, Relation ratio, New issue ratio, Intermediation ratio. Finance ratio is a micro analysis of an economy. The primary issues is known as the IPO. The Indian financial system can be classified as organised and unorganised sectors. The financial capability of the nation is highly influenced by many factors such evaluation of financial system, network of the rural banks, Industrial policy of the government. The organised sector of the financial system is controlled by the RBI and the Union Government. The unorganised sector of the financial system comprises Moneylenders, Indigenous bankers, lending pawn brokers, landlords,

Indian Financial System at Present

Intermediaries

I. Baking
- RBI
- Commercial bank
- Cooperative banks
- Urban cooperative banks
- Co-op. credit services
- Post office savings banks

II. Non-Banking
- Provident funds
- Small savings orgn.
- LIC
- GIC
- UTI
- Mutual funds
- Investment trusts
- Investment companies
- Finance companies
- Leasing companies
- Hire purchase companies
- Chits and Nidhis
- National housing
- HUDCO
- Venture capital
- Manufacturing companies
- Housing development finance company

Development Institutions
- IFCI
- ICICI
- IDBI
- EXIM
- NABARD
- SCICI
- TFCI
- RCTFC
- CWC
- REC
- NIDC
- NSIC
- SIDBI
- SFCs
- SWCs
- SIDC
- SIICs
- SSIDCs
- NCDCs
- IRBI
- Agricultural
- Finance
- Consultancy Ltd.

Regulatory

I. Regulatory
- RBI
- SEBI
- BIFR

II. Others
- ECGC
- DICGC
- TCOs
- SHCI
- CRISIL
- DFHI
- ILFS
- TDICI
- Merchant Banks
- Factoring companies
- Money Lenders
- Indigenous banks

Instruments & Marks

I. Instruments
- Equity shares
- Preference shares
- Debentures
- Bonds
- Capital gains bonds
- Government bonds
- Relief bonds
- National development bonds
- Indira Vikas Patra
- Kisan Vikas Patra
- National Savings
- NSC
- Insurance
- Units
- Participation cost
- CODs
- CP
- T Bills
- Comml. Bills
- Trade credit
- ICDs
- Hundis

II.Other/Markets
- Call money
- OTC
- Stock market
- Other market

Services
- Merchant banks
- Credit rating
- Re-Finance
- Brokers
- Syndicate
- Port folio manage-ment
- Leasing
- Under writing
- Bond transfer

Source: L.M. Bhole, *Financial Institutions and Markets*, p. 35, 1998, Tata McGraw, Delhi.

traders. The evaluation of financial system has the three distinct phases such as: phase I, II and III (1951 to 1990).

Savings are the most powerful weapons for the Capital formation in the Community. The capital formation leads to the investment activity in the country. The investment activities will enhance the growth of the economy. The important elements of the legislative measures adopted by the government are: Companies Act, SEBI, SCRA, MRTP, FEMA. The Indian financial system during the IIIrd phase is: Privatisation, Reorganisation, Investor protection. The privatisation is a part of the strategy. The government wants to reduce its liability from the public sector because of the mismanagement. The Indian financial system is undergoing an outstanding transformation and it can create wonders in the **capital market**, if it sticks on to a strong policy, the reorganisation of the institutional structure are made with the areas: Commercial banks, Non-banking Finance Companies, Mutual Funds, PFI and Capital Market.

ABBREVIATION

CWC	:	Central Warehousing Corporation
EXIM	:	Export and Import Bank of India
GIC	:	General Insurance Corporation
HUDCO	:	Housing and Urban Development Corporation
ICICI	:	Industrial Credit and Investment Corporation of India
IDBI	:	Industrial Development Bank of India
IFCI	:	Industrial Finance Corporation of India
IRBI	:	Industrial Reconstruction Bank of India
LIC	:	Life Insurance Corporation
NABARD	:	National Agricultural Bank for Rural Development
NIDC	:	National Industrial Development Corporation
NSIC	:	National Small Industries Corporation
RBI	:	Reserve Bank of India
RCTFC	:	Risk Capital Technology Finance Corporation.
REC	:	Rural Electric Corporation
SCICI	:	Shipping Credit and Investment Corporation of India
SFC	:	State Finance Corporations
SIDBI	:	Small Industries Development Bank of India
SIDC	:	State Industries Development Corporation.
TFCI	:	Technology Finance Corporation of India
UTI	:	Unit Trust of India

Regulatory

BIFR	:	Board for Industrial Financial Reconstruction
CRISIL	:	Credit Rating Information Services of India
DFHI	:	Discount and Finance House of India
DICGC	:	Deposit Insurance Credit Guarantee Corporation
ECGC	:	Export Credit Guarantee Corporation
ILFS	:	Infrastructure Leasing Financial Services
OTC	:	Over the Counter Exchange
RBI	:	Reserve Bank of India
SEBI	:	Securities Exchange Board of India
SHCI	:	Stock Holding Corporation of India
TDICI	:	Technology Development and Investment Corporation of India

NOTES

1. L.M. Bhole, *Financial Institutions and Markets* p. 13, Tata McGraw, 1998.
2. The rebirth of an economy, *Business Today*, Anniversary Issue, p. 24, 2002.
3. The Indian Economy, *Business Today*, Anniversary Issue, p. 27, 2002.
4. The Indian Economy, 1950-01, BT Anniversary Issue, p. 27, 2002.
5. The great IPO rush, *Business Today*, Anniversary Issue, p. 70, 2002.
6. The great IPO rush, *Business Today* Anniversary Issue, p. 70, 2002.
7. M.Y. Khan, *Indian Financial System*, Tata McGraw, p. 22, 2000.
8. The Economy—Crown Jewels or bleeding ulcers. *Business Today*, Anniversary Issue, p. 31, 2002.
9. Inspector Raj: The grant survivor, *Business Today*, Anniversary Issue, p. 50, 2002.
10. The Problem of NPA, *Business Today*. Anniversary Issue, p. 88, 2002.
11. The Mutual Funds Boom, *Business Today* Anniversary Issue, p. 69, 2002.

PART - II

- Financial Markets
- Primary Market
- Secondary Market
- Money Market
- Capital Market
- SEBI

2

FINANCIAL MARKETS

Introduction

Each and every business unit must operate within the financial environment. The financial system consists of a number of organisations, institutions and market. They secure the needs of the **consumers, firms and governments**. If a firm invests the idle funds temporarily in marketable securities, then it has to approach the financial market. Most of the firms use the financial markets to finance their investments in assets Financial markets can be defined as "All Institutions and procedures for bringing buyers and sellers of the financial instruments together".[1] They provide better facilities for buying and selling of all the financial claims and services. All the participants trade in the financial products in the markets either directly or through the brokers. Financial institutions, agents, brokers, dealers, borrowers, lenders and savers participate both on demand and supply sides of the financial markets. The demand for capital will be influenced by the business expectations regarding the future state of the economy. The demand for goods is highly influenced by the prices, government policies, profitability, availability of internal funds, cost of funds and technology changes. On the other hand, the supply of funds depends on its level of savings by the household sector, business sector and government sector in a given economy. The savings of the participants in the market are determined by a number of factors. The factors will depend on the level of current and expected income, distribution of income in the economy, degree of certainty in income, wealth, inflation provision for oldage, family members, rate of interest, availability of savings media with required investment characteristics. The development banks and financial institutions can also influence the supply of funds. The government will determine the volume of supply of funds, allocation of funds, cost of funds and other factors. The financial markets are said to be perfect when :

(a) a large number of savers and investors operate in the market.
(b) participants are rational.
(c) all players in the market are well informed and the information will be freely available to all of them.
(d) there are no taxes.
(e) there are no transaction costs.
(f) the financial assets are infinitely divisible.

The financial markets can perform proximate functions such as:

1. Enhancing liquidity of the financial assets.
2. Transformation of the financial claims to suit the needs of the participants.
3. Enabling the business concerns to exercise their time preference.
4. Diversification, distribution, and reduction of risk.
5. Better mode of operation of the payment mechanism.

The financial markets are characterised by many imperfections, restrictive practices, existence of transaction costs, lack of information, limited number of operators, direct and indirect intervention by the authorities and so on.

The financial markets may be categorised as the primary and secondary markets. The Primary market is also known as the Direct Market. The Secondary market is also known as the Indirect market. Further the Direct market is called as the "New Issue Market". The NIM deals with the new securities offered by the newly established concerns or the existing enterprises. On the other hand the Secondary market deals with securities that are already issued by the Companies. The primary market creates the capital formation in the country. It channelises the savings in a productive way. The secondary markets do not contribute directly to the supply of the additional capital. But it will provide liquidity to the primary market. Therefore the NIM and secondary markets have impact on each other.

The financial market are also classified as:

(a) Organised and Unorganised.
(b) Formal and Informal.
(c) Official and Parallel.
(d) Domestic and Foreign.

The financial transactions which arise in a systematic manner in an organised system are called as "Organised Markets". The financial transactions which take place outside the well-established exchange constitute the "Unorganised Markets". The Unorganised market refer to the markets in rural areas. The "Informal markets" constitute the financial transactions which arise between the individuals and small families.

The financial markets are further classified as:

A. Money market, and
B. Capital market.

There is no difference between these two markets. Both of them perform the same functions in the transferring of the financial assets. They provide a mechanism to sell the financial assets.

A. MONEY MARKET

The Money market is a market for the short-term funds. It provides funds for less than a period of one year. It is dominated by the Central Bank. The RBI is the watch-dog of the monetary system. It provides a channel for the exchange of the financial assets for money. The money market is of very great help in the financing industry and commerce for their working capital requirements. The money market includes money, capital and bill markets. Markets consists of both money and capital markets. In the money market, the fund is being sold and purchased at a certain price. It is like the commodity market. It refers to lending and borrowing activities of banking, financial institutions and individuals.

Definition of the Money Market—The Money market is defined by A. Crowther as "the money market is the collective name given to various firms and institutions that deal with various grades of near money."[2] It deals with the trade bills, promissory notes, and treasury bills for a short period. The RBI defined the money market as "the money market is a market for short-term financial assets that are close substitutes for money, facilitates the exchange of money for the new financial claims in the primary market and also for the financial claims, already issued in the secondary market."[3]

The Central Bank Act as a promotional and development banker in the money market. The money market can be organised as the organised sector and unorganised sector. The unorganised sector consists of indigeneous bankers and village moneylenders. The organised sector consists of the RBI, SBI, Mutual Funds, Companies, Cooperative Societies and Financial Institutions. Geographically, the money market may be located or associated with a particular place like Indian Money Market, New York Money Market, Bombay Money Market etc. In the Bombay Money Market, the short-term loanable fund is available for the whole India. The London Money Market, on the other hand is a market of international importance. It is known as the International Money Market. It attracts the short-term funds from all over the world for redistribution among the borrowers. The demand for the short period comes primarily from the Government, Business concerns and Private individuals. The Government has become probably the biggest borrower; everywhere money is being required to meet the current deficits. Individual and Commercial concerns borrow funds for working capital needs. Sometimes they borrow to enable to carry additional inventories. The other important private borrowers include the stock exchange brokers, dealers in the government and other security merchants, manufactures, farmers. Banks themselves may require additional funds and may borrow from the Central Bank or from each other. The supply of loanable funds in the money market comes mostly from the Central Bank of the country, the Commercial Banks and other finance companies. The Central Bank is the source of credit to the Commercial Banks while the latter constitute the most important source of the short-term credit to the individual houses, business houses and the brokers.

Characteristics of the Money Market

The following are the characteristics of the money market:

1. It involves in the arrangement of the short-term funds.
2. It is a tool for the preparation of the monetary policy and fiscal management.
3. It deals with the high liquid instruments.
4. The players in this market are the RBI, Commercial Banks and Companies.
5. It is subjected to the RBI regulations.
6. It tells about the trends in the liquidity and interest rates.
7. It provides funds at low transaction cost.

8. It suits the requirements of the borrowers for the short-term funds.
9. It encourages the open market operations.

Different sub-markets of a developed money market help in the proper functioning of the Central Bank. The money market and the short-term rates of interest serve as a good barometer for monetary and banking conditions in the country. Thus they provide a valuable guide in determining the Central Banking Policy. The developed money market being a highly integrated structure, enables the Central Bank to deal with the most sensitive sub-markets also.

The main borrowers of the short-term funds in the money market are:

1. Commercial Banks.
2. Central Government.
3. State Government.
4. Corporate Sector.
5. Local Bodies.

The money market is unable to meet the long-term requirements of the industries. It consists of Central Banks, Commercial Banks, Cooperative Banks, Savings Banks, Discount Houses, Acceptance Houses, bill market, bullion market etc. The existence of a well-developed money market ensures that the market instruments can be converted into money without incurring much loss.

The Need for a Money Market

1. It is a coordinator between borrowers and lenders of the short-term funds.
2. It provides the transmission of funds from surplus concerns to the shortage funds concerns.
3. It is a device of the Government to balance its cash inflows and outflows.
4. It is a weapon of the business firms to meet their short-term funds.
5. Money Market creates the minimum rate of return on the Idle fund lying at the disposal of the Corporate and Banking Sectors.
6. It is tool to the finance managers in more utilisation of the funds to enhance the share-holder's wealth.

The following chart shows the structure of the Indian Money Market:

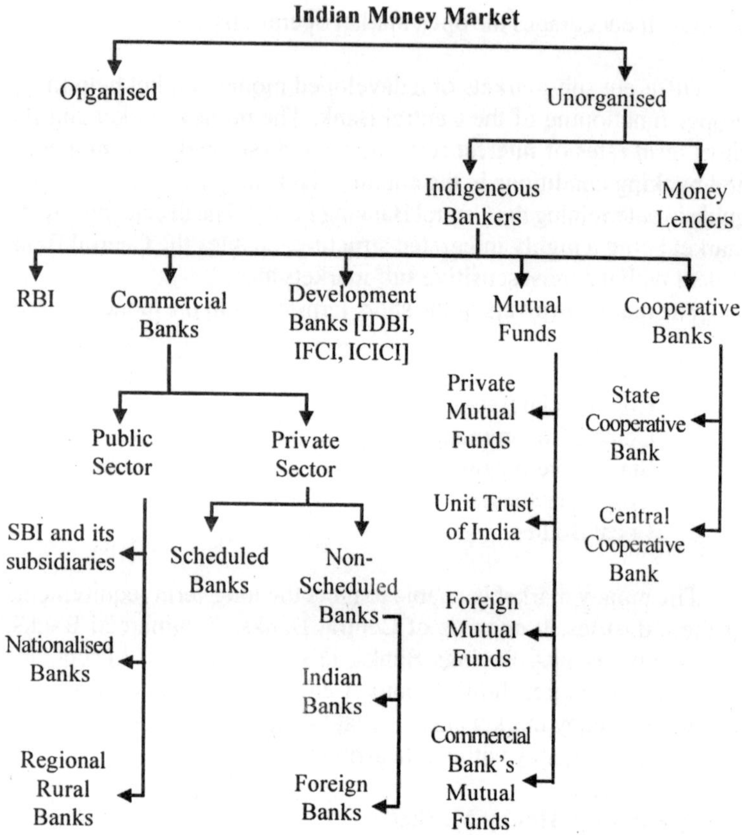

The Goals of the Money Market Investor

1. The main objective of the investors in the money market is about the safety and liquidity of the principal amount. They also think about some gains along with their amount.
2. The Money market is a parking place of an idle fund.
3. The Investor wisely escape from the long-term market risks.
4. Money market instruments generally offer more protection against the political risk and inflation risk.
5. In money market, the investor never face default risk.

On overall evaluation of the money market, we can find that it is entirely dominated by the RBI. All the policy matters of the sector will be finalised by the India's Central Bank. The SEBI and the other statutory organisations have been playing an important role in the smooth functioning of the Money Market. It is a powerful weapon in the hands of the Central Government. It is handled skillfully by the Ministry of Finance. Crores of rupees are available in the market at the disposal of various large organisations within few hours. Therefore the development of the Money Market can boost the wealth of a nation. It also encourages the capital market.

Recent Developments in the Money Market

The annual statement of the monetary and credit policy that was released on April 19, 2001 projected a GDP growth of 6 to 6.5 per cent for 2000-2001. This projection is based on the assumptions such as reasonable monsoon, good performance of exports and revival of the industrial sector.

The annual policy statement also indicated that under normal circumstance and boring emergence of any adverse and unexpected developments in domestic or external sectors, the overall stance of the monetary policy for 2001-02 will be:

(a) The average call money rate came down sharply from 8.6 per cent in early April to 7 per cent in mid October 2001. During this period, the repo rate also came down from 7 per cent to 6.5 per cent The CRR was reduced by the 50 Basis Points to 7.5 per cent on 19th May 2001, augmenting lendable resources of the banking system Rs. 4,500 crores. Responding to these operations, the interest rates in other money market instruments also showed a declining trend. The primary yield on 91 days treasury bills were declined by 150 Basis Points from 8.5 per cent to 7 per cent between April and mid October 2001. During the same period, primary yield on 364 days treasury bills fell by 168 Basis Points from 8.85 per cent to 7.17 per cent. The discount rates on the CP also showed a similar trend. At the long end of the market, the secondary yields on the government paper between 10-20 years have softened from 10.08 per cent to 10.70 per cent in April to 9.12 to 9.92 per cent by mid October 2001.

(b) The RBI issued fresh guidelines for the issuance of commercial paper on 10 October 2000, relaxing the terms and conditions and streamlining the procedures. As indicated in the annual policy statement of April 2001, Banks, FIs, PDs, Satellite Dealers (SDs) are now permitted to make fresh investments and hold the CPs only in dematerialised form effective from June 30, 2001. In this context, the fixed Income Money Market and the Derivatives Association of India circulated a "report on FIMMADA working group" primarily relating to the market conventions and guidelines for the CPs. The FIMMADA in consultation with the market participants, Depositories and the RBI prepared the related guidelines and made them public on 3 October 2001. These guidelines seem to be working reasonably well and no changes are being proposed at present.

(c) As announced in the annual policy statement, 14 days and 182 days Treasury Bills (TBs) have been withdrawn from the week beginning *i.e.* on 14 May, 2001. The notified amount of 91 days TBs has been simultaneously increased to Rs. 250 crores. It has also been ensured that both the 91 days and 364 days TBs mature on the same day to facilitate the availability of adequate fungible stocks of TBs varying maturities in the secondary market. Increased attractiveness of the TBs is evident from the fact that no development of the RBI has taken place in the TB auctions and the bid-coverage ratio, particularly in respect of 364 days TB.

(d) A Negotiable Dealing System (NDS) is being introduced with a view of facilitating electronic bidding in auctions and Secondary Market transactions in the Government securities and dissemination of information on trades. The technology infrastructure related to NDS has been tested with the involvement of all market participants in LAN and WAN environments. Parallel runs are expected in November 2001.

(e) The Clearing Corporation of India Ltd. (CCIL) was registered on 30 April, 2001 under the Companies Act, 1956, with the SEBI as the chief promoter. Initially the CCIL would clear all the transactions and the repos reported on the NDS of the RBI and also US/Rupee/dollar forex spot and forward deals. The operationalisation of the CCIL, linked to the NDS was expected to commence with a test run in November 2001.

The necessary amendments to the notification was issued by the Government for introducing the uniform price auction format for the auctions of the dated securities. With the approval of the Government, the new auction format will be introduced on an experimental basis.

(f) A scheme of retail participation including the middle segment encompassing the PFs. Trusts in the Primary market for the Government securities on Non-competitive basis has been finalised after consulting the market participation and the Technical Advisory Committee on Money Market and Government Securities Market. The details of the scheme is yet to be finalised by the RBI.

(g) The Satellite Dealer System was introduced in 1996 to serve as a second tie to the PDs in the Government securities market with the particular objective of promoting retail segment. The experience of the SDs confirm that impractice SDs role in retaining the Government securities has remained very limited. Even as complementary service, the SD system is perceived to result in higher transaction costs to the retail investors. As many of them are broker firms because of the limited capital strength and also wider presence in the non-government securities, business also raised some supervisory concerns.

(h) After the overall review of the present environment in the market, the RBI has decided to undertake a review of the SD system along with the SDs, PDs and TAC. The review will consider the role carved out for the SDs in the development of the retail market, particularly in the context of the expanding role of the PDs. They are emerging as an alternative mechanism of the retailing government securities on the screen-based trading in exchange and the supervisory concerns in monitoring the SDs operations. The review will examine the scope for establishing a better linkage between SDs and PDs and thereby improving the SD system as an effective distribution channel at a retail level for government securities.

(i) The Satellite System dealership was launched in 1996 to serve as a second tier to the primary dealers in retaining of G-secs. The RBI in its mid-term monetary and credit policy has tacitly accepted that the concept of the satellite dealers has not taken off as an efficient medium for retaining the government securities. The Central Bank has decided to review the entire system of the satellite dealers in the fixed income market. The RBI has decided to allow the players such as provident funds, trusts to participate in the government bond auctions on a non-competitive basis. This review would consider the role carved out for the satellite dealers in the development of the retail market. The review would focus on the building linkages among the primary and satellite dealers and improving the satellite dealership system.

(j) Call Money Market with an average daily gross lending improved to Rs. 19,600 crores between May-Sept. 2001 from Rs. 10,900 crores during the corresponding period of the previous year. Therefore the Central Bank feels that the planned phasing out of the non-banking participants from the call money market has not caused any strain on the market.

(k) Top rated corporates can now have the best of the both worlds. They can obtain a commitment from a bank for working capital funds by getting the cash credit limit sanctioned. Thereafter the banks can go for shopping the best sub-PLR rate available from other banks. If by any chance rates harden, they can always pull back the cash credit limit that has already sanctioned. Till now the banks could not shop for the funds after receiving the sanction, as 80 per cent of the sanctioned working capital funds has to be drawn immediately in the form of a loan. The remaining 20 per cent will be available. Now the RBI has given permission to the banks that they can offer 100 per cent of the sanctioned limits in the form of the cash credit.

ANNEXURE I

AVERAGE DAILY TURNOVER IN CALL MONEY MARKET

Fortnight ended	Turnover per day (Rs. in Crores)
May 5, 2000	Rs. 48056
May, 19, 2000	Rs. 39214
June 2, 2000	Rs. 40056
June 16, 2000	Rs. 38300
June 30, 2000	Rs. 38357
July 14, 2000	Rs. 42465
July 28, 2000	Rs. 39797
Aug. 11, 2000	Rs. 39275
Aug. 25, 2000	Rs. 35973
Sept. 8, 2000	Rs. 41797
Sept. 22, 2000	Rs. 42933
Oct. 6, 2000	Rs. 44635
Oct. 20, 2000	Rs. 45776
Nov. 3, 2000	Rs. 47321
Nov. 17, 2000	Rs. 46805
Dec. 1, 2000	Rs. 47310
Dec. 15, 2000	Rs. 46747
Dec. 29, 2000	Rs. 43568
Jan. 12, 2001	Rs. 50396
Jan. 26, 2001	Rs. 49039
Feb. 9, 2001	Rs. 50675
Feb. 23, 2001	Rs. 45987
Mar. 9, 2001	Rs. 51550
Mar. 23, 2001	Rs. 50314
Apr. 6, 2001	Rs. 44630
Apr. 20, 2001	Rs. 50957
May 4, 2001	Rs. 48008
May 18, 2001	Rs. 41395
June 1, 2001	Rs. 46156
June 15, 2001	Rs. 44790
June 29, 2001	Rs. 47052
July 13, 2001	Rs. 47071
July 27, 2001	Rs. 44597

Sources: RBI Bulletin, October 2001, P.No. 5997.

ANNEXURE II

DAILY CALL MONEY RATES (FROM 1-8-2001 TO 12-9-2001)

As on	Range of Rates		Weighted Average Rate	
	Borrowings	Lending	Borrowing	Lending
Aug. 1, 2001	5.47-7.10	4.92-7.50	6.90	6.92
Aug. 2, 2001	5.89-7.10	4.89-7.40	6.86	6.88
Aug. 3, 2001	5.85-7.10	4.85-7.00	6.92	6.87
Aug. 4, 2001	6.15-7.05	5.39-7.05	6.82	6.96
Aug. 6, 2001	5.80-7.05	4.80-7.10	6.78	6.80
Aug. 7, 2001	5.45-7.20	4.90-7.10	6.88	6.89
Aug. 8, 2001	5.70-7.65	5.10-7.90	7.11	7.12
Aug. 9, 2001	5.79-7.60	5.20-7.60	7.18	7.26
Aug. 10, 2001	5.94-7.50	6.25-7.50	6.93	6.97
Aug. 11, 2001	5.90-7.25	5.54-7.25	6.97	6.97
Aug. 13, 2001	5.21-7.25	4.97-7.90	6.92	6.99
Aug. 14, 2001	6.00-8.30	5.11-8.30	7.05	7.06
Aug. 16, 2001	5.59-7.30	5.09-7.30	7.04	7.08
Aug. 17, 2001	5.55-7.30	5.03-7.30	7.02	7.01
Aug. 18, 2001	5.96-7.15	6.50-7.25	6.97	7.00
Aug. 20, 2001	5.59-7.34	5.06-7.90	7.04	7.04
Aug. 23, 2001	5.61-7.25	5.06-7.25	7.04	7.08
Aug. 24, 2001	6.00-7.50	5.06-7.25	7.04	7.05
Aug. 25, 2001	5.86-7.20	5.42-7.80	6.86	6.88
Aug. 27, 2001	5.85-7.05	4.85-7.05	6.84	6.85
Aug. 28, 2001	5.30-7.30	4.75-7.10	6.74	6.75
Aug. 29, 2001	5.26-7.30	4.75-7.80	6.73	6.78
Aug. 30, 2001	5.44-7.40	4.89-7.10	6.90	6.93
Aug. 31, 2001	5.53-7.55	4.96-7.55	6.95	6.98
Sept. 1, 2001	5.92-7.10	6.10-7.15	6.91	6.92
Sept. 3, 2001	5.45-7.45	4.90-7.50	6.89	6.91
Sept. 4, 2001	5.85-7.00	6.00-7.15	6.85	6.86
Sept. 5, 2001	5.43-7.25	4.89-7.25	6.98	6.90
Sept. 7, 2001	6.00-7.95	5.89-7.95	7.14	7.17
Sept. 8, 2001	6.08-7.40	6.60-7.40	7.08	7.15
Sept. 10, 2001	6.05-7.75	5.05-7.75	7.02	7.15
Sept. 11, 2001	6.10-7.80	5.10-7.50	7.06	7.06

Source: RBI Bulletin October 2001, P.No. 5996.

B. CAPITAL MARKTET

Introduction

Capital Market is the market for long-term funds. It deals long-term and medium term funds. Capital market consists of shares, stocks, debentures and bonds. Securities dealt in capital market are long-term securities. The funds which flows into the capital market comes from the savers. It provides a market mechanism for those who have savings and to those who need funds for productive investments. It diverts resources from wasteful and unproductive channels to productive investments. Since 1951, the Indian Capital Market has been broadening slowly. There is a steady improvement in the volume of savings and investment. Many types of encouragement and tax relief exists in the country to promote savings. Many steps have been taken to protect the interests of the investors. The growth of capital market indicates the growth of Joint Stock Companies and corporate enterprises. In 1951, there were 28,500 companies with a paid up capital of nearly Rs. 7.5 crores and as on 31-3-1998, there were more than 2,00,000 companies with a paid up capital of nearly Rs. 1,37,959 crores. The growth of investment has been quite phenomenal in recent years in accordance with the accelerated tempo of development.

Definition

Capital Market can be defined as "the market for relatively long-term financial instruments."[4]

According to Arun K. Datta the capital market may be defined as "the capital market is a complex of institutions investment and practices with established links between the demand for and supply of different types of capital gains."[5]

Further F. Livingston[6] defined the capital market as "In a developing economy, it is the business of the capital market to facilitate the main stream of command over capital to the point of the highest yield. By doing so, it enables, control over resources to pass into the hands of those who can employ them must effectively thereby increasing production capacity and spelling the national dividend."

Capital market consists of gilt edged market and the industrial securities market. The gilt edged market refers to the market for government and semi-government securities backed by the RBI. The securities traded in this market are stable in value and are much sought after by the banker and other institutions. The Industrial securities market refers to the market for equities and debentures of old and new companies. The industrial securities market is further divided by the new issue market and further capital issue market. The new issue market refers to the raising of capital by the new companies in the form of shares and debentures. While further old issue capital deals with securities already issued by the existing companies. The two markets are equally important. But the NIM is much more important for the capital formation in the country. However, the functioning of NIM will be facilitated only when there are facilities for the transfer of the existing securities.

Considerable deregulation of financial markets whose taken place in India favouring the unbridled growth of financial services companies. The reforms have been increased competitiveness within the financial sector by means of, interest rates, allowing new financial institutions and instruments. As a consequence, the scope and activities of the banks, and non-banking finance companies have expanded rapidly due to the liberalisation drive, more particularly since 1991, the non-banking finance companies have been competing and complementing the services of the Commercial Banks. It has been observed that the growth of non-banking finance companies are more pronounced than banking companies.

Nature and Constituents

The capital markets consists of a number of individuals and institutions. The Government is also an important player in the capital market. The players in the capital market, canalise the supply and demand for the long-term capital. The constituents of the capital markets are, the stock exchange, commercial banks, co-operative banks, savings banks, development banks, insurance companies, investment trusts and companies etc.

The Growth of the Capital Market

The Indian financial system is both developed and integrated today. Integration has been through a participatory approach in granting loans as well as in saving schemes. The expansion in size and number of institutions has led to a considerable degree of diversification and increase in the types of financial instruments in the financial sector which are wholly owned by the government.

The development banks in the Indian financial system have witnessed vast changes in the planning periods. Now the development banks constitute the backbone of the Indian capital market. The relevant of the development banks in the industrial financial system is not merely qualitative, but they have overwhelming qualitative dimensions in terms of their promotional and innovational functions. The growth of the capital market is determined by the following factor:

1. Economic development.
2. Rapid industrialisation.
3. Level of savings and investment of the household sector.
4. Technological advances.
5. Corporate performance.
6. Regulatory framework.
7. Participation of foreign institutional investors in the capital market.
8. Development of financial services.
9. Liquidity factors.
10. Political stability.
11. Globalisation.
12. Financial innovation.
13. Economic and financial sector reforms.
14. International developments.
15. Agency costs.
16. Emergence of financial intermediaries.
17. Specialisation among investment managers.
18. Incentives.
19. Speed in acquiring, processing and acting upon information.
20. NRIs investment

Components of the Capital Market

In a capital market, banks and financial institutions are the important components. They act as catalysts in the economic development of any country. These institutions mobilise financial savings from household, corporate and other sector of the economy and channelise them into productive investments. They act as a **Reservoir** of resources and form the backbone of the economic and financial system. The banking industry has undergone a sea change during the last three decades. After the modernisation of banks, they not only lend for the social and economic causes but also participated in the development programmes of the central government and state government. The main components of the capital market in India are:

1. **New-Issue Market (Pubic issues) (Primary Market)**
2. **Secondary Market (Stock market)**

1. Public Issues (New Issue Market)

Public issue is known as primary market. The new issue market creates financial claims. It deals with those securities which have been made available to the public for the first time. Public issue can be defined as "sale of bonds or stock to the general public."[7] The flow of new securities from the issuer of securities to the buyer of securities. Therefore the new issue market deals with the new securities. The new issue market provides the issuing company with additional funds. It facilitate transfer of funds from saver to entrepreneur, the NIM does not have any physical distance. It facilitates the transfer of resources from saver to users. New securities may be floated both by the newly set up organisation or by the existing ventures.

The role of the new issue market and stock exchange is complimentary to each other in the infrastructure facilities provided for the sale and purchase of the securities in the market. The new issues of shares are subscribed to the corporate sector through the application forms before the date of closing of the issue.

Recent Developments in NIM

Public equity issues may be inactive at the present situation. According to the prime data base, the public issues for debt and equity issues just Rs. 1101 crore and Rs. 6 crore respectively in the first half of the current fiscal 2001-2002 period. The first half of the current year witnessed 118 institutions and corporates mobilised an amount of Rs. 22,673 crore through the private placement of debt. The amount raised by the private sector recorded a 31 per cent gain to reach Rs. 6234 crore compared to Rs. 4812 crore raised in first half of 2001-2002.[8]

Mega Issues

During the fiscal year 2001-2002 the leading pack of mobiliser is Reliance Petroleum Rs. 1061 crore and it is followed by GE Capital Rs. 520 crore, TISCO Rs. 350 crore and Tata Power Rs. 300 crore. In the case of PSU a 34 per cent improvement found with Rs. 4816 crores being mobilised from the market. The major mobilisers are REC Rs. 869 crore, Power Grid Corporation Rs. 761 crore, SAIL Rs. 700 crore, NTPC Rs. 575 crore and BPCL Rs. 445 crore respectively. On the other hand the mobilisation by state level undertakings (SLU) is by 51 per cent from Rs. 5858 crore to Rs. 2891 crore in the relevant periods 2000-2001 and 2001-2002 respectively.

According to the new RBI guidelines, the commercial banks can invest in the state government papers. It is found that the most of the funds raised by SLUs have been for the infrastructure sector, mainly power, roads and water resources. The leader in mobilisation during the 6 months (2001-2002) (upto Oct. 30, 2001) was Krishna Bhagy Jal Nigam Rs. 356 crore, followed by GEB Rs. 300 crore, Maharasthra Vikrikar Rs. 244 crore, IKSPDC Rs. 200 crore and GSRJC Rs. 200 crore.

Significantly a total of Rs. 12272 crore was raised by AAA rated paper on the other hand Rs. 2025 crore of paper was not rated at all during the 2000-2001 year. On an industrywise analysis, it was found that the financial services sector including banking and term lending, continued to dominate the market, collectively raising Rs. 10,736 crore, power sector ranked second with Rs. 3765 crore. The analysis of public issue during 2000-2001 further revealed that Maharashtra led the resources mobilisation activity at Rs. 9877 crore, followed by Delhi at Rs. 6778 crore and Karnataka at Rs. 1940 crore.

Functions of NIM/Public Issues

The main function of NIM is to facilitate the transfer of resources. The NIM can also be utilised for selling the existing concesus to the public. The NIM is a tool for the implication of the privatisation policy. According to R.F. Henderson the functions of the NIM can be categorised into two ways:

(*a*) Initial issues by new companies.
(*b*) Further issues by old companies.

These issues bear no relation to the age of the company. But these are based on the fact that listing of securities with stock exchange. Therefore the classification of these issues are concerned only with the flow of the money.

Another classification of issues are concerned with the flow of funds into the market and the flow of fresh capital. Issue of shares involving in the newly created share is called initial issue. The sale of securities which are already in existence and are sold by their holders can be classified secondary market. This classification excludes two types of issues from the category of new issues. They are bonus issues and exchange issues.

Therefore, the main function of the new issue market is channelising the investible funds, the NIM has the following three functions:

1. Origination
2. Underwriting
3. Distribution

1. *Origination*

Origination is the first step in planning a public issue. It refers to the task of investigation and analysis of new proposals. In this function, the specialised agencies would assess the capabilities of the issuing company. They will undertake a careful study of the technical, economic, financial and legal aspects of the issuing companies. The specialised agencies also advise the issuing company on the following aspects.

(*i*) Investment climate.
(*ii*) Determination of class of security to be issued.
(*iii*) Determination of issue price.
(*iv*) The timing and magnitude of issues.
(*v*) Method of flotation.
(*vi*) Techniques of selling

These functions of origination are mainly in advisory nature. The function of origination has been taken over in India by the specialised concerns of commercial banks. The commercial banks have created a separate division called the "Merchant Banking Division". Merchant

Banking would advice the companies about the viability of the project. They offer the services regarding pre and post public issue. A detailed discussion would be available in preceding pages regarding the merchant banking.

2. *Underwriting*

Underwriting has originated to face the uncertainties of the capital market when the company approaches the public issues. In NIM, if the issue remains unsubscribed, the directors cannot proceed to allot the shares. The director are required to return the money to the applicants consequently the project would fail. To overcome the situation, the companies are taking the precautions about the public issue for the successful completion. Underwriting is the arrangement, where the investment bankers too undertake for ensuring the full success of the issue of securities. The underwriters agrees to take a specified number of shares or debentures offered to the public in the event of non-subscription by the investors. In this situation, underwriter has to contribute the share capital for his assistance part. If the company gets success in the public issues, the underwriter is entitled to get a commission for this assignment. It is called as underwriting commission.

3. *Distribution*

Distribution is the most important aspect in the process of public issue. The sale of securities to the ultimate investor is referred to as distribution. It is a specialised task performed by the brokers and dealers in securities. They maintain regular and direct contact with ultimate investors. They know the pulse of the investors and able to influence them towards the mobilisation of share capital of the companies.

Mechanics of Floating New Issue

The following are the methods of new issues which are placed in the market:

1. Public Issue
2. Offer for sale
3. Private Placement.

Public Issue

The sale of shares and debentures through prospectus is known as **public issue**. It is the method of flotation of shares and debentures. The offer to the public is made directly through the intermediary at specific price. Intermediaries are not involved but they will help in the mobilisation of resources. But it is an expensive method of flotation of shares which approximately costs 10 per cent of public issue amount. The issuing company has to incur expenses on administration, advertisements, printing prospectus, press releases, bankers commission, underwriting commission, agents fee, legal charges, stamp duty, document fee, listing fee and registration charges.

Offer for Sale

In this method, the sale of shares is made indirectly by an issuing house. It involves the sale of securities through different steps:

I Step

Sale of shares by the issuing company to issuing house or broker.

II Step

The broker or issuing house will resell the shares to the public with a charged profit.

Offer for sale is not used for selling securities to the public, but to comply with certain stock exchange regulations at the time of listing the shares. This method is not used in India. But it is very popular in abroad.

Private Placement

Private placement refers to the direct sale of newly issued securities by the issuer to a limited number of investors. It is an indirect method of sale of shares. It is very popular in **United States, Canada, U.K., France, Sweden, Mexico and European** countries. It is subject to some regulations in the abroad. But in India this method is not bound by any regulatory system.

Private placement can be defined as "the sale of an entire issue of securities directly to one purchaser or a small group of purchasers."[9]

Features

The following are the important features regarding the private placement:

- **(a)** The transactions are very fast.
- **(b)** There are no legal hurdles in this method.
- **(c)** It can be tailored to the borrower's needs.
- **(d)** Financing can be consummated quickly.
- **(e)** Flexibility in borrowing/utilising the funds.

Private placement does not require the detailed compliance of formalities as required in public or rights issues. It is a cost and time effective way of raising funds for the corporate sector. In this method, for issuing the equity, companies are free to fix the quantum of placement and only follow the rule for pricing of preferential allotment as stipulated by the SEBI. These placements have no lock in period. There is no compliance system for the merchant bankers in private placement as in the case of public issues. Therefore, the method has become a favourable route for the corporates and the financial institutions in India for mobilising the resources during the last few years. The private placement market will be very active in future.

Public Issue Process

Public issue is essentially an exercise which involves the active participation of a number of agencies. The growth of the number of public issues has become more popular. The promoters should be able to coordinate effectively. The efforts of all the agencies makes success of the issue. There are different companies which approaches the NIM, for every type of organisation. There will be a separate legal formality that have to be fulfilled. The public issues can be made by[10] :

- (*a*) First issue of the new companies set up by the entrepreneurs without a track record.
- (*b*) First issue of the new companies set up by the existing companies with a **track record**.

(*c*) First issue by the existing closely held company.
(*d*) First public issue by the unlisted companies with **3 years track record**.
(*e*) First public issue by the unlisted companies without 3 year track record.
(*f*) Public issue for the closely held companies seeking **Disinvestment**.
(*g*) Public issue for the closely held companies seeking disinvestment without issuing a fresh capital.
(*h*) Public issues by the existing listed companies.

Therefore the public issue activities have been processed as follows:

(a) Pre-issue activities.
(b) Post-issue activities.

(a) Pre-issue Activities

The following process is required to make an issue as a success.

1. Approvals and clearances for the issue.
2. Appointment of agencies, drafting of prospectus.
3. Permission from RBI (for issues to NRI/FII)
4. Formalities related to banks.
5. Pre-issue stock exchange formalities.
6. Printing and distribution of stationery and advertising material.
7. Advertising and promotional compaign.
8. Preferential offer to shareholders/promoters.
9. Allotment formalities.
10. Board meeting.

(b) Post-issue Activities

This is the next stage after the completion of public issue. After closing the issue the following process should be involved to finalise issue:

1. Instructions to collect the amount from branches of bankers to the issue.
2. Receipt of applications and allotment of shares.

3. Monitoring daily collection and announcement regarding closure.
4. Feedback from collecting branches.
5. Registrars to make details about issue response.
6. Obtain certificate from the controlling branches.
7. Scrutiny of share applications by the Registrar.
8. Preparation of bank reconciliation statement by the registrar.
9. Allotment formalities.
10. Despatch of allotment letters with refund orders.

The another classification of process of public issues can be found as follows.

I step	→	Consent from the SEBI.
II step	→	Compliance with the Companies Act.
III step	→	Drafting of prospectus.
IV step	→	Approval from the RBI.
V step	→	Printing and distribution of stationery.
VI step	→	Marketing and advertising.
VII step	→	Bank coordination.
VIII step	→	Stock exchange formalities.
IX step	→	Post issue activities.

The important and annexures have been presented in next page.

LIST OF ANNEXURES

New Issue Market

Annexure 1	:	Back up documents from the promoters.
Annexure 2	:	Questionnaire to be filled by the lead manager.
Annexure 3	:	Applications to be filed with the SEBI with draft prospectus and list of documents. (*a*) Certificate of due deligence (*b*) Copy of interse allocation of responsibilities between the lead managers (*c*) MOU between issues and lead managers (*d*) Rights of the lead manager (*e*) Consequences of breach of MOU (*f*) Compliance certificate (*g*) Compliance certificates by the Company.
Annexure 4	:	Questionnaire to be filled at the site visit.
Annexure 5	:	Copy of prospectus
Annexure 6	:	List of documents required for listing along with a copy of listing form.
Annexure 7	:	Application for inviting bankers to act as collecting bankers and their consent format.
Annexure 8	:	List of documents to be filed to Registrar of Companies along with acknowledgement card.
Annexure 9	:	Copy of Form 2A
Annexure 10	:	Copy of compliance reports (Public issue)
Annexure 11	:	Copy of compliance reports (Rights)

ANNEXURE 1

Back up documents required from promoters

Part I

1. Collaboration agreement, if any.
2. Appraisal note.
3. Confirmed order slip.
4. Auditors tax benefits certificate.
5. Auditors report for the last five years.
6. Relevant papers of new industrial policy.
7. Memorandum in terms of new policy submitted.
8. RBI approval of foreign collaboration, if applicable.
9. RBI approval for issue of shares to NRIs.
10. Form 5 for authorised capital.
11. Amount of shares allotted and their respective dates of allotment.
12. Auditor's certificate for the amount bought in by promoters.
13. Promoters undertaking.
14. Promoters certificate for the total number of employees.
15. Promoters bio-data duly signed.
16. Company secretary's certificate.
17. Bio-data of technical and key management personnel.
18. Copy of letter of allotment/for the land covered in the project.
19. List of machines to be procured.
20. Details of orders placed for plant and machinery.
21. Letter with regard to sanctioned loan.
22. No objection certificate from state pollution control board.
23. Schedule of implementation of the project.
24. Deployment of funds and their resources.
25. Projections as envisaged by the company, if any.
26. Promoter's certificate for outstanding litigation.
27. Promoter's certificate for litigation.
28. Promoter's certificate for defaults.
29. Promoter's certificate for material development.
30. Promoter's certificate for miscellaneous aspects.

Part II

31. Consent of : (*a*) Lead manager, (*b*) Co-manager(s),

(*c*) Registrars, (*d*) Bankers to the Company, (*e*) Bankers to the issue, (*f*) Auditors (for inclusion of name, tax report and auditors reports), (*g*) legal advisors, (*h*) Company secretary(s), (*i*) Directors.

32. Form 32 for changes in directorship (C.S. Certificate)
33. For change in auditors, since incorporation (C.S. Certificates)
34. Minutes of special resolution pursuant to Section 81(1A)
35. Working Capital limits.
36. Applications made to any bank for enhancement of working Capital limits, if any.
37. Term loan sanction letters(s).
38. Letters of registrars regarding fees payable.
39. Letters of Lead managers regarding fees payable.
40. Promoters undertaking regarding interest of the promoters and directors.
41. Copy of power of attorney for Signing and Corrections in the prospectus.
42. Copy of Resolution under Section 293(d)(a), if any.
43. Copy of Resolution under Section 293 (1) (c) or 293 (1) (d), if any.
44. Copy of Board resolution authorising the registrar for accepting applications accompanied by stock invest.
45. Solicitors Certificate to the effect that these are no statutory ones dues/outstanding litigations/criminal prosecutions against the directors/company, it applicable.
46. Working results of the collaborators for the last five years.
47. Names of others partnership concerns managed by the promoters.
48. Banker's report of promoters.
49. Profile/bio-data of any foreign directors.

ANNEXURE 2

Questionnaire for work—in clients
(Answer: Yes/No)

Q.1. Do promoters have any past experience in the same industry? If "yes", then please specify the numbers of years.
Q 2. Are the promoters new to the investing public?
Q 3. How was the response to the promoters previous issue (if any)? Rating! (Kindly rate it on a Scale 1-10, 1 means excellent and 10 stands for poor).
Q.4. Were the promoters able to achieve the result as mentioned in the prospectus, in the previous issue?
(*a*) Upto 90 per cent and above.
(*b*) 75 per cent and above.
(*c*) Below 25 per cent.
Q.5. Are these any outstanding liabilities? If "Yes", then please specify
(*a*) Contingent liabilities.
(*b*) Personal liabilities of the promoters.
(*c*) Any others.
Q.6. What is the promoters' state in the present project 20-25/ 25-40/above 40 per cent?
Q.7. Did the promoters sell any part of their holding in the past 12 months?
Q.8. Name a few issues of similar industry, which went public recently (in the past six months) and rate them, as per the investors response (Rating scale: 1-10).
Q.9. Has the project been appraising? If 'yes' then
(*a*) Name the appraising agency and its states.
(*b*) Cost of the issue.
(*c*) Means of finance.
(*d*) Date of commencement of operations.
Q.10. At what capacity utilisation would the Break Even Point (B.E.P.) be achieved?
(*a*) 20-30 per cent
(*b*) 31-40 per cent
(*c*) Above 40 per cent
Q.11. Is the project an export oriented/import substitution?

Q.12. What is the gestation period?
(*a*) 1-2 years
(*b*) 2-4 years
(*c*) 5 years and above

Q.13. What is the status of the land? Owned by the company/or lease?

Q.14. What is the status of the plant and machinery?
(*a*) Indian/Imported
(*b*) Already ordered/to be ordered/received at the site.

Q.15. What is the source of raw material?
(*a*) Near the factory premises.
(*b*) Far away from the factory.
(*c*) Imported.

Q.16. Is the debt-equity ratio high? (more than 2:1)

Q.17. Has the company detained the consent of the bankers with whom it is enjoying the limits?

Q.18. Has the project received all the government approvals!

Q.19. Has the Company obtained the RBI's permission for NRI's participation in the issue (if any)?

Q.20. Has the company got the increase in the authorised capital registered with the ROC?

Q.21. Has the Company tied up for the working capital requirement?

Q.22. What kind of technology is used in the project?
(*a*) New
(*b*) Time tested
(*c*) Foreign collaboration

Q.23. Has the Company entered into any marketing tie up for its product? If "Yes", then is it an MOU/agreement?

Q.24. Is the project liable to receive any concession/benefit/incentive/from the government? If "Yes" then, please specify.

Q.25. The pricing of the issue is based on:
(*a*) Past EPS
(*b*) Net profits
(*c*) Corporate Image
(*d*) Any other.

Q.26. Is the pricing of the issue being done keeping in mind the current trend/scenario?
Rating: (Kindly rate it on a scale of 1-10).

Q.27. Does the listing arrangements provide adequate liquidity?
Rating. (Kindly rate it on a scale of 1-10)

Q.28. If the company is a listed one please give:
  (*a*) The stock market data for the last 6 months.
  (*b*) The past 3 years' financial performance.

Sales Net profit EPS

Also kindly furnish the bankers' confidential report.

ANNEXURE 3

Application to the SEBI along with the list of documents while filing of the draft prospectus.

Securities and Exchange Board of India.
Kailash Building, 4th Floor
Kasturba Gandhi Marg,
New Delhi-110001

Reg: Public issue of (number of equity shares) equity shares of Rs. (face value) each for cash at par aggregating to Rs. (amount in lakh) by (name of the company)

Dear sir,

We formed herewith the undermentioned documents for your scrutiny and approval:

1. Draft prospectus.
2. Certificate of due diligent alongwith annexure.
3. Statement of *inter se* allocation of responsibilities.
4. Confirmation and compliance of the SEBI guidelines.
5. Undertaking from company regarding: (*a*) redressal of investors' grievances, (*b*) provision of funds to registrar for despatch of refund order/tellers of allotment/certificates by U.P.C./registered post, (*c*) getting the instruments of the proposed issue listed within the prescribed time period, (*d*) Promoters' contribution to be brought in full before the subscription list opens.
6. Copy of the MOU entered into between the company and us.
7. Undertaking from Lead manager(s) to get the public issue fully underwritten and to include details thereof in the final prospectus.

We shall arrange to get the issue underwritten and shall finalise the underwriters list/the bankers to the issue/co-managers to the issue keeping in view the SEBI guidelines issue for this purpose.

Kindly accord your approval at an early date.

Yours faithfully,

For (Names of the merchant banker)
(Name of the person concerned and designation)

ANNEXURE 3(A)

Copy of the Due Diligence

Securities and Exchange Board of India
Kailash Building, 4th Floor
Kasturba Gandhi Marg
New Delhi-110001

Dear Sirs,

Certificate of due diligence of Public Issue of Equity Shares of XYZ Limited.

We, the undernoted lead manager(s) to the above mentioned forth coming issue, state as follows:

1. We have examined various documents including those relating to litigation like commercial disputes, patent disputes with collaborators, etc., and other materials in connection with the finalisation of the draft prospectus pertaining to the said issue.
2. On the basis of such examination and the discussion with the company, the directors and other officers, other agencies, independent verification of the statements concerning the objects of the issue, projected profitability, price justification and the contents of the document mentioned in the annexure and other papers furnished by the company.

We confirm that:

(*a*) The draft prospectus forwarded to the SEBI is in conformity with the documents, materials and papers relevant to the issue.

(*b*) All the legal requirements connected with the said issue as also the guidelines, instructions, etc., issued by the SEBI, the Government and any other competent authority in this behalf have been duly complied with; and

(*c*) The disclosures made in the draft prospectus are true, fair and adequate to enable the investors to make a well informed decision as to the investment in the proposed issue.

3. We confirm that besides ourselves, all the intermediaries named in the prospectus are registered with the SEBI and that till date such registration is valid.
4. We have satisfied ourselves about the worth of the underwriters to fulfil their underwriting commitments;

For,

Name of the Merchant Banker and the name of the person concerned.

Annexure to the due diligence Certificate:

1. Memorandum and articles of association of the company.
2. Letter of intent/SIA registration/foreign collaboration approval/approval for import of plant and machinery, if applicable.
3. Necessary clearances from governmental, statutory, municipal authorities, etc., for implementation of the project, wherever applicable.
4. Documents in support of the track record and experience of the promoters and their professional competence.
5. Listing agreement of the company for existing securities are the stock exchange.
6. Consent letters from company's auditors, bankers to the issue, bankers to the company, lead managers, brokers and where applicable, proposed trustees.
7. Applications made by the company to the financial institutions/ banks for financial assistance as per object of the issue and copies of relative sanction letters.
8. Underwriting letters from the proposed underwriters to the issue.
9. Latest audited balance sheet of the company.
10. Auditors' certificate regarding tax benefits available to the company, members and NRIs.
11. Certificate from architects or any other competent authority or project implementation schedule furnished by the company, if applicable.
12. Reports from government agencies/expert agencies/ consultants/company regarding market demand and supply for the product, industrial scenario, standing of foreign collaborations, etc.

13. Documents in support of the infrastructural facilities, raw material availability etc.
14. Auditors report indicating summary of audited accounts for the period including that of subsidiaries of the company.
15. Stock exchange quotations of the last three years duly certified by the regional stock exchange in case of an existing company.
16. Application to the RBI and approval thereof for allotment of shares to non-residents, if any, as also for collaboration terms and conditions.
17. Minutes of the meeting of board and general body of the company for matters which are in the prospectus.
18. A certificate from a director (for particulars of directorship).
19. Revaluation certificates of company's assets given by Government values or any approved values.
20. Environmental clearance as given by pollution control board of the state government as the central government, as applicable.
21. Certificate from company's solicitors in regard to compliance of legal provisions of the prospectus as also applicability of FERA/MRTP provisions to the company.
22. Other documents, reports, etc. as are relevant, necessary for true, fair and adequate disclosures in the prospectus.
23. True copy of the board resolution passed by the issuer authorising a representative of the registrars to act on behalf in relation to handling of stock-invests.

Place: For ABC Merchant Bankers Ltd.
Dated:

ANNEXURE 3(B)

Statement of *Inter se* Allocation of Reponsibilities between the Lead Managers

Reg: Public issue of (number of equity shares) equity shares of Rs. (face value) each for cash at par aggregating to Rs. (amount in lakh) by (name of the company).

We are the sole lead managers to the capital issue. The *inter se* allocation responsibilities as follows:

(*a*) Capital structuring with the relative components and formalities such as composition of debt and equity, type of instruments, etc.

(*b*) Drafting and design of prospectus and of advertisement of material including newspaper advertisement and brochure. The designated lead manager shall ensure compliance with stipulated requirements and completion of prescribed formalities with stock exchange, registrar of companies and the SEBI.

(*c*) Marketing of the issue, which will cover, *inter alia*, formulating marketing strategies, preparation of publicity budget, arrangement for selection of (*i*) advertisement media, (*ii*) bankers to the issue, (*iii*) collection centres.

(*d*) Tieing up underwriting arrangement and invoking underwriting obligations.

(*e*) Selection of various agencies connected with the issue, namely registrars to the issue, printers and advertising agencies.

(*f*) Following up with bankers to the issue to get quick estimates of collections and advising the issues about closure of the issue, based in the correct figures.

(*g*) The post-issue activities will involve essential follow-up steps, which must include listing of certificate and refunds, with the various agencies connected with the work such as registers to the issue and the bank handling refund business. Even if many of these activities would be handled by others intermediaries, the designated lead manager shall be responsible for ensuring that these agencies fulfil their functions and enable him to discharge his responsibility through suitable arrangement with the issuer Company.

For ABC Merchant Bankers Ltd.

ANNEXURE 3(C)

Memorandum of understanding between the Lead Manager to the issue and the Issuer

Where as:

1. The Company is taking steps for the issue of (number of shares) equity shares of Rs. each for cash at par aggregating to Rs. lakh to the public, the said issue of shares here in after referred to as "The Issue", and
2. The Company has approached the lead manager to manage the issue and the lead manager has accepted the engagement *inter alia* subject to the company, entering into a memorandum of understanding for the purpose here in presented.

Now, therefore, the Company and the lead manager do hereby agree as follows:

(*i*) Besides the lead managers, the co-managers/advisors to the issue, if any, will be appointed at a later date.

(*ii*) The company hereby declares that it has complied/will comply with all the statutory formalities under the Companies Act, guidelines for disclosure and investor protection issued by the SEBI and other relevant statutes to enable it to make the issue and in particular in respect of the following matters.

Statutory Requirements:

(*a*) Conversion of the company from private limited to public limited.

(*b*) Shareholders' resolution under Section 81(1)(a) of the Companies Act, 1956.

(*c*) Approval of memorandum and articles of association from the stock exchange upon alteration of relevant clauses such as capital clause, names clause, etc.

(*d*) SEBI acknowledgement of the draft prospectus.

(*e*) Compliance with the provisions of the Companies Act regarding the appointment of each director/each change in the board of directors since its incorporation.

(*f*) Compliance with the Companies Act, regarding the appointment of auditor/each change in auditors since incorporation.

(*g*) Filing initial listing application with the stock exchange along with the initial listing fees.
(*h*) Filing the draft prospectus and a copy of all material contracts and documents as detailed in the prospectus with the ROC and obtaining an acknowledgement from ROC.
(*i*) Compliance with the stipulations made by stock exchanges vide announcement of issue, security deposit, stationary requirement, etc.

3. The Company undertakes and declares that any information made available to the lead manager or any statement made in the offered documents would be complete in all respects and would be true and correct, and that under no circumstances it would give or withhold any information or statement which is, likely to mislead the investors.
4. The Company also undertakes to furnish complete audited annual report(s), other relevant documents, papers, information relating to pending litigations, etc., to enable the lead manager to corroborate the information and statements given in the offer documents.
5. The company shall, if so required, extend such facilities as may be called for by the lead manager(s) to enable him to visit the plant site, office of the company or such other place(s) to ascertain for himself the true state of affairs of the company including the progress made in respect of project implementation, status and other facts relevant to the issue.
6. The company shall extend all necessary facilities to the lead manager to interact on any matter relevant to the issue with the solicitors/legal advisors, auditors, co-managers, consultants, advisors to the issue, the financial institutions, banks or any other organisation and also with any other intermediaries who may be associated with the issue in any capacity whatsoever.
7. The Company shall ensure that all advertisements prepared and released by the advertising agency or otherwise in connection with the issue confirm to the regulations, guidelines, etc., issued by the SEBI and instructions given by the lead manager(s) from time to time and that it shall not make any misleading, incorrect statement in the advertisement, press releases, or in any materials relating to the issue or at any press/brokers/investors' conference.
8. The Company shall not, without prior approval of the lead manager, appoint other intermediaries or other persons such as

registrars to the issuing bankers to the issue, refund bankers, advertising agencies, printers for printing application forms, allotment advices/allotment letters, share certificates/debentures certificates, refund orders or any other instruments, circulars or advices.

9. Whenever required, the company shall, in consultation with the lead manager, enter into a memorandum of understanding with the concerned intermediary associated with the issue, clearly setting forth their mutual rights, responsibilities and obligations. A certified true copy of such memorandum shall be furnished to the lead managers.
10. The company shall take such steps are necessary to ensure the completion of allotment and refund orders to the applicants including NRI's, soon after the basis of allotment has been approved by the stock exchanges and in any case not later than the statutory time limit and in the event of failure to do so pay interest to the applicants or provided under the Companies Act, 1956.
11. The company shall take steps to pay the underwriting commission and brokerage to the underwriters and stock brokers etc. within a responsible time.
12. The Company undertakes to furnish such information and particulars, regarding the issue as may be required by the lead manager to enable him to file a report with the SEBI in respect of the issue.
13. The company shall keep the lead manager informed if it encounters any problems due to dislocation of communication system or any other material adverse circumstances which is likely to prevent or which has prevented the company from complying with the obligations, whether statutory or contractual, in respect of the matters pertaining to allotment, despatch of refund orders/share certificates/debenture certificate, etc.
14. The company shall not resort to any legal proceedings in respect of any matter having a bearing on the issue except in consultation with and after receipt of advice from the lead managers.

ANNEXURE 3(D)

Rights of Lead Manager(s)

1. The lead manager reserves the right to withdraw from the issue in the capacity of lead manager if it is found at any point of time that the disclosures made by the company are not correct, incomplete or involve misrepresentation of facts.
2. The lead manager also reserves the right to withdraw from the issue of it is found that the company has intentionally or otherwise concealed information which is not in the interest of the company, investors and/or the lead manager.
3. The company will decide the issue opening date in consultations with the lead manager and will abide by the decision of the lead manager. In the event, the company decides to go against such decision, the lead manager reserves the right to notify and agencies connected with the issues, underwriters and the SEBI of the breach.
4. The fees payable to the lead manager, will be Rs.......... which is to be paid in the following manner:
   (*i*) Rs............. of the time of filing of prospectus with the SEBI.
   (*ii*) Rs.............at the time of filing of prospectus with ROC.
   (*iii*) Rs............. on closure of the issue.
   Over and above the issue management fees and incidental fees, the company shall also reimburse all, out-of-pocket expenses incurred by the lead manager, in the event of any breach by the company in the above mentioned manner of payment, the lead manager reserves the right to advise the collecting banker to withhold the issue proceeds.
5. The Company will be required to obtain a written statement from the lead manager in respect of the date of closure of the issue. The advertising agency will release the closing advertisement only on the advice of the lead manager. The lead manager reserves the right to notify the SEBI of any breach on the part of the advertising agency as well as of the company. If the company proceeds with the closing of the issue at a date not agreed upon mutually with the lead manager, the lead manager will not be responsible for the consequences resulting out of such a decision.

6. The lead manager shall be released of all obligations towards the company if the company acts upon a decision at any point of time in any manner contrary to the terms agreed with the lead manager.

ANNEXURE 3 (E)

Consequences of Breach

1. In the event of breach, in addition to the consequences stated above, the lead manager shall reserve the right to represent the case to the SEBI, the stock exchange, the ROC and other regulatory bodies against the company and/or any other agencies corrected with the issue or the matter under dispute.
2. The lead manager can also represent the case to the concerned legal authorities against the company and/or any other agencies connected with the issue on the matter under dispute.
3. The lead manager, if he finds it appropriates, shall advise the collecting banks to withhold the issue proceeds until such time that the dispute has been clarified. The lead manager can also represent the matter to the SEBI, if it feels so, for an intervention from the SEBI in respect of the dispute.
4. The underwriting commitment of the lead manager shall stand withdrawn if the company decides upon the issue closure date on the own and the issue is not filling subscribed.

For ABC Co. Ltd.	For XYZ Merchant Bankers Ltd.
Managing Director	Director
Date:	
Place:	

ANNEXURE 3(F)

Compliance Certificates by the Lead Manager

Securities and Exchange Board of India
Kailash Building, 4th Floor
Kasturba Gandhi Marg
New Delhi-110001

Dear Sirs,

Reg: Public issue of (number of equity shares) equity shares of Rs. (face value) each for cash at par aggregating to Rs. (amount in lakhs) by (name of the Company).

With respect to the above, we hereby confirm that the SEBI, guidelines in respect of disclosure and investor protection and all the clarifications issued by the SEBI till date, have been complied with.

Yours faithfully,
For XYZ Merchant Bankers Ltd.

ANNEXTURE 3(G)

Compliance Certificate by the Company

To,
Name and address of the Lead Manager

Dear Sir,

I, ... in my capacity as managing director of ABC Company Ltd. hereby undertake that requisite funds will be made available by the company to the registrars to the issue for the purpose of despatch of allotment letter(s)/refund order(s)/share certificate(s) by U.P.C./registered post as applicable.

For ABC Ltd.

....

Managing Director

To,
Name and Address of the Lead Manager

Dear Sir,

I, ..., in my capacity or managing director of M/s. ABC Ltd. do hereby undertake that all investors grievances and complaints, received in respect of the issue would be attended to expeditiously and satisfactorily.

For ABC Ltd.

....

Managing Director

To,
Securities and Exchange Board of India
Kailash Building, 4th Floor
Kasturba Gandhi Marg
New Delhi-110001

Proposed Public Issue of ABC Co. Limited.

I, ..., in my capacity as managing director ABC Ltd., do hereby undertake that the equity shares of the proposed public issue shall be listed on stock exchanges within the prescribed time period and all necessary steps be taken and compliance be made to this effect.

For ABC Ltd.

....

Managing Director

To,
Name and address of the Lead Manager

Dear Sir,

The undersigned in my capacity as the promoter/director of ABC Ltd. do hereby undertake the following:

1. Once the SEBI acknowledgement card is issued, no advertisement relating to the issue shall be released without giving risk factors in respect of the concerned issue.
2. Issue advertisement shall not certain any matter or matters which is/are extraneous to the contents of the offer documents.
3. The all advertisements, equal treatment in all respects shall be given to the risk factors and highlights.
4. No advertisement would include any issue slogans and brand names in the issue except the normal commercial name of the company or commercial brand names of the products already in use. The advertisements shall also not make use of models/ celebrities etc.
5. In case there is a reservation for NRIs, the issue advertisement shall specify the same and indicate the source in India from where the individual NRI applicant can procure application forms.

6. We shall also strictly comply with the instructions (*i*) Non-publishing of any advertisement in newspapers to the effect/ of the nature that the issue has been over subscribed, and (*ii*) advertisement between the date of announcement of the issue and the date of closure of the issue.
7. I shall release the following advertisements at least in two all India newspapers.

   Advertisement giving full details relating to over subscription, basis of allotment, number, value and percentage of applications received along with stock investment, number, value and percentage of successful allotees who have applied through stock invest, date of completion of despatch of refund orders, date of despatch of certificates and date of filing of listing application. Such advertisement shall be released by us within 10 days from the date of completion of the various activities.
8. Recommendation and approval of the lead manager will be sought before releasing any issue related advertisement to the print India.

For ABC Ltd.
Managing Director

ANNEXURE 4

Questionnaire to be got filled by the promoters during the site visit. (Yes/No)

Q.1. (*a*) Do the promoters have any past experience in the same line? If 'Yes', then please specify the number of years.
(*b*) What kind of products would be manufactured?
(*c*) What is the plant capacity? (please also specify the units).
(*d*) What is the plant situated?
(*e*) How much manpower is in use/would be there skilled, semi-skilled; unskilled?

Q.2. Were these any labour problems in the past? If 'Yes', there are they solved now?

Q.3. How do you sale the market potential for the product? Rating: (Kindly rate it as a scale of 1-10; 1 means excellent and 10 stands for poor).

Q.4. Funds collected by the issue would be utilised for (*a*) expansion, (*b*) diversification (*c*) modernisation, (*d*) any other.

Q.5. Do you have interest in the management of any other listed/ unlisted company? (If Yes, please specify.)

Q.6. What would be your participation in the project, 25 per cent/ 26-40 per cent/above 40 per cent?

Q.7. Has the project been appraised? If "Yes", then name the appraising agency and its stoke.

Q.8. At what capacity utilisation is the B.E.P. achieved: (*a*) 20-30 per cent, (*b*) 31-40 per cent (*c*) above 40 per cent?

Q.9. Is the project an export oriented/import substitution are?

Q.10. Did the promoters sell any part of their holding in the past 12 months?

Q.11. What is the gestation period: 1-2 years/2-4 years/5 years and above?

Q.12. What is the status of the land: owned by the company/leased?

Q.13. What is the status of the plant and machinery: (*a*) Indian/ imported, (*b*) already ordered/to be ordered/received at the site?

Q.14. Has the project received all the government approvals?

Q.15. Have the assets been revalued for issue of the bonus issue? If 'Yes', then please specify the bonus ratio?

Q.16. Has any change been brought about in the accounting policies of the company? If 'Yes' then please specify.

Q.17. What is the source of raw materials: near the factory premises/far off place/imported?

Q.18. Is the debt-equity ratio high (more than 2:1)?

Q.19. Has RBI given the required permission for the foreign collaboration?

Q.20. What kind of technology is used in the project: New/time tested/foreign collaboration?

Q.21. Has the company entered into any marketing tie-up for its product? If 'Yes', then is it an MOU/agreement?

Q.22. Is the project liable to receive any concession/benefit/incentive/from the government?

Q.23. What kind of instrument would you like to propose: equity shares/preference shares/debentures? If debentures is your choice, then what could you prefer FCD/PCD/NCD? So please specify the rate of interest.

Q.24. If the company is a listed one, please give:

(*a*) The stock market data for the last 6 months.

(*b*) The past 3 year financial performance:

Sales	Net profit	EPS

Kindly also furnish the bankers confidential report.

NOTE

Annexure 5 deals with "prospectus" of issuing company. There is no specific model for incorporating in this context. It should be prepared by the issuing company as per Section 2(36) of the Companies Act. It appears in Annexure 9.

ANNEXURE 6(A)

Documents and information required from Secretarial department for Listing

1. Fifteen copies of memorandum and articles of association of the company.
2. Copies of statutory advertisement.
3. Copy of the statement in lieu of prospectus.
4. Fifteen copies of the balance sheet with directors report for the last five years.
5. Certificate of expenses.
6. Certificate of allotment made according to the basis of allotment.
7. Certificate of defacement for non-transferable shares.

ANNEXURE 6(B)

Application for Listing on Exchange for New Companies

LETTER OF APPLICATIONS
(APPENDIX-C TO REGULATION-2)
REGULATION-1

From: Date:

To

Dear Sir,

In conformity with the listing requirements of the stock exchange, we hereby apply for admission of the following securities of the company to dealings on the exchange.

ANNEXTURE 7

Request and Consent of the Collecting Bankers

To,
(Name of the banker concerned and address)

Reg: Public issue of (Number of equity shares) equity shares of Rs. (face value) each for cash at par aggregating to Rs. (amount in lakh) by (name of the company).

Dear Sir,

We are pleased to inform you that we are acting as sole lead managers to the captioned issue which is expected to open on the (date). We have already received the SEBI acknowledgement card for the issue.

In view of our long association with you, we will be pleased to appoint you as one of the bankers to the issue. Kindly give your acceptance at the earliest. Please also furnish a certificate and your consent in the enclosed formats.

Thanking you.

Yours faithfully,
(Name of the Merchant Bankers)
(Name of the person concerned and designation).

To,
The Lead Manager

Reg: Public issue of (number of equity shares) equity shares of Rs. (face value) each for cash at par aggregating to Rs. (amount in lakh) by (name of the company).

Dear Sir,

With reference to the captioned subject, we hereby confirm as under:

(*a*) We are authorised to act as bankers to an issue in accordance with the provision of sub-section (i) of Section 12 of the SEBI Act, 1992.

(*b*) We will accept applications accompanied by stock invest.
(*c*) We will perform all duties connected with the work of bankers to an issue, including preparation of collection statement, reconciliation and listing separately instrument-wise applications.

Yours faithfully

....

(Bankers)

To,
The Board of Directors
(Name of the Company and address)

Reg: Public issue of (number of equity shares) equity share of Rs. (face value) each for cash at par aggregating to Rs. (amount is lakh) by (name of the company).

Dear Sir,

We hereby give our consent to act as bankers to the issue for the captioned public issue and our name to be included in the prospectus as bankers to the issue.

We further authorise the company to deliver a copy of this consent to the Registrar of Companies, Delhi and Haryana at New Delhi pursuant to Section 60 of the Companies Act, 1956.

Thanking you.

Yours faithfully,

(Banker)

ANNEXURE 8

Documents required for filing the prospectus, with ROC

1. Consent of:
   (*a*) Lead manager(s), (*b*) Co-manager(s), (*c*) Registrars, (*d*) Bankers to the Company, (*e*) Auditors, (*f*) Bankers to the issue, (*g*) Legal advisors, (*h*) Company secretary, (*i*) Directors, (*j*) Underwriters.
2. Copies of power of attorney for signing and corrections in the prospectus.
3. Copy of the board resolution authorising the registrar for accepting applications accompanied with stock-invest.
4. RBI approval for issue of shares to NRIs (if applicable).
5. Stock exchange approval of MOU and Articles of Association (AoA) and draft prospectus where the listing is proposed.

ANNEXURE 9

FORM 2A

Memorandum containing salient features of the prospectus [see Section 56(3)]

I. General Information: (*a*) Name and address of registered office of the company; (*b*) Issue listed at (name of the stock exchange); (*c*) opening, closing and earliest closing dates of the issue; (*d*) Name and address of Lead managers; (*e*) Name and address of trustees under debenture trust deeds (in the case of debentures/issue); (*f*) Rating for the debenture/ preference shares, if any, obtained from crisis and any recognised rating agency.

II. Capital structure of the Company
   (*a*) Issued, subscribed and paid-up capital;
   (*b*) Size of present issue giving separately reservation for preferential allotment to promoters and others;
   (*c*) Paid-up capital; (*i*) after the present issue, (*ii*) after conversion of debentures (if applicable).

III. Terms of the Present Issue—(*a*) Authority for the issues terms of payments and procedure and time schedule for allotment and issue of certificates; (*b*) How to apply availability of forms, prospectus and made of payment; (*c*) special tax benefits to company and shareholders under the Income-tax Act, if any.

IV. Particulars of the Issue—(*a*) Objects of the issue, (*b*) Project cost, means of financing (including contribution of promoters).

V. Company, Management and Project—(*a*) History, main objects and present business of the company; (*b*) Background of promoters, managing director/wholetime director and names of nominees of institutions, if any, on the board of directors; (*c*) Location of the project; (*d*) Plant and machinery, technology, process etc.; (*e*) Collaboration performance guarantee, if any, or assistance in marketing by the collaborators; (*f*) Infrastructure facilities for raw materials and utilities like water, electricity, etc; (*g*) Schedule of implementation of the project and progress made so far, giving details of land acquisition, execution of civil works, installation of plant and machinery, trial production, date of commercial production, if any; (*h*) the products: (*i*) Nature of product(s); consumer/ industrial and end-users; (*ii*) Existing, licensed and installed capacity of the product, demand of the product as existing, and estimated in the coming years as estimated by a Government authority and by any other reliable institution, giving source of the information, (*iii*) Approach of marketing and proposed marketing set up. In case of Company providing services, relevant information in regard to nature/extent of services, etc., to be furnished. Prospectus—the expected year when the company would be able to earn net profit, declare dividend.

VI. Financial Performance of the Company for the Last Five Years (Figures to be taken from the audited annual accounts in tabular form):
   (*a*) Balance sheet data: equity capital, reserves (State revaluation reserve, the year of revaluation and its monetary effect on assets) and borrowings;
   (*b*) Profit and loss data: sales, gross profit, net profit, dividend paid, if any;
   (*c*) Any change in accounting policies during the last three years and their effect on the profits and the reserves of the company;
   (*d*) Stock market quotation of shares/debentures of the company, if any (high/low price in each of the last three years and monthly high/low price during the last six months).

VII. Whether all payments/refunds, debentures, fixed deposits, interest on fixed deposits, debentures interest, institutional dues have been paid upto date, if not, details of the arrears if any, to be stated.

VIII. Following particulars in regard to the listed companies under the same Management within the meaning of section 370(B) which made any Capital issue in the last three years:
   (*a*) Name of the company;
   (*b*) Year of issue;
   (*c*) Type of issue (public/rights/composite);
   (*d*) Amount of issue;
   (*e*) Date of closure of issue;

(*f*) Date of dispatch of shares/debentures certificate completed;
(*g*) Date of completion of the project, where project of the issue was financing of a project;
(*h*) Rate of dividend paid.

IX. Management Perceptions of risk factors:(*e.g.*, sensitivity to foreign exchange rate fluctuations, difficulty in the availability of raw materials or in the marketing of products.

If the company does not receive application money for at least 90 per cent of the issued amount, the entire subscription will be refunded to the applicants within ninety days from the date of closure of the issue.

If there is delay in the refund of application money, by more than 8 days after the company, becomes liable to pay the excess amount, the company will pay interest for the delayed period, at prescribed rates in sub-section (2) and (2a) of Section 73. No statement made in the form shall contravene any of the provisions of the Companies Act, 1956, and the rules made thereunder.

Place: Signatures of Directors
Date:

ANNEXURE 10(A)

Public Issue: 3-Day Monitoring Report

Subscription status: (subscribed/unsubscribed)

Responsibility; Post-issue lead manager (to be submitted in duplicate within 3 days from closure of the public issue)

1. Name of issuer company
2. Issue opening date
3. Earliest closing date
4. Actual closing date
5. Date of filing prospectus with ROC
6. Issue details (as per the prospectus):

6.1. Nature of instrument: (Equity/FCD/PCD/NCD/other)

6.2. Offer price per instrument for different categories

6.3. Amount per instrument on application for different categories

6.4. Issue size (Rs. Lakh) : (*a*) (*i*) Promoter's contribution, (*ii*) Date of submission of auditors certificate to the SEBI for receipt of promoter's contribution; (*b*) (*i*) Amount through offer document (including reserved categories and net public offer), (*ii*) Reserved category: Amount reserve (Rs. Lakh): (*iii*) Net public offer.

	Firm basis	Competitive basis
Mutual Funds		
FIs/Banks		
FIIs		
NRIs/OCBs		
Employees		
Others (Please specify)		

7. (a) Provisional subscription: Details of net public offer (including unsubscribed position of reserved categories): (*i*) Total amount to be collected on application (Rs. lakh); (*ii*) Amount collected on application, (Rs. lakh); (*iii*) Percentage subscribed, i.e. of (*ii*) to (*i*).
8. Please tick mark whether 90 percentage minimum subscription of the amount through offer document is collected.

(*i*) Yes (*ii*) No

Lead Manager(s)
(Name, Signature and Seal)

Date:
Place:

Note: It is the responsibility of the lead manager(s) to give correct information after verifying it from the company and the Registrar to the issue.

ANNEXURE 10(B)

Public Issue: 78 Day post-issue Monitoring Report

Subscription status: (Subscribed/under subscribed)
Responsibility: Post-issue Lead Manager(s)
(To be submitted in duplicate within 78 days from the closure of the public issue).

1. Name of the Company:
2. Issue opening date:
3. Actual closing date:
4. 3-day report: (*i*) Due on, (*ii*) Submitted on
5. Number of collecting banks. Also specify number of bank branches.
6. Bank-wise names of branches which did not submit final consolidated certificate within 21 days from closure of issue and mention the dates when they actually submitted.
7. Subscription details:
   (*a*) Public offer (net) [including unsubscribed position of resourced category added back to net public offer] [Rs. Lakh]:
      (i) Number of applications received.
      (ii) Number of instruments applied for.
      (iii) Amount of subscription received (Rs. Lakh).
      (iv) Number of times issue subscribed, Number of instruments applied for/Number of instruments under net public offer category.
      (v) Number of applications accompanied by stockinvests.
      (vi) Number of instruments applied through stockinvests.
      (vii) Amounts of subscription received through stockinvests (Rs. Lakh)
      (viii) Percentage of subscription through stockinvests in total subscription.
   (*b*) Information relating to reserved categories:

Reservation to	Number of applicants	Number of instruments applied	Amount subscribed
NRIs			
FIs			
FIIs			
MFs			
Employees			
Others (specify)			

8. The firm allottees who did not meet their commitments through mentioned in the prospectus (please give their names and amount and whether the promoters have subscribed to that amount before opening of the issue).
9. Actual date of finalisation on the basis of allotment (enclose copy).
10. Allotment details:
    10.1 Number of successful allottees per 1 lakh shares.
    10.2 Number of successful allottees from stockinvest applicants.
    10.3 Number of instruments allotted to stockinvest applicants.
    10.4 Percentage of stockinvest allottees in total allottees.
    10.5 Number of unsuccessful allottees: (*a*) Refund order, (*b*) Cancelled stockinvest, (*c*) Certificate/allotment letter, (*d*) Certificate/allotment letter against application by stockinvest, (*e*) Reasons for delay in despatch, if any, (*f*) Whether interest paid for delayed period, if so, for which period.
11. If there is a reservation for NRI, date(s) of completion of despatch of:
    11.1 Refund orders
    11.2 Cancelled stockinvests
    11.3 Certificate/allotment letters.
    11.4 Reasons for delay in despatch, if any.
    11.5 Whether interest paid for delayed period.
    11.6 Date of submission of application to the RBI for approval for despatch of share certificates.
    11.7 Date of approval received from RBI.
12. Amount of refund due (Rs. lakh).
13. Refund banker(s) (name and address).
14. Date of transfer of refund amount to refund bankers, if any.
15. Date of completion of despatch of refund orders/cancelled stockinvests.
16. Name of regional stock exchange.
17. Name of other stock exchange where listing is sought.
18. Date on which application was filed with each stock exchange for listing of instruments.
19. Date when listing and trading permission given by each stock exchange (enclose copies of permission letters of stock exchanges).

20. Reasons for delay in listing for trading, if any.

To be filled up in case of under subscribed issue only

1. If the issue is underwritten, mention the amount of issue underwritten.
2. Extent of under subscription on the date of closure of the issue: (*a*) percentage, (*b*) amount.
3. Total number of underwriters.
4. If devolvement notices had not been issued, mention how the shortfall was met.
5. Number of underwriters to whom development notices had been issued.
6. Date of issue devolvement notices.
7. Number of underwriters who did not pay devolvement (please give names, amount of underwriters and reasons for not paying).
8. In case of default from underwriters, mention how the shortfall was met.
9. In case where FIs/MFs had subscribed to make up shortfall not as underwriter (*a*) Name of FI/MF, (*b*) Number of instruments applied for, (*c*) Amount received.

Certified that the information given above and also in the enclosures are true to the best of our knowledge and no refund order/allotment letters/certificates are pending for despatch in respect of the issue.

Certified that shares to be locked-in are duly inscribed with the words. Share cannot be hypothecated/transferred till.........

Date: Lead Manager(s)

Place: (Name, Signature and Seal)

Note: It is the responsibility of the lead manager(s) to give correct information after verifying it from the company and the registrar to the issue.

Please enclose:

Certificate from the refund bankers that the amount of refund due from the company to investors is deposited in a separate account giving details of the total amount deposited in the account and date of deposit.

ANNEXURE 11(A)

Rights Issue: 3-day Monitoring Report.

Subscription Status: Subscribed/unsubscribed.

Responsibility: Post-issue lead manager.

(To be submitted in duplicate within 3-days from closure of rights issue).

1. Name of the Company
2. Issue opening date
3. Actual closing date.
4. Date of filing letter of offer with the stock exchange.
5. Issue details (as per the letter of offer):
   - 5.1 Basis of offer (ratio)
   - 5.2 Nature of instrument: (Equity/FCD/PCD/NCD/Others, etc.)
   - 5.3 Offer price per instrument.
   - 5.4 Amount per instrument on application.
   - 5.5 Issue size (Rs. Lakh)
6. Record date.
7. Provisional subscription details of the issue:
   - (*i*) Total amount to be collected on application (Rs. lakh).
   - (*ii*) Amount collected on application (Rs. lakh).
   - (*iii*) Percentage subscribed, *i.e.*, percentage of (*ii*) to (*iv*).
   - (*iv*) Please tick mark whether 90 per cent minimum subscription collected: (*i*) Yes, (*ii*) No.

Date: Lead Manager(s)

Place: (Name, Signature and Seal)

Note:

It is the responsibility of the lead manager(s) to give correct information after verifying it from the Company and the registrar to the issue.

ANNEXURE 11(B)

Rights Issue: 50-Day Post-Issue Monitoring Report
Subscription Status: Subscribed/unsubscribed
Responsibility: Post-issue lead manager.

(To be submitted in duplicate within 50 days from closure of rights issue).

1. Name of the Company:
2. Issue opening date:
3. Actual closing date:
4. Issue details (as per the letter of offer):
   4.1 Basis of offer
   4.2 Nature of instrument: (Equity/FCD/PCD/NCD/etc.)
   4.3 Offer price per instrument.
   4.4 Amount per instrument on application.
   4.5 Issue size (Rs. in lakh)
5. 3-day report (*i*) due on; (*ii*) submitted on.
6. Number of collecting banks (also specify number of bank branches).
7. Bank-wise names of branches which did not submit final consolidated certificate within 21 days from closure of issue and mention the dates when they actually submitted.
8. Details of subscription: (*i*) Percentage of rights taken up by (*a*) promoters, (*b*) other shareholders; (*ii*) percentage of rights renounced by (*a*) promoters, (*b*) others; (*iii*) Percentage of rights taken by shareholders/renounces; (*iv*) percentage of the disposal of the board; (*v*) Out of the unsubscribed portion as in; (*vi*) above, taken by (*a*) promoters, (*b*) others.
9. Promoters shareholders: Number of shares, percentage (*a*) prior to the issue, (*b*) on expanded capital after the rights issue.
10. Date of finalisation of allotment (enclose copy on the basis of allotment).
11. (*a*) Name and address of refund banker, (*b*) amount of refund due, (*c*) date of transfer of refund amount to refund banker, if any.
12. Actual date(s) of completion of despatch of (*a*) refund orders, (*b*) certificate/allotment letters, (*c*) reasons for delay in despatch, if any, (*d*) whether interest paid for delayed period,

if so, for which period.

13. Name of regional stock exchange.
14. Names of other stock exchanges where listing is sought.
15. 42nd day from the date of closure of the issue.
16. Date on which application was filed with each stock exchange for listing of instruments.
17. Date when listing and trading permission given by each stock exchange (enclose copies of permission letters of stock exchanges).
18. Reasons for delay in listing for trading, if any.

    Issue only:

    (*i*) Extent of under subscription to be filled up in case of under subscribed on the date of closure of the issue (*a*) Percentage, (*b*) amount.

    (*ii*) Details of stand by assistance, if any (*a*) Number of under writers, (*b*) Number of underwriters who did not pay devolvement (please give names, amount underwritten and reasons for not paying).

    (*iii*) In case where FIs/MFs had subscribed to make shortfall not as underwriter (*a*) Name of FI/MF, (*b*) Number of instruments applied for, (*c*) Amount received.

Certified that the information given above and also in the enclosures are true to the best of our knowledge and no refund orders/allotment letters/certificates are pending for despatch in respect of the issue certificate that shares to be locked in are duly inscribed with the words "share cannot be hypothecated/transferred/sold till.........

Date: Lead Manager

Place: (Name, Signature and Seal)

Note: It is the responsibility of the lead manager(s) to give correct information after verifying it from the company and the registrar to the issue.

Please enclose:

Certificate from the refund banker that the amount of refund due from the company to investors is deposited in a separate account giving details of the total amount deposited in the account and date of deposit.

B. SECONDARY MARKET

Introduction

The Secondary Market is an important component of the capital market. The stock exchanges are known as the secondary markets. They play an important role in the securities trading. In the stock exchanges, the government securities, municipalities, investment trusts, port-trusts and other public and financial instruments are traded.

The stock exchange is a medium of transfer of resources for the securities. In the stock exchanges, securities issued in the primary markets are bought and sold. It does not create any financial claim. Purchases and sales of the existing stocks and bonds occur in the secondary market. Transaction in the secondary markets do not provide funds to the Corporate Sector. But the strong secondary market movements create a high demand for the New issue market. The **NIM and the stock exchanges** inter-link and work together. They cannot be demarked as two separate units. In this market, the public can buy and sell the securities. It is the resale market for shares and bonds. It represents an organised market in trading the securities. In the Stock exchange the trading is carried on by the member of the exchange. It is an association or organisation of members to carry on trade in the securities. The securities are traded under certain set of rules and regulations. The definitions of the stock exchange are:

The Securities Contract (Regulation) Act, 1956—"Stock exchange means an association, organisation or body of individuals whether incorporated or not; established for the purpose of assisting, regulating and controlling the business in buying, selling and dealing the securities."

According to **J. F. Pyle**: "Security exchanges are the market places where the securities that have been listed there on may be bought and sold for either investment or speculation."

Functions of the Stock Exchange

The stock exchange is established for the purpose of providing a market place. The members of the stock exchange deal with the securities according to the rules and regulation laid down by the Act. It protects the investors' interest. The functions of the stock exchange are as follows:

1. It provides liquidity to the securities.
2. It ensures the safety and transparency.
3. It facilitates the marketability.
4. It brings the companies and investors together.
5. It ensures a wider ownership to the securities.
6. It provides capital to the profitable sectors.
7. It allows the companies to float their shares on the market.
8. It provides an orderly regulated market for the securities.
9. It facilitates a ready market for buying and selling of the securities.
10. It promotes the savings and capital formation.
11. It facilities a continuous market for the securities.
12. It motivates the companies to enjoy the goodwill in the stock market.
13. It encourages the corporate sector to improve the performance for converting various group of shares in the stock exchange.

Origin and Growth

The stock exchange is an organised place, where the securities are purchased and sold. The organised stock exchange in India are of recent origin. The stock markets are highly specialised institutions in India. Our stock exchanges are competing with the global stock exchange. India is a **Sleeping lion** and Asia's tiger in the world market. Now India is in transformation stage where it enters from an old economy to the **Digital economy.** India has an excellent technical skills in the Information Technology. With the help of the **IT,** India can become a 24 hours stock market. India can teach lessons to the western market. India has an excellent potential and talented manpower to construct the **Technology courses.**

The first stock exchange was set up in India under the name of the Native Share and Stock Brokers Association of Bombay in 1875. At present there are **23** recognised stock exchanges under the Securities Contract Act, 1956. All the stock exchanges operate under the rules, bye-laws and regulations duly approved by the government. The objective of the Securities Contract Act 1956 are as follows:

1. to control the malpractices in the stock exchanges.
2. to regulate the stock market.
3. to protect the investor's interest.
4. to improve the working conditions of the stock exchange.
5. to create an efficient securities market.

The stock exchanges in India should work within the framework of the act. The stock exchanges involve in accordance with the following laws:

1. **Companies Act, 1956.**
2. **Income Tax Act, 1961.**
3. **Foreign Exchange Management Act.**

The Bombay Stock Exchange has been granted a permanent recognition. The other stock exchanges are recognised for a period of 5 years. There is no uniform structure in respect of the organisation pattern of the stock exchange in India. There are different stock exchanges which follow different patterns. Some are Public limited companies and the others are limited by guarantee or voluntary non-profit making organisation. The Organisation patterns of the recognised stock exchanges in India are presented below:

Sl. No.	Name of the	Year of Est. Stock Exchanges	Type of Association
1.	Bombay	1875	Voluntary
2.	Ahmedabad	1894	,,
3.	Calcutta	1908	Public Limited Co.
4.	Madras	1908	,,
5.	Indore	1930	Voluntary
6.	Hyderabad	1943	Limited by Guarantee
7.	Delhi	1947	Public Ltd. Company
8.	Bangalore	1957	,,
9.	Cochin	1978	,,
10.	Kanpur	1982	,,
11.	Pune	1982	,,
12.	Ludhiana	1983	,,
13.	Gauhati	1983	,,
14.	Jaipur	1984	,,
15.	Kanara	1985	,,
16.	Magadh	1986	,,
17.	Bhuvaneswar	1989	Ltd. by Guarantee
18.	Saurashtra	1989	,,
19.	O.T.C.	1989	,,
20.	Vadodara	1990	,,
21.	Coimbatore	1991	,,
22.	Meerut	1991	,,
23.	NSE	1992	,,

The stock exchanges are self-regulatory organisations supervised by the Ministry of Finance under the Securities Contract Regulation act. Stock exchange regulation cover the entire operations. They are:

(a) The enrolment of members.
(b) The listing of securities.
(c) The disciplinary actions.

Regulations on trading are largely confined to some specified shares. The specified shares and transactions could be forwarded from one settlement period to another. Several committees examined and made recommendations to reform the organisation of the stock exchanges.

1. G.S. Patel Committee (1985)
2. L.C. Gupta Committee (1991)
3. Pherwani Committee (1991)
4. Varma Committee (1997)

Organisation

A stock exchange is managed by the governing board. The governing body consists of a president, a vice-president, an executive director, elected directors, public representatives and nominees of the government. The board will look after all the affairs of the stock exchange. The stock exchange affairs are monitored through various committees. They are like:

(a) Listing Committee
(b) Clearing House Committee
(c) Defaulters Committee

Listing of Securities

Listing of shares means admitting a scrip to trade on the floor of a stock exchange. Every security issued by the companies cannot be traded at a stock exchange. The stock exchange will admit a share for listing under certain requirements. The following information should be submitted to the exchange for listing the security:

(*a*) Memorandum and Articles of Association.
(*b*) Prospectus or statement in lieu of prospectus.
(*c*) Copies of balance sheets and audited accounts.
(*d*) Copies of agreements with promoters, underwriters, brokers.
(*e*) Consent letters from the SEBI.
(*f*) Details of the capital structure.
(*g*) Particulars of bonus and dividends.
(*h*) Brief particulars about the companies.
(*i*) Agreement with the MD.
(*j*) An undertaking regarding the compliance of various provisions i.e. Companies Act, 1956; SCRA, 1956.
(*k*) A list of the highest top-ten holders of each class or kinds of securities of the company.

The stock exchange has the authority to withdraw or suspend the trading of a security if the company violates any rules and regulations. The securities are classified into the following categories:

1. **Group A shares (Specified Securities).**
2. **Group B shares.**
3. **Permitted Securities.**
4. **Cleared Securities.**
5. **Non-cleared Securities.**

Listed Securities are classified as cleared or specified or Group A Securities.

Group A shares are allowed in the forward trading. These shares are included in the cleared list of the exchange. The shares which satisfies the following conditions may be classified as 'A' shares:

(a) The shares should be fully paid up equity shares.
(b) The Company's paid up capital should be atleast **Rs. 5 crores.**
(c) The Company should have a growth potential.
(d) The Company should be a dividend paying one.
(e) The shares should have been actively traded on the screen.
(f) The Company's shares should have the market capitalisation of atleast **Rs. 10 crores.**

Group B shares are traded on cash basis. They are known as the cash scrips. The carry-forward facility is not available to this group.

Permitted Securities are listed by some of the recognised stock exchanges. The recognised stock exchanges will permit the scrips even if they are not listed by them. These scrips are known as the permitted securities. The permission is granted as per the rules and regulations of the stock exchange.

Cleared Securities are traded for fortnightly settlement. The payment and delivery will be completed in the 3rd week following the fortnightly clearing. The cleared securities are also known as the **"Specified Securities"**. Speculation activities is permitted only such shares. The concerned stock exchange has the power to pass special resolutions specifying the securities which may from time to time be included in the specified securities list.

Non-cleared Securities are traded among the brokers. These securities are not cleared through the stock exchange clearing house. The securities are not permitted to carry over facilities.

Advantages of Listing

The listing of securities has some advantages:

1. Listing creates liquidity to the security.
2. It enhances the marketability.
3. Listed Securities command higher collateral value for the purpose of bank credit.
4. It facilitates prestige to the company.
5. Listed securities enjoy more public confidence.
6. It provides greater publicity for the concerned company.

Dealings on the stock exchange are subjected to the bye-laws and rules of the stock exchange. The trading floor of the stock exchange will carry out the operations through the authorised members. The members or authorised clerks are permitted to enter the exchange during the fixed working hours. The trading on the floor can be done in two ways. They are:

1. **Ready Delivery Contract**
2. **Forward Delivery Contract**

Ready Delivery Contract is also known as cash trading or cash securities. They are to be settled either on same date or within a short period of time. If the payment and delivery of the securities is on the same day or on the next day, it may be called as **spot delivery contract.** The ready delivery contracts can be made in respect of all the securities.

The **Forward Delivery Contract** enjoys the facility of carryover. These contracts are discharged on fixed settlement days which occur at periodical intervals. These contracts are confined to those securities which are placed on the forward list.

Procedure for Dealing at the stock exchange

The Investors are not allowed to enter the stock exchange for buying and selling of the securities. They have to approach the brokers. The brokers are the members of the stock exchange. The dealing in the stock exchange can be done only through them. The following procedure is followed for the dealings at the stock exchanges.

1. Finding a good broker
2. Placing order
3. Making the contract
4. Contract note
5. Settlement

Broker is the most important person in the stock exchange. Each and every transaction should be performed through the members only. The investors should find a best broker for the execution of their transactions. The intending investor or seller may approach his banker for the purchase of securities. The banker can appoint his own broker at the exchange. The brokers contact for dealings on behalf of their customers. Instructions from the bank will be followed by the broker and the clients' account is opened by the broker. The bank assures about the financial strength of the client. Therefore, the broker will be introduced by the banker.

Placing order with the broker is the second step in the process. After selecting the broker, the client places an order for the purchase or sale of the securities. The broker provides all the information about the corporate sector and the economy. He guides the client about the type of securities to be purchased and the proper time. If the client approaches for the selling of securities, he must tell him about the favourable time for sale. However, it is not advisable to depend upon the broker's advice. In India, most of the investors are buying and selling scrips only on the advice of the brokers. They simply hand over the cheque to the broker for their commitment. But the investor's should know the information about the **economy, industry growth, company sales, company product, company market share, gross profit, Net profit, profit before tax, profit after tax, EPS, PE ratio, market capitalisation etc.**

Making the contract is the third step in the process. After taking the order, the broker goes to the stock exchange and fulfils the investor's desire by making the deals with his counter parts. He will make enquiries and bargains on behalf of the investor.

The brokers will prepare the notes after their mutual consent. The seller broker will send the selling note and the buyer will send the buying note. They provide in the note about all the details of the trading.

Settlement is the last step in the process of buying or selling of the securities in the stock exchange. Settlement is the process between two brokers. All the transactions between them will be settled in the exchange.

The stock exchange contracts are categorised into two kinds. They are the ready delivery contracts and the forward delivery contracts. The settlement of the ready delivery contracts is done between 3 to 7 days of the transactions. This contract is further classified as liquidation and square up. In their liquidation settlement process, the securities will be delivered on receipt of cash. The other method is known as "squaring up". The dealings are squared by adjusting the price difference.

The settlement of forward delivery contracts can be done through the stock exchange. These delivery contracts are done for speculative purposes. In this category, the active securities are traded. The settlement of forward delivery contracts can be done in the following ways:

(a) **Liquidation in full.**
(b) **Liquidation by the payment of differences.**
(c) **Carryover.**

Liquidation in Full

In this method, the securities are delivered and payment will be received immediately. The amount will be adjusted after crossing all the intermediate purchases and sales.

Liquidation by the Payment of Differences

Under this category the purchase and sales are offset at the ruling price by paying or receiving the difference amount. Therefore, the securities are not delivered. But the difference amount will be paid. The price difference will be adjusted between the two parties.

Carry Over

If the buyer party does not want to settle the contract but wants to carry it to a further date then, it is called as the carry over. For this the buyer party will have to pay certain amount to the seller party. The payment of consideration is called as **Badla or Contango charges**.

Types of Speculators

The purchase of assets for profit is called as the **"speculation"**. It is a short-term activity. It is an inspiration to the stock market. It is the oxygen to the capital market. We can say that without the speculation, there is no stock market. It is different from investment. Investment is long-term in nature. It creates the capital formation in the country by encouraging the savings. Investments are useful for the present and future consumption. Investment leads to more income and larger capital appreciation.

Speculation aims at only short-term trading gains. It involves in buying and selling off the securities for the short-term purpose. It is double edged sword either to get profit or loss. It may lead to profit sometimes and loss at other times. Persons who are involved in the speculation are called as the **"speculators"**. The speculators will balance the share price movements in the market. The speculators are classified according to their nature and working. They can be categorised as follows:

(a) **Bull**
(b) **Bear**
(c) **Stag**
(d) **Lame Duck**

Bull

A bull is also known as Tejwala. Bull is an operator who expects rise in the prices of the securities in future. The bull always thinks that the future will be very bright. He purchases the shares with the intention to sell at higher prices in future. He is not interested to take the delivery of shares which he has purchased. He deals with the **differences of prices**. The speculator is called a bull because his behaviour resembles like a bull. He is an optimist. He tries to raise the prices of the securities by making heavy purchases. The market is called as for **Bullish Market** when all the bulls enter the market at once. In the bullish market, there will be pressure for buying the securities. In this market, the supply of shares will be scarce and demand will be more. The scarcity of scrips may lead to rise in the share prices. The bulls are the creators of liquidity to the securities market.

Bear

A bear is known as **Mandiwala**. He expects that the prices will fall in future and sells the securities at present. He purchases the securities at lower prices and sells securities at higher prices. He is interested to purchase in the down-market and sell in the up-market.

When all the bears enter the market, it is known as the **Bearish Market**. A bear does not take the delivery of securities but takes the difference, if the prices fall. In case the prices increase, he will have to pay the difference. If the market is dominated by the bears, it is known as the **Bearish phase**. The **bearish phase** tends to force down the prices of different securities. When all the bear operators start selling the securities, the pressure gradually forces down the prices. The bear is a pessimist. If the prices do not fall, they may start spreading the rumours to pull the prices downwards. This situation is known as the **Bear raid**. The bear is quite opposite to the bull speculator.

Stag

A stag is another speculator in the market. He is a cautious speculator. He concentrates on the primary market. He applies for the shares in the new companies and expects to sell them at a premium if he gets an allotment. The stag selects only those companies whose shares are in more demand and are likely to carry a high price. He sells the shares before being called to pay the allotment money. He does not indulge in buying and selling of shares in the market. He depends on the securities that are allotted to him.

Lame Duck

Lame Duck is a speculator who behaves like a duck. If a bear speculator fails to fulfill his commitments, then he is called as "struggling like a lame duck".

The following transactions reveal the speculative nature:

Bull Deal

For Example: A bull asks his broker to buy 100 shares of ABC Ltd., at Rs. 10 each. Then the broker executes the deal. At the time of settlement, the market price of shares of ABC Ltd. will be Rs. 35 each. The bull would instruct his broker to sell the shares and takes the difference in prices.

(a)	Sale proceeds of 100 shares @ Rs. 35/-	Rs. 3500
(b)	Purchase Consideration 100 × 10	Rs. 1000
(c)	Bull's profit	Rs. 2500

Bear Deal

A bear is instructed to sell 100 shares of X Ltd., at Rs. 50 each. At the time of settlement of transactions, the actual price of the share is Rs. 40 each. He would instruct the broker to purchase the shares of X Ltd., and enjoys the difference in prices.

(a)	Sale proceeds of 100 shares @ Rs. 50/-	Rs. 5000
(b)	Purchase price 100 × 40	Rs. 4000
(c)	Bear's profit	Rs. 1000

The speculation assumes the risk of loss with a view to make profits. Speculation needs the full information about the capital market. It requires the best expertise on the part of the speculator. The main aim of the speculation is to achieve the profits through the price changes. Speculation may be categorised as:

Constructive Speculation
Destructive Speculation

The **constructive speculation** is based on predicting the future trends of prices. It requires high talent, skill, fore-sight and intelligent analysis of the securities market. The **destructive speculation** hardly depends on the evaluation of the security market. The speculation has the following advantages and disadvantages:

Advantages

1. It creates liquidity to the market.
2. It creates stability in prices.
3. It encourages the forward trading.
4. It provides continuity in the market.

Disadvantages

The speculation is a high intelligent activity. It requires a lot of skill. It also requires a perfect knowledge about the capital market trends. Even though it is useful to us, it creates problems. If the speculators' skills do not match with the speculation tool, it may be a misfire. The investors will have to face many problems.

Types of Speculative Deals

The speculative dealings in the capital market are presented below:

(a) Manipulation
(b) Rigging
(c) Arbitrage
(d) Kerb deal
(e) Cornering
(f) Wash Sales

Manipulation is one of the speculative dealings in the stock market. It is the most important activity. It involves in the creation of false opinion and spreads rumours. Manipulation means the purchase and sale of the securities by a group of speculators to create an impression that such transactions are the result of the natural phenomenon. It artificially twists the prices of the securities in the market.

Rigging is another speculative dealing method. The speculator places orders to different brokers at different prices. He places orders for buying and sellings of the securities. It is done artificially to stimulate the market. It will effect the demand and supply of the securities.

Arbitrage is a highly specialised activity. It requires a lot of talent and skill. These transactions are carried out by the speculators to earn profit at different prices in different markets. The speculator make purchases in the cheaper market and sells it in the dearer market. This situation creates artificial ups and downs in the prices of the securities.

Kerb deal means the purchase and sale of securities before or after the official hours of business of the stock exchanges. Trading before or after the official hours is called as **kerb trading**. It is an unfair practice of dealing.

Cornering means the speculators some times create a scarcity of a particular scrip by purchasing a large amount of shares. They create an artificial demand for a scrip. The particular scrip circulation will be controlled by the speculators. If the velocity of the scrip is more, it will lead to high prices. It is an unhealthy practice of trading.

Wash sales means the speculator make purchase and sale of shares at the same time. This situation may create an illusion of great activity, and it gives misleading position about the value of a security. It creates an incorrect value of a particular scrip in a market.

Membership

The stock market consists of the issuing companies, financial intermediaries and brokers. The brokers are the most important persons who match buying and selling orders from the investors. In the stock exchange, only the members are allowed to trade the securities at the floor of the stock exchange. To become a member in the stock exchange, one has to satisfy many rules and regulations laid down by the Act. The following are the important provisions as per the **Rule 8 of the Securities Contract Act, 1957**.

1. The following conditions must be satisfied by every member of the stock exchange:

   (a) He must be 21 years of age.
   (b) He must be a citizen of India.

(c) He must be solvent.
(d) He should not be convicted in any offence involving fraud.
(e) He should not be expelled at any time from the exchange.
(f) He should not be declared as the defaulter by any other exchange.
(g) He should maintain better relations with the creditors.

2. The member is eligible for admission as a member if he works for two years as a partner or he must be either worked as a authorised assistant or authorised clerk.
3. The Corporate bodies are also eligible to become the members in the stock exchange, if they fulfill the following conditions:

   (a) The corporate body is established in compliance with the provisions of **Section 322** of the said Act.
   (b) The majority of the directors are the share holders of such company and are also members of that stock exchange.

Types of Operators

The following operators involve in the stock exchange operations. They are:

(*a*) Jobbers
(*b*) Brokers
(*c*) Tarawaniwalas
(*d*) Budiwalas
(*e*) Arbitrageurs
(*f*) Odd lot dealers

Jobbers play an important role in the stock market operations. They are the dealers in the securities in the stock exchange. They buy and sell the securities for themselves. They buy securities at lower price and sell them at higher prices. The difference between the two prices is known as the Jobbers task. They cannot buy the shares on behalf of the public.

Brokers are the most important intermediaries in the stock exchange. They are commission agents. They work for their commission. They transact the business in the securities either for their customers or for other members. The brokers who work for their customers are called as the commission brokers. The brokers who purchase for other members are known as **the floor brokers**. They charge commission from both the parties for their services. The investors who do not know anything about the stock markets are greatly benefited by the expertise of the brokers.

Tarawaniwalas handle the transactions on a commission basis for other brokers. They are like Jobbers. They make purchase and sale of the shares on their own account. They act as brokers on behalf of the public.

Budiwalas are the financers in the stock exchange. They provide loans to the parties for a short period *i.e.* 2 to 3 weeks. They charge the fee which is known as **Cantago**. The Cantago may be called as Seedhabadla and backwardation or **undhbadla**. They grant credit facilities to the needy parties. They act as financers of the market.

Arbitrageur is a dealer. He enters into the dealings with the securities in different stock exchange centres at the same time. It is a highly specialised activity which requires a great talent. They work to take the advantage of the price differences in the same market or different markets.

Odd lot dealers specialises in handling the odd lots. In the stock exchanges, the prescribed round lots are traded. Anything less than the market lot is the odd lot. The broker who specialises in the odd lots is called as the odd lot dealer. An odd lot arise from the issue of rights or bonus. The stock exchanges have been making the alternative arrangements for handling the odd lots.

Types of Orders

In the stock exchange, the broker buys and sells the securities on behalf of his customers. Various orders can be made by the broker for his clients. They are:

1. Net rate order.
2. Best rate order.
3. Limited order.
4. Stop order.
5. Market rate order.
6. Discretionary order.
7. Matched rate order.

A **Net rate order** means the fixed rate of a particular scrip. It includes the brokerage payable to the broker. The order will be placed by the client to the broker.

The **Best rate order** means the order will be placed by a client to the broker to buy or sell at the best price immediately available in the market. If the instruction is for the purchase of the share, the broker must try for the lowest prices. **If it is for the sale of the share,** the broker must sell at the highest possible price. This type of orders will be placed by the clients in the **actively trading shares**.

A **limited order means** the investor will instruct the broker to buy or sell at a stated price or better price. This order clearly indicates the maximum or minimum price that the investor is willing to accept for his trade transactions. The broker protects the customer against paying more or selling for less than the intended. In this type of order, the rate depends upon the broker and client.

A **stop order** means it is an order used to restrict the loss. It also protects the amount of capital gains. It is also known as the stop loss order. These orders will be useful to the broker and client.

A **market rate order** means the investor will pay the brokerage separately. The investor will order for a fixed rate which is based on the market conditions.

A **discretionary order** means the investor does not specify the price of securities to be bought but the transactions are left to the brokers.

A **matched rate order** means the investor sometimes appoints two brokers. The speculator instructs one broker for buying and another for selling. These transactions are called "matched rate orders".

Stock Exchange in India

The growth of the stock exchange depends upon the growth of the corporate sector in India. In India there have been 5937 companies listed on the bourses in 2001. Every stock exchange follows its own methods of working. The stock exchange in India follow some important provisions of the Act. The provisions can be discussed as follows:

(a) Recognition of the Stock Exchange.
(b) Control of the Government.
(c) Curbing the Speculation.

The securities can be traded only at the stock exchanges recognised by the Union Government in compliance of the Securities Contract Act. The recognition of the stock exchange depends on the following situations:

1. The bye-laws of the applicant stock exchange should ensure fair dealings and must be transparent.
2. The stock exchange should protect the interests of the genuine investors.
3. The stock exchange should give consent to the conditions that may be imposed by the Union Government from time to time.
4. The Government should grant the recognition to the stock exchange in the interest of public and trade.

The Act empowers the Central Government to control the working of the stock exchanges. The controlling powers of the government are presented below:

The Central Government controls the stock exchanges such as preventing undesirable transactions in the securities. The act empowers the government relating to the regulation of the procedure for the recognition of the stock exchanges, their management, power to make rules, bye-laws or amendments, power to withdraw the recognition granted.

The Central Government can curb the speculative transactions of an exchange. The government has banned the option dealings in the securities. The government declared the kerb trading as illegal. Trading outside the stock exchange is known as the **'Kerb Trading'**. The government reduces the life period of a blank transfer to the extent of **two months**. The powers so far exercised by the Central Government have now been transferred to the SEBI. Thus the SEBI now regulates the stock market through various regulations.

Brokers

Generally every stock exchange runs through its members. The member of a stock exchange is known as the stock-broker. The stock-broker of a recognised stock exchange buys and sells the securities on behalf of his clients. The person who wants to become a stock-broker, is required to get a registration certificate from the SEBI. The SEBI is the most powerful organisation to control, regulate, monitor and guide the market from time to time. The SEBI is empowered to grant the registration certificate to the eligible brokers. The SEBI has the authority to impose conditions before granting the registration to a broker. A person who is granted the status of the broker by the SEBI, must abide by the rules. The broker is required to pay a prescribed fee to the SEBI. The brokers are responsible for the redressal of the investors' complaints. They should bring into the notice of the SEBI regarding the nature of the complaints received by them. In India, the brokers are categorised into two. They are:

1. **Indian Brokers, and**
2. **Foreign Brokers**

Indian Brokers

The stock-brokers in India should move according to the guidelines issued by the SEBI from time to time. The SEBI guidelines are the most important guidelines to the brokers. The SEBI has taken the monitoring function to prevent the malpractice in the trading and also to protect the rights of the investors. The function also includes the submission of the report by the stock exchanges and registration of the brokers. The broad regulatory frame-work of the stock exchanges contain the major organisational reforms in respect of **stock-brokers, sub-brokers, foreign brokers, custodial services, depository system and stock lending scheme**. The following steps are required to fulfil the legal formalities by the stock-brokers:

(a) Registration
(b) Fee
(c) Code of Conduct
(d) Capital Adequacy Norms
(e) Sub-brokers

A stock-broker in a recognised stock exchange has to get the registration with the SEBI. The stock-broker should apply to the SEBI through his recognised stock exchange. The stock exchange may forward the application with their comments to the SEBI regarding his candidature. On receipt of the application from the stock exchange, the SEBI will enquire the matters regarding such broker. For granting the registration, the SEBI should consider many factors such as membership in a recognised stock exchange, capability of the broker, his man-power and infrastructure facilities, his past experience, his discipline and suitability. The SEBI will grant the Certificate of Registration to the stock-broker if he satisfies and fulfills all the norms that are required. The selected broker should undergo some process to get the registration certificate.

The selected broker has to pay the fee to the SEBI as the registration fee. The registration fee will be based on the annual turnover of the broker. The annual turnover means the quantum of sales and purchases of the securities received and receivable by the stock-broker on his own account and as well as his clients a/c during any financial year. The grant of registration will be valid for five years. The registration fee should be paid by the broker, if his annual turnover is found to be Rs. one crore, then he should pay Rs. 5000 to the SEBI. If his turnover exceeds Rs. One crore, then he should pay Rs. 5000 + 1 per cent excess to the excess of 1 crore turnover. The broker turnover should be certified by the auditors of the concerned stock exchange. After the completion of five years, if the broker keeps it in force, he should pay Rs. 5000 for this purpose. If a stock-broker fails to pay the fee within the specified period, he would be liable to pay the interest at 15 per cent per annum for each month of delay. If the individuals or firms convert into a corporate body, then the fee would be exempted for the conversion period. It should pay the fee on the basis of turnover, for the purpose of calculating the turnover, the underwriting and collection of deposits are not taken into consideration. On the execution of orders, the brokers are charged with 1/4th of the fee payable on the other items of the turnover. In case of the turnover on accounts of the transactions in **PSU bonds, Mutual Funds, Unit Trust, and the Government securities** are subjected to 1/10th of the fee payable on the other items of the turnover. In case of the carry forward transactions, two entries are made by the stock exchange from one settlement to another. Therefore only **one entry** should be counted for the purpose of assessment of the turnover.

Every broker who registered with the SEBI should abide by the code of conduct as presented below. The following formalities should be fulfilled by the stock-broker for the smooth functioning of the stock market:

- **(a)** Transparency
- **(b)** Service to the Investors
- **(c)** General Obligations
- **(d)** Inspection
- **(e)** Default

Every stock broker has to maintain best relations with the investors. The broker should maintain high standards of integrity, promptness and fairness. He should have adequate skills, care and intelligence for discharging his duties. The broker should be transparent at the price consideration in dealing with the investors. The broker should not involve in manipulative, fraudulent transactions or schemes or spread rumours with a view to make personal gains. The broker should be honest while dealing with his customers. The business of the broker mainly depends upon his degree level of his honest nature. The investors always think about the credibility of the broker before he commits his investment decisions. The broker or his colleagues should not create false market. He should not involve himself in excessive speculative activities. At last but not the least, he has to abide by all the rules and regulations of the SEBI Act. The broker should follow the rules which are issued by the Government of India from time to time. The stock exchanges can also issue the rules and directions to the brokers which have to be followed by them.

The fundamental duty of the broker is to provide a better quality of services to the investors. The brokers should work for the satisfaction of the investors. The brokers must be in a position to provide any services related to the dealings in the securities to the investors. The following duties should be provided to the investors by a registered broker:

- **(a)** While dealing with the public, the broker must be transparent in all aspects.
- **(b)** The broker should execute the orders faithfully in buying and selling of the securities.
- **(c)** He should always provide the securities at the best available market prices.
- **(d)** The broker cannot show the partiality between the big and small investors.
- **(e)** He should promptly inform his client about the execution and non-execution of an order.
- **(f)** The broker should issue a contract note to the client without any delay according to the specifications of the stock exchange.
- **(g)** He should not reveal about the personal investment of his client to another investor. He should maintain the confidentiality in this aspect.
- **(h)** He should not encourage sales or purchases of the securities with the sole objective of earning the brokerage or commission.
- **(i)** He should deal with the investor who defaults with another broker knowingly or unknowingly.

(j) The broker should not behave against the advantage of the investors. He should not create any conflict of interest between him and his client.

(k) The broker should not give investment advises to the investor unless he has reasonable grounds for believing the information.

(l) The broker should have excellent trained staff with competent skills and outstanding abilities to render services to the clients with fairness and promptness.

(m) The stock-broker should maintain a cordial relationship with other fellows.

(n) The stock-broker should cooperate with each other when the unmatched transaction arise.

(o) He should not willfully or knowingly make bad deliveries.

(p) The broker should cooperate with other fellows in replacement of documents in case of bad deliveries.

(q) The broker should cooperate with others in case of investor's rights, dividends, blank shares, and any others related to such securities.

(r) Every broker should cooperate in the settlement of transaction.

(s) The stock-broker can make wide publicity only with the permission of the stock exchange.

(t) Every stock-broker should submit the annual reports to the SEBI in a stipulated time.

(u) A stock-broker should not neglect or refuse the instruments of the SEBI.

(v) The broker should be a member of a recognised stock exchange. He should submit the required returns to the stock exchange.

General Obligations

The stock-broker is required to maintain the books and records as per the Act. Every registered broker should maintain the following books:

(a) Sauda book (Register of transactions)
(b) General ledger
(c) Client ledger
(d) Cash book
(e) Ledger
(f) Pass book
(g) Documents Register

- **(h)** Register of accounts of sub-brokers
- **(i)** Margin Register
- **(j)** Members agreement book
- **(k)** Client's consent letters register
- **(l)** Confirmation register
- **(m)** Agreement register of sub-brokers

All the above books should be maintained by every broker. The books and records must be preserved for a period of **five years**. The SEBI has the full authority to verify all the books which are maintained by every broker. The SEBI is empowered to appoint an inspection committee. It consists of one or two members to inspect the books of accounts, records and other documents of the stock broker. The inspection committee should ensure that the broker has maintained all the records as per the stipulated Act. The committee may also ensure that the broker has in compliance with all the provisions of the Act. The committee may investigate whether the broker had fulfilled the Securities Regulation Act or not. The committee is empowered to look into the affairs of the investor's complaints. It should also verify about the complaints from other brokers and sub-brokers. The SEBI has the suo moto to investigate the affairs of the investor's interest. In some situations, the SEBI can also appoint a qualified auditor to carry out the investigation into the records of the broker. On submitting the report by the inspection committee, the SEBI can direct the broker to take effective measures as desired by the inspection committee. A stock-broker who fails to take measures or recommendations will be liable to the punishment as per the Act. The broker can be punished, if he violates the conditions of the grant of registration. He will be punished, if he contravenes any of the provisions of the SEBI Act, SCRA, Bye-laws and stock exchange regulations, the broker's licence will be cancelled or suspended for a specific period of time.

Suspension

The SEBI has the authority to suspend the registration of a broker on the following grounds:

- **(a)** If the broker violates the SEBI provisions.
- **(b)** Violation of the conditions for the grant of registration.
- **(c)** If the broker does not follow the code of conduct.
- **(d)** If the broker involves in price rigging or cornering.

(e) If the broker is guilty of misconduct, improper business or unprofessional conduct.
(f) If the broker fails to furnish any information required by the SEBI.
(g) If the broker fails to pay the annual fee.
(h) If the broker does not cooperate at the time of inspection.
(i) If the broker furnishes false information or wrong information to the SEBI.
(j) If the broker fails to submit the periodical returns within the stipulated time.
(k) If the broker fails to resolve the investor's complaints or fails to give a satisfactory explanation to the SEBI.
(l) If the stock exchange suspends the membership of a broker, then the SEBI suspends his registration.

Cancellation

The SEBI has the authority to cancel the registration of any broker. The SEBI should indicate in writing about the defaults of the broker. It has the power to cancel the registration in case of repeated defaults. The following situations may cause the cancellation of registration of a broker:

1. Violation of any provisions of takeover regulations and insider trading.
2. Involves in a guilty offence or in conviction for a criminal offence.
3. Cancellation of membership by the recognised stock exchange.

The suspension or cancellation of registration of a member can be done only after holding a thourough enquiry as laid down by the Act. If the SEBI decides to cancel the registration of broker or suspend the registration, it must be published in atleast two daily newspapers. On publication of this order, the broker is prohibited to buy and sell the securities in the market. If a broker dissatisfies with the SEBI orders, he can approach the **Securities Appellate Tribunal** for justice.

Capital Adequacy Norms

Every registered broker in India should meet the capital adequacy requirements as per the Act. The Capital Adequacy norms contain two important components. They are:

(a) **Minimum Capital Level.**
(b) **Additional Capital.**

Minimum Capital

Every broker who is a member of a recognised stock exchange should pay a minimum amount of deposit to the concerned exchange. It depends on the status of the stock exchange. A member in Mumbai Stock Exchange should deposit Rs. Five lakhs in the stock exchange. The Calcutta Stock Exchange also requires a minimum amount of Rs. 5 lakhs as deposit. The Delhi and Ahmedabad Stock Exchange command Rs. 3.5 lakhs as deposit without relation to the turnover of the broker. The other regional stock exchanges require Rs. 2 lakhs. The deposit which is kept by the brokers in the stock exchange forms a part of the base. From the base capital 25 per cent should be in cash with the stock exchange and another 25 per cent should be in the form of FDR with a bank and the rest of the balance may be in the form of securities with 30 per cent margin. The value of the securities will be reviewed by the stock exchange for every 2 months. If any amount shows the deficit, the broker-member should bring some amount additionally to meet the capital adequacy norms.

Additional Capital

The Additional Capital brought by the member broker at any point of time should be together with the base minimum capital. It should not be less than **8 per cent** of the gross outstanding business in the exchange. The gross business turnover means the buying and selling of the securities. It also includes the inter client business which does not arise on the floor of exchange. The gross outstanding business should not exceed **12.5 times** than the base and additional capital requirements. If the outstanding business exceeds **10 times** the base and additional capital requirements, the broker should intimate the stock exchange. If the gross business outstanding reaches **12.5 times** the base and additional capital requirement, the broker should bring the additional capital. Until then, he would not be allowed for trading in the stock exchange. The member of the stock exchange should always fulfill the capital adequacy requirements. The capital of a broker is computed by adding capital and reserves **minus** non-allowable assets. The non-allowable assets can be as **Member's cards, bad deliveries,**

fixed assets, pledged securities, doubtful debts and advances, tangible assets, and 30 per cent of marketable securities. The brokers who do not submit their audited accounts should be liable to deposit the additional capital in the form of cash in the stock exchange. Every broker should submit the audited accounts quarterly indicating the net liquid capital with the member of the stock exchange. The stock exchanges are required to adjust the margin requirements on daily basis to facilitate the working capital management of the member brokers. Every broker should submit the quarterly reports to the concerned stock exchanges for meeting the capital adequacy norms. For this effect, he should submit a auditor's certificate to the exchange within one month of the end of every quarter. **(ending March 31st, June 30th, Sept. 30th and Dec. 31st)**. If any broker fails to meet the requirements of the capital adequacy, he deserves a penalty including fines and suspension from trading. The bye-laws of the stock exchange indicate that if any broker fails to inform the stock exchange on reaching the prescribed limits, he is punishable accordingly. The transactions which are to be delivered within **48 hours** would be exempted from the capital adequacy requirements.

Client and Broker

The transactions between the client and broker should be regulated. Every broker should keep his own money and his client's money in separate accounts. The broker should not utilise the client's money for his own purpose. But however, the member has any lieu set off counter-claim or otherwise claim against the money standing to the credit of the client's accounts. The broker should purchase the securities from the market only on receipt of **20 per cent margin** on the price of the security. The margin amount would be exempted for purchase of shares meant for **FIIs, MFs and Financial Institutions**. The member should sell the securities on behalf of his client only on receipt of **20 per cent margin** on the price of securities. But the Mutual Funds, FIIs and FIs are exempted from this restriction.

Generally the member must issue a contract note to the client within **24 hours** for buying or selling a scrip. The broker can close a transaction if the client fails to make the full payment for the execution of the contract within **two days** for the cash shares. The time limit for the specified group shares would be **seven days** within the delivery of the contract note. If any loss arises in this transaction, it should be adjusted from the margin of the client. The same process will be applied for the sale of shares by the client.

Sub-brokers

The sub-broker is an agent of the stock-broker. He acts on behalf of a stock-broker. He assists the investors in buying and selling of the securities in the market. He himself is not a member of the stock exchange. He should get a registration certificate from the SEBI. The SEBI is empowered to grant the certificate of registration under the following conditions:

- **(a)** The fee should be payable by the sub-broker.
- **(b)** Authorisation should be given in writing by a broker.
- **(c)** The sub-broker should make adequate steps for the redressal of the investors' grievances.

The provisions of the Act prescribes the following process to act as a sub-broker:

- (a) **Registration of Sub-brokers**
- (b) **General Obligations.**
- (c) **The Relation between Sub-broker and Broker.**
- (d) **Regulatory Authorities.**

Registration of Sub-brokers

Every sub-broker should register with the SEBI. He should apply to the exchange for the registration in a prescribed form. He must submit the application along with the recommendation from the stock-broker with whom he affiliates. He should also submit two references including his banker. On receipt of the application, the stock exchange should verify the information contained in it. It should also certify that the applicant is eligible for registration. His age should not be less than **21 years**. The sub-broker should not convict himself in any offence which involves fraud or dishonesty. He should at least pass +2 standard or an equivalent examination from a recognised institution. The educational qualification may be relaxed by the **SEBI** after considering the past experience. The concerned stock exchange should forward the application to the SEBI **30 days** from the date of receipt of the application.

General Obligations

Every sub-broker who registers with the SEBI should pay **Rs. 1000/-** as the annual fee for an initial period of **5 years**. After the completion of 5 years, every sub-broker should pay **Rs. 500/-** as long as the registration is in force. The broker and sub-broker should make an agreement between themselves specifying the role of the sub-broker. The sub-broker should maintain all the books of account on par with the stock-broker. He should follow the code of conduct. He should maintain high standard of integrity, fairness, transparency and skill. He should take care and due diligence in the business activities. He should behave smoothly with the general public and clients. Brokership mainly depends upon the characteristics of an individual. The investors and general public closely watch the affairs of the sub-broker activities. The business will be based on personal reputation, a strong belief in the public and confidence. He should faithfully execute the orders in buying and selling the securities. He should make purchases to his clients at the best available market and promptly inform the information about the execution and non-execution of the orders. The sub-broker should issue promptly to his clients.

(i) Purchase/Sale notes through the main-broker
(ii) Scrip-wise particulars purchase/sale
(iii) Clientwise particulars.

A sub-broker should maintain the confidentiality of the information about the clients. He should not disclose any information or make improper use details for the personal investments. He should not deal or encourage or execute either directly or indirectly with a defaulted person. He should not take advantage while dealing with his clients. He should not encourage the investors to earn brokerage or commission. He should not charge more than **one percent and a half of one percent** of the value mentioned in the respective sale or purchase contract. He should not give a false information or mislead the clients. He should not recommend any particular scrip to his clients (who might expect to rely there on to acquire or dispose off a retain securities unless there are reasonable grounds for believing that recommendation). The sub-broker should have sufficient staff with high skill and competent in their profession. The services should be fair, prompt and transparent to his clients. He should maintain cordial relation with other brokers. He should cooperate with others in the finalisation of unmatched transactions. He should provide his best services in locating the bad deliveries. He should protect the investors' interest regarding their right to dividends, bonus shares, or any other related information. He should carryout his transactions with the stock-broker more effectively and promptly. He should not show negligence in completing the transactions with the broker. A legal agreement should be made between the broker and sub-broker. Both the parties should behave accordingly. The contract should clearly specify the rights and obligations of both the parties. He should not involve in the Advertising Campaign unless he gets the permission from the concerned stock exchange. He should not procure the clients from his counterparts. He should comply with all the regulatory bodies. He should not indulge in any unfair practices or dishonest or disorder or willfully obstruct the business of the stock exchange. He should not involve in any excessive speculation activities. The inspection and punishment process will be the same on par with the broker status.

2. Foreign Brokers

The entry of the Foreign Institution Investors led to the emergence of the foreign brokers. The SEBI has taken an initiative step to encourage the FIIs, a different set of guidelines issued by the SEBI. The guidelines issued by the SEBI are presented below:

(a) **Registration**
(b) **Transactions**
(c) **Market Operations**

Registration

Every foreign broker has to register with the SEBI. He has to disclose all the information regarding his abroad registration particulars in a stock exchange. He should also submit an undertaking that he would operate and assist only on behalf of the registered FIIs. He should not deal the securities on his own account as principal in India. The SEBI and the RBI accords an approval to him to open a foreign currency denominated bank-account and a rupee-account with a designated bank branch. The foreign broker has to appoint a registered custodian on whose behalf, he should place the order with a member of the Indian Stock Exchange.

Transactions

As per the approval of the SEBI and the RBI, the foreign broker should open an account in the foreign currency denominated account. The amount of the funds that he had brought to India should be deposited in this account. He is entitled to pay the initial amount against the purchase contracts on behalf of the registered FIIs. The rupee account will be credited with the brokerage or commission earned by him in India. The fulfillment of purchase contracts may also be paid from the Rupee account. The initial amount of payment would be reimbursed by the Custodian of the FII or by the designated bank. The brokerage or commission earned by the broker will repatriate the foreign currency denominated account under the payment of taxes. The earned commission could be convertible to foreign currency and it would be transferred to the own country of the foreign broker.

Market Operations

A foreign broker cannot deal in the securities for his own purpose. He can operate only on behalf of the FIIs. The orders which are placed by the FIIs can be executed through a member of a recognised stock exchange. The foreign broker has no freedom in the market. His position is strictly restricted in the stock market. The other particulars need not be mentioned while placing a contract notes. The contract notes should be given to the custodian for the smooth functioning of the affairs. The payment for the purchases of the securities are made by the foreign broker from his rupee account. The sale proceeds of the securities should be credited to the rupee account of the FII for the tax purpose through a broker. The scrips which are purchased/sold should be delivered within **four hours** to the custodian. The FII has no freedom in repatriation of the sale proceeds. Repatriation of the surplus can be made only after the completion of such reconciliation. The custodians and the designated bank branches should submit their reports to the SEBI and the RBI. The custodian should also submit the monthly returns to the SEBI and the RBI with full information about the transactions which they have made. The particulars should be regarding the volume of transactions, number of scrips purchased, the date of receipt of the delivery, etc. The SEBI has the authority to inspect the books of accounts of the foreign brokers. Any violation of the guidelines lead to severe punishment.

BOMBAY STOCK EXCHANGE (BSE)

Introduction

The first stock exchange was set up in India under the name of the **Native and Stock Brokers Association of Bombay** in 1875. It was established as a voluntary non-profit organisation. It is managed by an executive or governing body. It is the premier stock exchange in India. It is the old market and has been recognised permanently. The other exchange in India are renewed for every five years. Its business is not confined to Mumbai alone, there are 100 other cities in which it has set up its business. It is a great surprise that the BSE membership fee in 1857 was just Re. 1 (One rupee only). Now it commands more than Rs. 2 crores. The BSE has introduced online trading system on 19-1-1995. It provides a quote driven automated trading facility to the investors.

The Market Indices have always been of great importance in the Security analysis. People have been observing the stock market fluctuations through market indicators. The investors use the market index as a bench mark. The Economists and Statisticians also use the index to study the trend of growth patterns in the economy. The investors use various indices for their analytical purpose. They also compute and compile the index numbers. The indices are equal weighting approach/ price weighted/value weighted approaches. All these methods are used in the calculation of the index. The **Price Weighted Index** is a simple arithmetic average. It is the concept of indexing which involves the comparison of currently computed averages with some basic value. There are two forms of indices. They are **the Paasche Index and the Laspeyres Index**. These two methods are used for determining the consumer price index. They measure the price inflation by taking the quantity as constant.

$$\textbf{Paasche Price Index} = \frac{\Sigma P_1Q_1}{\Sigma P_0Q_1} \times 100$$

$$\textbf{Laspeys Index} = \frac{\Sigma P_1Q_0}{\Sigma P_0Q_0} \times 100$$

$$\textbf{Fisher's Ideal Index} = \sqrt{\frac{\Sigma P_1Q_0}{\Sigma P_0Q_0} \times \frac{\Sigma P_1Q_1}{\Sigma P_0Q_1}} \times 100$$

The BSE started publishing an index number of equity prices from 2nd January, 1986 with the base year 1978-79. It is known as the

"BSE Sensitive Index". The equity shares of 30 companies have been selected on the basis of market activity with due representation to the major industries. The shares selected and the industrial group to which they belong for compiling the index are presented below:

Components of Sensex

Sl. No.	Name of the Company	Industry Group
1.	Hindustan Lever Ltd.	FMCG
2.	Reliance Industries	Synthetic Textiles
3.	Infosys Technologies	Computers
4.	I.T.C.	Tobacco, Hotels
5.	Reliance Petroleum	Refinery
6.	SBI	Banking
7.	HPCL	Petroleum
8.	Ranbaxy	Pharmaceuticals
9.	MTNL	Telecom
10.	Satyam Computers	Computers
11.	HCL Technology	Computers
12.	Dr. Reddy Lab.	Pharmaceuticals
13.	Hero Honda	Automobile
14.	Zee Tele Film	Entertainment
15.	Cipla	Pharmaceuticals
16.	Hindalco Industries	Aluminium
17.	ICICI	Banking
18.	Bajaj Auto	Automobiles
19.	Nestle	FMCG
20.	L & T	General Engineering
21.	BHEL	Heavy Electricals
22.	TISCO	Steel
23.	Gujarat Ambuja Cements	Cements
24.	TELCO	Automobiles
25.	BSES	Powers
26.	ACC	Cement
27.	Grasim Industries	Textiles
28.	Glaxo Smithkline	FMCG
29.	Castrol	Lubricants
30.	Colgate Palmolive	FMCG

The method of complication of the Sensex is based on Standard and Poor, U.S.A. The S &P is a value weighted index of 400 Industrial

Stocks, **40** Utility Stocks, **20** Transportation stocks and **40** financial stocks. The calculation of the Sensex is computed as follows:

$$\text{Sensex} = \frac{\Sigma P_{it}\ \Sigma Q_{it}}{\Sigma P_{io}\ \Sigma O_{io}} \times O$$

P_{it} = Period of stock *i* in period *t*,
Q_{it} = Number of shares outstanding for stock *i* in period *t*,
P_{io} = Price of stock *i* in the base period O, and
Q_{io} = Number of shares outstanding for stock in base period O; the base period 1978-79 has been chosen.

The sensex components are 30 companies from both specified and non-specified groups. The BSE has launched 30 more indices and some of them have taken some shine off the sensex. But the index retains its gold standard reputation. The highest is 6,150.69 in intra trading on Feb. 14, 2000. The lowest is 956.11 on Jan. 25, 1991. But we cannot rather dwell on that.

The BSE has seen several changes. The number of Companies listed on the BSE has grown from 197 in 1946 to 5,937 today. In 2000-01, the average daily volumes were Rs. 4775.8 crores. Still, the exchange has lost much of its former glory with the creation of the NSE.

Statement Showing the Average Daily Turnover[11]

(Rs. in crores)

Year	Turnover (Average daily)
1989-90	134.80
1990-91	188.54
1991-92	332.50
1992-93	238.00
1993-94	387.78
1994-95	292.02
1995-96	215.79
1996-97	517.85
1997-98	851.00
1998-99	1283.95
1999-2000	2728.20
2000-2001	4775.77

Statement Showing the Number of Companies Listed in BSE[12]

Year	No. of Companies Listed
1988-89	2275
1989-90	2247
1990-91	2471
1991-92	2601
1993 Dec.	3263
1994 Dec.	4413
1995 Dec.	5399
1996 Dec.	5999
1997 Dec.	5843
1998 Dec.	5860
1999 Dec.	5863
2000 Dec.	5937

The BSE Sensex can be compared with the NYSE Dow Jones. The Sensex movement is presented below:

Statement Showing the Movement of Sensex[13]

Year	Sensex Average	Highest for the Year
1986-87	570	659
1987-88	455	536
1988-89	613	719
1989-90	730	798
1990-91	1050	1559
1991-92	1845	4285
1992-93	2899	4286
1993-94	2895	4467
1994-95	3975	4631
1995-96	3289	3598
1996-97	3469	4069
1997-98	3812	4548
1998-99	3295	4281
1999-2000	4659	5934
2000-2001	4270	5542
2001-2002	–	3742

SECURITIES AND EXCHANGE BOARD OF INDIA (SEBI)

Introduction

The Government of India set up the SEBI on April 12, 1998 for the regulation and orderly function of the capital markets. It is likely to measure the fair trading in the securities and to protect the rights of the investors.

Initially the SEBI was established as an interim body under the administrative control of the **Finance Ministry**. Later it was given the statutory powers. The SEBI is the most powerful organisation in the security industry. It is the watch dog of the stock market. The tremendous growth in the capital markets led to the establishment of the SEBI. Until May 1992, the issue of capital by the Companies was controlled by the Central Government through the office of the Controller of Capital Issues. The CCI regulated the pricing of the issues. These controls were removed with the repeal of the Capital Issues Contract Act on May 1992.

The SEBI has emerged as an important constituent of the Indian Financial System (IFS). The powers of the IFS have been delegated to the SEBI. The constituents of the IFS; the Companies Act, 1956; the Securities Act 1956, the Capital Issues Act, 1947. The Companies act deals with the financial and non-financial aspects of the corporate sector. The aim of the act is to develop an integrated relationship among the promoters, investors and company managements. The act seeks to protect the interest of the share holders. The act contains specific provisions of the regulations such as issue of share capital, dividend distribution, capital structure, voting rights, Inter corporate investments shareholders meetings, format of the annual accounts, allotment process of shares, issue of share certificates, issue of shares at premium, par or discount. Issue of non-voting shares, buyback of their own shares. The Act is administered by the Department of Company Affairs and the Company Law Board. All these wings are working under the control of **The Ministry of Law, Justice and Company Affairs**. The provisions of the Companies act from section 55 to 68A relate to the issue of prospectus. If any prospectus is issued in **Contravention** of section 57 or 58, the Company and every responsible person would be punishable with a fine upto Rs. **5000**. The Registrar of Companies will not register the prospectus unless it satisfies with the requirements of Sec. 55 to 58. The shares allotment of a company should be in accordance with the **Sections 76, 77, 78, 79, 80, 80A, 81, 85, 86, 113** of the Companies Act. **The Securities Contract Act, 1956** deals with the Secondary Market operations. Section 3 deals with the recognition of the Stock Exchanges. Any stock exchange for the purpose of recognition should apply to the Central Government in a prescribed proforma. It should be accompanied by a copy of the **bye-laws** of the stock exchange. The Central Government is empowered under Section 4 to grant the recognition. According to Section 5, the Central Government has the power to withdraw the recognition. According to the **SCRA**, every recognised stock exchange should submit its annual report before 31 January of every year. The Annual report should contain all the activities of the stock exchange, about its trading securities, change in rules, bye-laws, changes in the governing body, admission or re-admission, resignation of members, defaults, securities delisted etc. The SCRA lays down the rules and regulations about the listing of securities in the stock exchanges. A company is defined public limited under the Companies Act if it desires to get its securities listed in a recognised stock exchange, should apply to the Central Government along with its application and required documents. The powers under the SCRA are transferred to the SEBI. The SEBI is empowered to control, regulate and monitor all the activities of the secondary market. The SEBI is the most powerful organisation in controlling, monitoring and evaluating the primary and secondary markets of the Capital Market in India.

The Capital Issues Control Act, 1947 has been playing an important role in the functioning of the Indian Capital Market since 1947. Its provisions are administered by **The Controller of Capital Issues** in the Ministry of Finance, Department of Economic Affairs. The SCRA mainly regulates the Secondary Market. The primary market is mostly regulated by the Capital Issue Control Act, 1947. The objectives of the act are to protect the investors, no mal-practice by the Corporate sector, better financial position, no undue congestion of public issue, to monitor the foreign investment. The Capital Issue Control act provisions have now become the power and functions of the SEBI. The CCI was repealed and the office was abolished in **1992**. Certain powers and sections of the SCRA and the Companies Act were delegated to the SEBI. The regulatory power of the SEBI have increased the Securities laws. The SEBI has now become a very important constituent of the financial regulatory framework in India. It was established on the same pattern of the **Securities Exchange Commission** in USA.

Organisation of the SEBI

The SEBI restructured its organisation. It has divided its activities into the following seven departments, each headed by officials of the rank of Executive Directors. All these departments are further sub-divided.

1. **Primary Market Department,**
2. **Issue Management and Intermediaries Department,**
3. **The Secondary Market Department,**
4. **The Secondary Market Department (Administration),**
5. **The Institutional Investment Department,**
6. **Legal Department, and**
7. **Investigation Department.**

The Primary Market Department deals with the policy matters. financial intermediaries, investors grievances etc. The Issue Management takes care of prospectus, registration, regulation and monitoring of issue related to the financial intermediaries.

The Secondary Market Department involves in the preparation of policy matters, stock exchange operations, control of secondary market trading activities, development of the new innovative financial products, price manipulations, monitoring, market surveillance, insider trading etc. It also involves in the inspection of the non-member intermediaries and stock sub-brokers. **The Institutional Investment Department** concentrate on the Mutual funds and foreign institutional investment affairs. It looks after the corporate mergers and acquisitions. It fully involves in Research, Publications and international affairs. **The legal department** undertakes all the legal affairs of the SEBI. It guides the SEBI on legal litigations, which are faced by it in the routine activities. The Investigation department works under the chief of the investigation. It carries out inspection and investigation activities. The SEBI is the member of **The International Organisation of Securities Commission (IOSCO).** It is an international organisation. It consists of security regulators from over 100 countries. The SEBI is an active participant in the development committee of the IOSCO.

Objectives of the SEBI

The SEBI is constituted by the Central Government as a supervisory body to regulate and promote the securities market. The objectives of the SEBI are:

- **(a)** To promote fair dealings by the issuers of the securities.
- **(b)** To provide a better market place for the corporate sector to raise the funds at a low cost.
- **(c)** To provide investor's protection and safeguard their rights and interests.
- **(d)** To regulate and develop the skills of the financial intermediaries to make them more competitive and professional in spirit.
- **(e)** To regulate the securities market.

Powers of the SEBI

The SEBI cannot act independently. It is governed by the Central Government. It is obliged to make an annual report to the Union Government every year. The annual reports should be laid down before the Parliament. The SEBI is entrusted with the following specific powers/functions:

1. Regulating the Securities market.
2. Regulating the affairs in the stock exchanges.
3. Power to call the periodical returns from the recognised stock exchanges.
4. Power to call for any information from the stock exchanges.
5. Power to grant the approval to the bye-laws of recognised exchanges.
6. Registering and regulating the work of the stock-brokers.
7. Registering and regulating the work of the bankers, registrars.
8. Registering and regulating the work of the Merchant bankers, underwriters.
9. Registering and regulating the work of the Portfolio managers and Share Transfer Agents.
10. Power to prohibit the insider trading.
11. Power to promote the investor's education.
12. Power to levy the fee.

13. Power to make or amend the bye-laws of recognised stock exchanges.
14. Power to prohibit the unfair trade practices.
15. Power to regulate the acquisition of shares and take over of companies.
16. Registering and regulating the work of the Depostories, Custodians, FIIs, credit rating agencies etc.
17. Registering and regulating the work of the venture capital funds.
18. Power to call for information, undertaking inspection, conducting enquiries and audits of the stock exchanges, financial intermediaries, mutual funds and self regulatory organisations.
19. Power to prescribe the maintainence of certain documents by the stock exchanges.
20. Compel a public company to list its shares in the exchange.
21. Power to give directions to the stock exchange.
22. Power to suspend the business of a recognised stock exchange.
23. Power to grant the recognition to the stock exchanges.
24. Power to withdraw the recognition to the stock exchanges.
25. Regulating and controlling the business dealings in the spot delivery contracts.
26. Power to prohibit the contracts in certain cases.
27. Licensing the dealers of securities in certain cases.
28. Power to declare the applicability of Section 17 of SCRA in any state or area; and to grant licences to the dealers in securities.

SEBI Act, 1992

The SEBI Act provides for the establishment of a board to protect the interests of the investors in the securities, to promote the development and to regulate the market. **Chapter I** deals with the preliminaries and definitions. **Chapter II** deals with the establishment; incorporation and management of the board; terms and conditions of the services of the chairman and members, removal process of member from the office, the procedure for conducting the meetings, appointment process for the officers and employees of the board. **Chapter III** contains the process of transfer of assets and liabilities of the existing board. The substantive part of the powers and functions of the board are incorporated in **Chapter IV.**

The Registration process of stock brokers, sub-brokers, share transfer agents, banker to an issue are presented in **Chapter V. Chapter VI** deals with the grants provided by the government to the board, maintainence of the fund, accounting procedure and audit of the board. **Chapter VII** contains all the miscellancous factors regarding the powers of the Central Government to issue the directions, powers of the central government to supercede the board, returns reports, delegation of powers, appeals, savings, employees of the board who are treated as public servants, penalties, exemptions from tax on wealth, income, cognizance of offences by courts, offences by companies, power to exempt, power to make rules and regulations etc.

Constitution of the SEBI

The SEBI as a regulatory and development board, has wide and varied powers. Its efforts include measures of efficiency, reforms and transparency in the market. The SEBI is a body of **six members**. It consists of a chairman, two members from the Central Government who deals with **Finance and Law Ministries**. Two members who are professional experts in the securities market and one member from the **RBI**. All these members except the RBI nominee are appointed by the Central Government. It has the full authority regarding the appointment of its members, terms of office, tenure conditions of service, removal of a member from the office etc. It is the supreme authority to supercede the SEBI in public interest. The general superintendence, the direction and management of the board's affairs vest in the board of members. The board of members and the chairman exercise all the powers that are done by the board. **The chairman and other members** should be the persons of ability, integrity and have a special knowledge or experience in law, finance, economics, accountancy, administration etc. The term of office and other conditions are prescribed by the Central Government. It has the full authority to terminate the services of **the Chairman/member** before the expiry period. The government should give him notice before 3 months or 3 months salary and allowances in lieu thereof; The chairman or a member in such case has the right to relinquish his office at any time before the expiry period. It has the authority to remove a member from his office if he—

(a) is or at any time been adjudicated as an insolvent,
(b) is of unsound mind and stands so declared by a competent court,

(c) has been convicted of an offence which involves a moral turpitude, and

(d) in the opinion of the Central Government, so abused his position as to render his continuation in office detrimental to the public interest.

The SEBI formed two advisory committees namely **The Primary Market Advisory Committee and Secondary Market Advisory Committee.** These committees are constituted among the market players, investors association recognised by the SEBI and eminent persons in the capital market. They are non-statutory in nature and the SEBI need not bound to its advice. It has recently opened its regional offices in **Kolkata, Chennai, Delhi** and the head-office in **Mumbai.** The regional offices help the investors in their complaints and with their issuers, intermediaries and stock exchanges. All the approvals are centralised at the head office.

The SEBI endeavours to provide a regulatory framework which would facilitate an efficient mobilisation and allocation of resources through the securities market. The SEBI has issued the following guidelines for the smooth functioning of the Securities market:

1. SEBI Guidelines, 1992 (Disclosure and Investor Protection, 1992).
2. SEBI Merchant Bankers, 1992.
3. SEBI Debentures Trustee Rules and Regulations, 1992.
4. SEBI Stock-brokers and Sub-brokers Rules and Regulations, 1992.
5. SEBI Insider Trading Regulations, 1992.
6. SEBI Guidelines for FII, 1992.
7. SEBI Registrars and Share Transfer Agents Rules and Regulations, 1993.
8. SEBI Underwriters Rules and Regulations, 1993.
9. SEBI Portfolio Managers Rules and Regulations, 1993.
10. SEBI Mutual Funds Regulations, 1993.
11. Guidelines for Foreign Brokers, 1993.
12. Advertising Code Primary Issues, 1993.
13. Guidelines for MMMFs.
14. SEBI Bankers to the Issue Rules and Regulations, 1994.
15. Guidelines for Disclosure and Investors Protection.

16. Guidelines for Peferential Allotment by Listed Companies to FIIs, 1994.
17. Guidelines for Advertisement of Schemes of the Mutual Funds, 1994.
18. SEBI Significant Acquisitions and Takeovers Regulations 1994.

Registration

The SEBI has the power to grant the certificate of registration to the Stock-brokers, Registrars, Sub-brokers, Merchant bankers, Underwriters, Share Transfer Agents, Lead Managers, Portfolio Managers, Investment Advisors and such Other Financial Intermediaries. The other intermediaries like **depository, custodian, FII, credit rating agency** commence their business after obtaining the Registration Certificate from the SEBI. No intermediary will be allowed without the certificate from the SEBI. It has the authority to order, suspend or cancel the certificate of registration in such a manner determined by the regulations.

Financial support from the Government

The Central Government will look after the financial needs of the SEBI. The Government has the authority to provide sufficient funds for the smooth functioning of the board. It may after the due appropriation made by the Parliament by law, on its behalf make the grants to the board. A fund should be constituted as **the SEBI General Fund**. This should be credited by all grants, fees and charges received by the board, penalties realised under the Act, and any other sources as decided by the government. The SEBI General Fund should be utilised for the payment of salaries, allowances and also for the remuneration of the members, officers and other employees of the board. The expenses should be made according to the specifications of the Act. The SEBI should maintain proper accounts and other relevant records. The board should prepare the annual statement of the accounts in such a form as prescribed by the government. The Central Government may direct the SEBI after consulting the Comptroller and Auditor General of India, for maintaining of books of accounts. The Accounts should be audited by the **Comptroller and Auditor General of India** at a specified schedule. The Audit expenses should be borne by the SEBI. The **CAG** or his nominee has the right to demand for the production of books, accounts, concerned vouchers and other documents. The audited accounts should be submitted to the Central Government which in turn submits in the House of Parliament.

Penalties

The SEBI has the whole authority to levy penalties and impose fines if a person/intermediary fails to obey the specifications of the act. Every financial intermediary/person who is associated with the Securities market must honour the rules and regulations issued by the SEBI from time to time. If any person who fails to furnish any document, return or report is liable to a penalty not exceeding **Rs. 1.50 lakh** for each such failure. If any person fails to file any return or furnish any information, books or other documents within the time specified, he is liable to a penalty not exceeding **Rs. 5000** per day during which the failure continues.

If any person fails to maintain the books of accounts or records, he is liable to a penalty not exceeding **Rs. 10,000** for every day during which the failure continues.

If any financial intermediary registers with the SEBI but fails to enter into an agreement with his client is liable to a penalty not exceeding **Rs. 5,00,000** for every such failure. If any financial intermediary registers with the SEBI but fails to redress the investors' grievances is liable to a penalty not exceeding **Rs. 10,000** for each such failure.

Every person should obtain the certificate of registration from the board for commencing the business. Without obtaining the certificate, he is liable to a penalty not exceeding **Rs. 10,000** for each day from the date of his activities or he should pay **Rs. 10,00,000** whichever is higher. If any person/financial intermediary registers with the board, but fails to comply with the terms and conditions of the certificate, he is liable to pay a penalty not exceeding **Rs. 10,000** per day or **Rs. 10,00,000** at a time.

If any person/intermediary fails to make an application for listing its schemes as provided in the regulations governing, such listing is liable to a penalty not exceeding **Rs. 5000** per day or **Rs. 5,00,000**. If any person who registers but fails to dispatch unit certificates of any scheme in the specified manner, he is liable to a penalty not exceeding **Rs. 5000** per day.

If any person who registers with the SEBI and fails to refund the application money paid by the investors within the period specified in the regulation, he is liable to a penalty not exceeding **Rs. 1,000/-** for day during which such failure continues.

If any person who registers with the SEBI fails to invest the money collected by him in the same manner, he is liable to a penalty not exceeding **Rs. 5,00,000** for each such failure.

If any **Asset Management Company** of a registered mutual fund fails to comply with any of the regulations, such AMC is liable to a penalty not exceeding **Rs. 5,00,000** for each such failure.

If any person who registers as a stock-broker fails to issue contract notes in the prescribed manner is liable to a penalty not exceeding **five times** the amount.

If any broker fails to deliver any security or fails to make the payment for the amount due to the investor, he is liable to a penalty not exceeding **Rs. 5,000** for each day during which such failure continues.

If any person who registers with the SEBI, charges an excess amount of brokerage as specified in the manner, he is liable to a penalty not exceeding **Rs. 5,000 or five times of the excess brokerage charged.**

If any Insider who deals with the securities of a body corporate or any stock exchange on the basis of any unpublished price sensitive information or communicates any unpublished price sensitive information to any person then he is liable to a penalty not exceeding **Rs. 5,00,000.**

If any person who fails to disclose the aggregate of share holding in the body corporate before he acquires any share of that body corporate or make a public announcement to acquire the shares at a minimum price, he is liable to a penalty not exceeding **Rs. 5,00,000**.

For the purpose of adjudicating under Section of the above failures by the concerned persons/intermediaries, the board should appoint any officer not below the rank of division chief as an adjudicating officer for holding an enquiry. The enquiry should be done in a prescribed manner. The adjudicating officer should think about the quantum of penalty after considering the following factors:

1. The repetitive nature of the default.
2. The amount of loss caused to an investor as a consequence of default.
3. The amount of disproportionate gain or unfair advantage.

Appellate Tribunal

The SEBI has acquired the statutory status. The study of various regulations of the Act gives this impression. The Central Government has the authority to establish the **Appellate Tribunal**. It consists of only one person who is to be appointed through a notification by the Central Government. **The presiding officer of a Securities Appellate Tribunal should be a Judge of a High Court; he should be a member of the Indian Legal Service and held a post in Grade I for atleast 3 years.** He should work as the presiding officer of a tribunal for atleast 3 years. He should hold the office for a term of **5 years.** He should hold the office until he attains the age of **65 years.** The Tribunal fixes the salary and allowances payable and also the terms and conditions. The presiding officer should not be removed from his office except by an order from the Central Government; he can be removed on the ground of proved misbehaviour or incapacity after the enquiry made by a Judge of the Supreme Court. The Central Government may investigate about the misbehaviour or incapacity of the presiding officer. The staff of the SAT should discharge its functions under the general superintendence of the presiding officer. The SAT should have the discharging functions under this Act, the same powers as a **Civil Court** under the Code of Criminal Procedure, 1908 while trying a suit in respect of the following matters:

- **(a)** Summoning and enforcing the attendance of any person.
- **(b)** Requiring the production of documents.
- **(c)** Receiving evidence of affidavits.
- **(d)** Issuing Commissions for the examination of witness.
- **(e)** Dismissing an application for default.

Government Control

The Central Government has the authority to make rules and regulations to monitor the activities of the SEBI. The power of the Central Government to issue the directions are as follows:

1. Regarding the policy matters of the SEBI, the Central Government may give directions in writing to it from time to time. The Board should as far as practiceable, be given an opportunity to express its views before any direction. The decision of the Central Government is final in any matter.

2. The Central Government may by notification supercede the board for such period not exceeding **six months** as specified in the notification.
3. The Central Government consider the publication of a notification regarding **superceding** the board that:

   (a) all the powers, functions and duties may by or under the provisions of this Act, be exercised or discharged by or on behalf of the board until the board reconstitutes.
   (b) all the members from the date of suppression vacate their own offices.
   (c) all property owned and controlled by the board should vest in the Union Government until the board reconstitutes.

4. After the expiry of the **Supersession** specified in the notification, the Government may reconstitute the board by a fresh appointment. In such çase, any person or persons who vacated their offices under the regulation of the Act, should not be deemed disqualified for appointment. The Central Government may take any action before the expiry of the supersession.

Step taken by the SEBI to reform the Capital market

The Capital Market in India has witnessed a spectacular growth during the decade. The trend has been overwhelming till recently. The market is being broadened further with the listing of securities. Therefore the SEBI has taken several initiative steps to promote, develop and regulate the capital market. These reforms include Primary and Secondary Markets. They are presented below:

1. Abridged prospectus.
2. Proportional allotment might be allowed in case of over subscribed issues.
3. Insider trading is illegal.
4. All the financial intermediaries are to be registered with the SEBI.
5. Credit rating is made compulsory.
6. Underwriting for issues is made mandatory.

7. Deployment of Issue proceeds.
8. Fixation of promoters' contribution.
9. Risk factors are to be disclosed in the prospectus.
10. Lock in period for promoters' quota shares.
11. Capital adequacy norms are to be prescribed for the stock-brokers.
12. Circuit breaker system should be introduced at the exchange.
13. Forward trading and carry over system are banned.
14. Uniform settlement system.
15. Flexibility in Issue pricing.
16. Guidelines for the DFI for disclosures and investors protection.
17. Brokers should keep the client's money in a separate bank account.
18. Audit inspection on the books of the Stock Exchange members.
19. Norms for multiple membership in the stock exchanges.
20. Introduction of **Jumbo transfer deeds**.
21. Precautions in the transactions between clients and brokers.
22. Guidelines for preferential allotment of shares.
23. PSU bonds should be brought under the purview of the SEBI.
24. Private Mutual Funds should be permitted.
25. Constitution of the governing councils of the stock exchanges.

Buyback securities

The SEBI has allowed the Companies to buy-back its own securities by the following methods:

1. **Buyback through tender offer.**
2. **Buyback through open market.**

Tender Offer

According to the rules and regulations, a Company can buy its securities from the existing share-holders or any other through negotiated deals. A company may also buy its shares through any private arrangement. The SEBI would not permit the insider trading in this aspect. If any company is interested to buy its own securities from any source, a special resolution should be made. The copy of the special resolution should be filed with the SEBI and the concerned stock exchanges within **Seven days** from the date of passing the resolution. The notice for the special resolution should be served along with the company's explanation regarding the buyback of its shares. The explanation document contains the following matters:

1. The date of approval of the proposal at the meeting.
2. The situation for the buy back of the shares.
3. The mode of buy back of the companies securities.
4. The sufficient provision of money for buy back the securities.
5. The base point for the fixation of the buy back price.
6. The number of securities to be purchased by the company.
7. The intention of the promoters regarding this scheme.
8. The details regarding the repayment of loans to FI/Banks.
9. The details regarding the refunding of fixed deposits, debentures etc.
10. The auditors' report addressed to the board of directors.
11. The details regarding the repayment of **Preference shares.**
12. The assurance of the board of directors regarding the company affairs.
13. The details regarding the general meting of the share holders.
14. The board of directors should give assurance that its state of affairs would not become **insolvent** within a period of **one year** from that date.

The tender method of option to buy back its own securities from the exiting securities holders on proportional basis, in addition to the above information, they should furnish some additional information regarding the buy back price of the securities. If a company wants to buy back its shares, it should make a public announcement in at least **one English daily, one Hindi and one regional language**. The announcement should contain the following information in the media:

1. Full information about the offer.
2. The schedule time for opening and closing of the process.
3. The details about the authority for the offer of the buy back.
4. The full details and complete disclosure of all material factors.
5. The environment for the buy back.
6. The methodology to be adopted for the buy back.

7. The maximum amount to be invested in this method.
8. Information about the Company.
9. The Auditor's report for the last three years.
10. The full details of the capital structure of the company.
11. The full information about the statutory approvals obtained.
12. The lead manager should ensure that the financial data should be latest.
13. The details about the collection and bidding centres.
14. The public announcement date should be confirmed by the board of directors.
15. Present Capital structure and the share holding pattern.
16. The information regarding any change in the management structure.
17. The other disclosures as may be specified by the SEBI from time to time.
18. The details about the persons who are in the control of the company.
19. Thc full information about **thc cscrow account**.
20. The information regarding the financial ratios as specified by the SEBI.
21. The listing details of the company's scrip with the stock exchange.
22. The stock marketing data regarding **high, low and average** market price of the scrip.
23. The monthly high and low prices for 6 months from the date of announcement.
24. The information regarding the number of securities are traded on the above (23) period.
25. The market price immediately after the date of approving the buy back.
26. The volume of securities are traded in each month during 6 months preceding the date of the public announcement.
27. The specified data must be earlier than **30 days** and not later than **42 days** from the date of the public announcement.
28. The draft letter of offer should be submitted with the prescribed fee to the SEBI.
29. The SEBI will charge the following fee for a proposed buy back of the securities **transactions**.

Size of the buy back offer	*Fee*
If the issue size is more than Rs. 500 crores	Rs. 5,00,000
" " " between Rs.100–500 "	Rs. 2,00,000
" 50–100 "	Rs. 1,00,000
" 10–50 "	Rs. 75,000
" 5–10 "	Rs. 50,000
upto Rs. 5 crores	Rs. 25,000

According to the Companies Act **Section 77A**, the Company should file along with a draft letter of offer and declaration of solvency in a prescribed manner.

The buy back of the securities must be opened to the share holder for a minimum period of **15 days** and maximum period of **30 days.** The buy back offer should not be earlier than 7 days or later than 30 days after the specified date of the buy back securities. After the process of completion, a communication should be made within **15 days** from the closure of the offer.

Escrow Account

Before the commencement of the buy back process, the company should deposit some amount in the Escrow Account. It is an account for which the bank acts an uninterested third party to ensure compliance with the terms of the deed between two parties to fulfill some stated conditions. After that it operates. The bank hold such account in which the funds thus accumulated have to pay **taxes, insurance on mortgage property etc.** The escrow Account consists of :

(a) Cash deposited with a schedule bank.
(b) The bank guarantee in favour of the Merchant banker.
(c) A deposit of margin with the merchant banker.

The Company should keep the amount in the Escrow Account and make it available to the Merchant banker. The merchant banker is empowered to operate the Escrow Account according to the situation. On payment of consideration to all the share-holders who have accepted the offer and after the completion of all the formalties of the buy back, if any amount remains in the Escrow Account, it should be released to the Company. The SEBI has full authority in case of **Non-fulfillment** of obligations under these regulations. The Company can forfeit the Escrow Account either in full or a part. The amount of the forfeited sum can be distributed on pro-rata basis amongst the security holders who accepts the offers. If there is any balance, it would be deployed for the investors protection.

Payment of the Consideration

After the closure of the offer, the company is required to open a special account with a banker and there in deposit such sum together with the amount lying in the **Escrow Account**. This must be utilised the payment of consideration in cash to those security share holders whose offer has been accepted or returned.

Destruction of the Share Certificates

After the payment of consideration to the accepted shareholder, the company may collect the shares by hand and destroy the security certificates bought back in the presence of a merchant banker/STA/ Registrar and the statutory auditor within 7 days from the date of acceptance of the securities. If the buyback securities are in the form of **"Dematerialised"**, they should be extinguished and destroyed according to the act of the SEBI **(Depositories and Participants)** Regulation 1996 and bye-laws. The company should submit a certificate to the SEBI signed by a Registrar/Merchant banker and MD with the statutory auditor of the Company within **7 days** of the extinguishment and destruction of the certificates. The company should maintain a separate account for cancelled and destroyed certificates. The destroyed certificates should be submitted to the concerned stock exchange within **7 days.**

Buyback from the Open Market

A Company can buy its own securities through the Open Market. The shares may be further categorised as:

(a) Book Building Process
(b) Stock Exchange
(c) From Odd-Lot Buyback

(a) Book Building Process

The buy back of securities through the book building process can be made by the company with a special resolution. The company should pass a special resolution by specifying the maximum price. The Company should make a public announcement at least **7 days** prior to the commencement of the buy back. The Company has to appoint a Merchant Banker for this purpose. It has to deposit in **the Escrow account** before the date of public announcement. After the announcement of the book building process, the company has to submit a copy to the SEBI along with the specified fees within two days. The public announcement should reveal the following matters:

1. **The methodology of book building process**
2. **The manner of acceptance**
3. **The format of acceptance**
4. **The details of the bidding centres.**

The book building involves with the latest technology and transparency. For this, the company should arrange the bidding centres with a minimum number of **30**. There should be a computer terminal connecting all the bidding centres. The offer should be open to the security holders for a period of **15 days** but should not exceed **30 days**. The company should decide the buy back price along with the Merchant banker's opinion. The offer price should be paid to all the holders who accepts the buy back method.

(b) Stock Exchange

The shares are repurchased by the company through the stock exchanges. For this purpose, a special resolution should be passed by the company. The resolution should specify the maximum offer price. The shares cannot be purchased from the promoters or interested parties. If a company wants to buyback its shares through the Stock Exchange Process, it should make a public announcement atleast **7 days** prior to the commencement of the buy back. The Company has to appoint a Merchant banker. A copy of public announcement should be submitted to the SEBI within two days along with the specified fees. The announcement should reveal all the information regarding the details of the brokers and stock-exchanges etc. The buy back should be made only through:

1. **the stock exchange which has an electronic trading facility or**
2. **matching mechanism.**

The Merchant banker and the company should furnish the information to the concerned stock exchange on a daily basis regarding the developments of the process. The furnished information should be published in a national daily newspaper. The company identity should appear on the electronic screen. The process for destroying the share certificate should be applicable on par with the earlier methods. The company should complete its legal formalities within **15** days of the payment.

(c) From Odd Lot Buyback

The rules and regulations pertaining to the buy back scheme through the odd-lot method are applicable in the same manner which the earlier methods followed:

General Obligations

The Company can buyback its own securities either through tender offer method or through open market system. The method to be adopted by the company depends on the decision of the company. The company should fulfill the obligations in the following manner :

- **(a)** The company should furnish true, factual information in a letter of offer or in a public announcement or any other advertisement, circular, brochure or publicity material.
- **(b)** The announcement should indicate that the information is true and the board of directors have to accept the responsibility of the information.
- **(c)** The Company should ensure that during the offer period no bonus issue will be made under these regulations.
- **(d)** The Company should pay consideration only in the form of cash.
- **(e)** The Company should not withdraw the offer, after the announcement.
- **(f)** If the Company announces the offer to buy back its own securities through any of the sources, the promoter or the person in control should not involve in the securities of the company in the stock exchange during the offer period.

(g) The Companies Act does not allow the buy back offer of the companies if the **amalgamation** method is in pending.

(h) The Company should appoint a compliance officer for redressing the investor's problems.

(i) The particulars of the destroyed security certificate should be furnished by the company to the concerned stock exchange within 7 **days** of destruction.

(j) The Company should not buy back its own securities in the following situations:

(1) Locked in securities

(2) Non-transferable securities till the pendency of the lock in period.

(k) The Company should issue an advertisement in the national daily within two days of the completion of the process by disclosing the following factors :

1. The number of securities bought under this offer.
2. The price of the security which the offer is made by the company.
3. The total amount paid in consideration of the securities.
4. The full details of the security holders who have offered their securities under this process exceeding one percent of the total securities.
5. The Company should also reveal about the consequences of the capital structure before and after the buy back of the securities.
6. The Company should follow all the rules and regulations of the SEBI in addition to the Company Act and other applicable laws.

Obligations of the Merchant Banker

The Merchant banker plays an important role in the buyback process. The Merchant banker is also responsible for fulfilling all the formalities by the offer made company being a client to him. He has to ensure that:

(a) The offer will be implemented by the company without any hurdle.

(b) The obligations of the Company towards the **Escrow A/c**.

(c) Payment of consideration in the form of cash.
(d) The announcement of the buy back should be done according to the legal formalities.
(e) The letter of offer should be filed with the SEBI.
(f) The contents of information regarding the public announcement should be fair and true.
(g) The compliance of the Section 77A, 77B of the Companies Act and any other laws are necessary.
(h) Fulfillment of the obligations of the **Escrow A/c** must be maintained by the Company.
(i) A final report should be furnished in a specified manner within **15 days** from the closure of the buyback offer.
(j) If the Merchant banker fails to comply with the obligations of these regulations, immediate action should be taken against the financial intermediary.

Penalty Procedure

The SEBI is the most powerful organisation in India and it controls the activities of all the financial intermediaries like Registrars, Merchant bankers, Underwriters etc. The penalties imposed by the SEBI are as follows:

(a) Power to order Investigation
(b) Power to Issue Directions

The SEBI has the power to order the investigations on the ***Suo moto*** or upon the information received by it, to conduct the affairs of any person associated with the process of the buy back. The SEBI is empowered to appoint an officer for the following:

(a) to monitor the activities of any person who involves in malpractice.
(b) to investigate into any complaint of these regulations.
(c) The suspected person should produce before the SEBI the things required *i.e.* books, accounts, documents.
(d) The suspected person should extend cooperation to the investigating officer for examining the books of accounts and other documents.

(e) The investigating officer has the full powers to summon and enforce the attendance of the persons.

(f) After completion of the investigating process, the investigating officer should submit a report to the SEBI.

(g) On receipt of the report from the investigation officer, the SEBI takes an initiative action depending upon the degree of guiltyness of such person.

The SEBI has the power to issue directions in the interest of the securities market and investors.

(a) It has the power to direct the concerned person not to participate in any activities which lead to the violation of the Companies Act.

(b) It has the power to direct the concerned person not to involve in any further deal in the securities in any manner.

(c) It can direct the concerned person to divert or sell the shares which are acquired by violating the rules and regulations of the act.

(d) It has the power to take an action against the registered financial intermediary.

(e) Any person who involves in the Insider Trading against the provisions should be dealt in accordance with the provisions of the **SEBI Insider Trading regulations, 1992; and SEBI (Prohibition of Fradulent and Unfair Trade Practices) Regulations, 1995.**

Therefore the SEBI has been set up to protect the interests of the investors. It is the watchdog of the market. It is empowered to look after the welfare of the Individual investors, Institutional investors, financial intermediaries and corporate sector. It has now full powers to regulate the primary and secondary markets.

Takeover SEBI Regulations

At present, the takeover wave is sweeping the country. It is known fact that there have been a number of takeover bids. It became a quite common phenomenon. It can be defined as "the acquisition of another Company that may take the form of a friendly or unfriendly merger."[14] The shareholders of the target company realise an appreciable increments in wealth relative to the market value of their holdings prior to take over activity. The appreciation in wealth is possible only due to the premium paid by the acquiring company. Once the announcement has been made to the takeover of a particular company, the target company's stock tends to raise in the market. Usually in the takeover process, the acquiring company's simply pay too much. Therefore the acquiring company worth decreases. All acquisition may not be fruitful but some are worthy. Some elements enhance the value of the worth. The combination of these two companies is treated either as a **purchase or a pooling of interest**.

The benefits of a takeover company depends on the availability of ready-made manufacturing facilities, well-established brand, market share and potential, no need of licences and well-planned distribution network. The takeover is a device for the companies which try to enter into the new business areas or expansion in the same time of activity. The various acts like **FEMA, MRTP, IRDA** have further added the needed impetus. It is also known as **"unwanted undertakings" or buying up their competitors**. The BIFR became a facilitator of **M&A deals**. After the introduction of the SEBI regulations, the legal hurdles dismantled. The Government is in the attitude of non-interference in the takeover process. The availability of the cheap funds in the Global and domestic markets strengthened the takeover method.

The takeover is a method of amalgamation of Companies. In amalgamation, one company makes an offer to purchase the shares of another company's members.

The takeover is different from the merger in approach. It is a unilateral step and the offer company decides the maximum price by considering the existing rules and regulations. It takes a less time while the merger requires a time consuming method. Various things influence the takeover decision such as goodwill of the company, large scale production, increase in the earning capacity by acquiring the same line sector company, a high calibre to meet the R&D expenditure. Acquisition is the purchase by one Company of a controlling interest in the share capital of another existing company. The acquisition may arise in the following situations :

(a) Agreement with the majority share holders in the company.
(b) Buying of shares in the open market.
(c) Buying of new shares by private treaty.
(d) An offer to the existing shareholders.

(e) Payment of consideration in the form of **cash, debenture and issue of shares.**

Amalgamation is defined by **Halsbury** as "a blending of two or more existing undertakings into one undertaking the shareholders of each blending company becoming substantially the shareholders in the company which is to carry on the blended undertaking."

Amalgamations and Mergers process

Amalgamation means the creation of a new organisation by combining two ore more units. In the process of amalgamation two or more companies may liquidate themselves under the law and sell their assets and transfer liabilities to a new company which issues its own stock in exchange for the **new worth** of property received from the amalgamating companies. No one company can exist after the completion of the amalgamation. The Merger is also known as **"Absorption".** The absorbing company retains its identity and expands its size through a merger. **Reconstruction** means purchase of one undertaking by the other, transfer of shares from one undertaking to the other, and an order of the Central Government in the regulation of **Section 394, 395, 396** of the Companies Act, 1956. According to the Section 391 of the Companies Act, 1956, a compromise should be done with the creditors to carry out the scheme of reconstruction or amalgamation. The court may order for a compromise or arrangement or by a subsequent order makes provision to facilitate the reconstruction or amalgamation.

The following steps are involved in the scheme of **amalgamation**:

(a) The acquirer prepares a scheme of amalgamation.
(b) Defining the transferor and transferee.
(c) Authorised, issued and subscribed capital of transferor and transferee companies.
(d) Basis of scheme-evaluation report, transfer of assets and liabilities, specified date, consolidation of capital.
(e) Change of name, object and accounting year.
(f) Protection of employment.
(g) Dividend position and prospects.
(h) Conditions of the scheme.

The Mergers, Acquisitions and Takeovers are regulated by the SEBI. The SEBI Regulations. 1994 deals with the substantial Acquisition of Shares and Takeovers. The Act contains 5 chapters indicating the rule position regarding the takeover methodology. **Chapter I** reveals the preliminary aspects such as definitions and concepts of various terms. **Chapter II** deals with the disclosures of share holdings as per Regulations 5 to 8. **Chapter III** indicates the applicability of the regulation for takeover process. **Chapter IV** contains the bailout takeover process. **Chapter V** discloses the information regarding the investigation process as per the Regulations 33 to 40.

Exemptions

According to the regulations from **9 to 25**, the takeover provisions are not applicable to the acquisitions of shares in the following cases. **(exempted cases)**

- **(a)** Application of shares are made in pursuance of a prospectus issued shares (Public Issue).
- **(b)** Underwriting arrangement.
- **(c)** Share acquired under **Sections 391 and 394** of the Companies Act.
- **(d)** The shares acquired under **Section 18** of the Sick Industrial Companies Act, 1985.
- **(e)** Acquisitions of shares in the general course of business by a registered stock-broker.
- **(f)** The shares of unlisted companies.
- **(g)** The SEBI is empowered to grant exemption.

Minimum Offer Price

The Minimum Offer Price is regulated by the SEBI provisions under **Regulation 19**. It deals with the declaration of the minimum price by the acquirer. He should make the public announcement atleast in one English newspaper and one in regional newspaper. An acquirer who holds shares carrying **10 per cent** or less voting rights should not acquire further shares from the open market which when taken together with his existing holding would carry more than **10 per cent** of the voting rights unless he makes a public announcement. The purchasing offer should be made through a registered merchant banker. The take over announcement copy should be furnished to the SEBI atleast **24 hours** before its issuance. The **Regulation 17** of the SEBI Act reveals that the acquirer should submit the draft of a letter to the board for the approval within **14 days** of the public announcement. A certificate should be submitted by the merchant banker. The acquirer should pay a fee of **Rs. 25,000/-** to the board. The letter of offer should be sent to all the shareholders of the company for the purpose of acquisition. Under the regulations, the minimum offer price may be payable in cash or by exchange of shares or by combining the both. According to the **Regulation 9**, the minimum offer price is the negotiated price or quoted price on the stock exchange though it will be **higher**. Under the **Regulation 10** of the Act, the minimum offer price is the highest price in the open market or quoted on the stock exchange whichever is higher. The **Regulations 21, 23 and 25** deal with the number of shares to be acquired, competitive acquisition and withdrawal of offer respectively. The **Regulation 20** indicates the general obligations which are to be fulfilled by the acquirer. They are presented below:

- **(a)** The acquirer company should be able to implement the offer.
- **(b)** The acquirer should submit a letter of offer to the board of directors of the company whose shares are being acquired.
- **(c)** The acquirer should indicate the period of offer.
- **(d)** The acquirer should declare accepting the responsibility for the information presented by him.
- **(e)** The acquirer should also give an assurance for not making any further public announcement for the acquisition of shares in **succeeding 6 months.**

Bailout Takeover

Bailout takeover means the promoter who takeover a financially weak company in pursuance of the rehabilitation scheme approved by a public financial institution or schedule bank. The provisions pertaining to the bailout takeovers would not apply to the **Sick Industrial Companies.** The Sick Industrial Companies are governed by the **Sick Industrial Companies (Special Provisions) Act**. The financially weak company may not be a sick company. According to the **Regulation 26** of the Act, financially weak company means, a company which accumulates losses at the end of the previous financial year and results in the erosion of more than **50 per cent** but less than **100 per cent** of its net worth. The net worth of the company is the sum total of the **paid up capital and free reserves**. This regulation excludes the Sick Industrial Unit. For understanding the context in a better way, we must know the difference between sick company and financially weak company. The Sick Company has been defined by the **Sick Industrial Companies (Special Provisions) Act 1985** "an industrial company (being a company registered for not less than five years) which has at the end of any financial year, accumulates losses equal to or exceeding its entire net worth."

Substantial acquisition means a total acquisition of not less than **20 per cent** or more of the shares. The **Regulation 30** reveals that substantial acquisition held by the public should be less than **20 per cent** of the paid up share capital of such company. The lead financial institution appraises the company in financial viability, assess fund requirements for revival and draw up of the **rehabilitation** scheme. The rehabilitation scheme should also provide the details of any change in the management. It may provide for the acquisition of shares in a financially weak Company in the "outright purchase of shares or exchange of shares or a combination of both." According to the Rehabilitation programme, the lead institution should invite offers for the acquisition of shares from atleast **Three Parties**. The lead institution would have to select one party among the three, based on the managerial competence, technical capability of the person/party, adequacy of the financial resources etc. It should provide necessary information to any interested person regarding the present management capability, technology, range of products, share holders pattern, financial holding, five years balance sheets and any other information desired by that person. It evaluates the bids received with reference to the purchase price or exchange of shares, track record, financial muscle, goodwill of the management of the person acquiring the shares. After the evaluation, the financially weak company accepts one of the bids. The selection of the bid-decision should be informed to the lead institution which in turn invite the acquirer for determining the offer price. The promoter of the weak company, financial institutions and also other shareholders together determine the offer price by a mutual negotiation between the person acquiring the shares and the lead institution.

The acquirer should make a pubic announcement of his intention *i.e.* about the acquisition of shares. The announcement should contain relevant details about the offer process. Therefore the acquisition process should be completed as per the procedure laid down in the Act.

The SEBI has the full authority to investigate the affairs of the acquired company as per the SEBI Act. **Chapter V** of the SEBI Act deals with the investigation process about the affairs of the acquired company.

SEBI and Insider Trading

Insider Trading is an unfair and unhealthy practice. The SEBI prohibited the Insider Dealing or Trading. It may be defined as the "sale or purchase of securities by the persons who possess the price sensitive information about the company."[15] It damages the integrity of the market. Insider trading may be a brain child of the brokers and top level management of the corporate sector. The favourable and unfavourable trends of the particular company lead to the Insider Trading. The favourable trends for a particular Company are **Takeover and Diversification and Takeover**. The Unfavourable trends are the occasions of the poor performance and loss of earnings. The unpublished price sensitive information occupies an important role in the Insider Trading. **For example** financial results, interim and final dividends, rights issues, bonus issue, mergers, amalgamation, takeovers. The company executives, journalists, banks, financial institutions, top level management have access towards this information. Insider Trading is considered as committing an offence. The SEBI has the full authority to investigate the mal-practice on the basis of complaints from the investors/ intermediaries/***suo-motu***. The SEBI can carry on the inspection on the books of account, other records and document of a suspected person. It has the power to issue directions to the suspected person not to involve in the securities in any specific manner. According to **Section 24** of the SEBI Act, it has the power to initiate criminal prosecution against the responsible person. The Securities act also imposes the penalty upto **Rs. 5.00 lakhs** for indulging in the Insider Trading. It can be curbed only through effective enforcement of the Act. The effectiveness can be established through the strict actions like **fine, withdrawal of licenses etc.** and also treating such activities as criminal cases. But the criminal case requires a high standard of evidence. Therefore the Insider Trading could be watched and controlled by those who holds more than **5 per cent of stock**.

Prohibition of Fraudulent and Unfair Trade Practices

The Insider Trading is extremely difficult to **Pindown**. It includes the market manipulation. Market manipulation means no person should buy or sell the securities in a fraudulent manner or no person should indulge in any unfair trade practices. No person should take part or enter either directly or indirectly in the transactions of securities, which are likely to have the effect of artificially raising/depressing/stabilising the prices of securities. No person should involve in creating a **false or misleading** appearance of trading on the securities market. No person should involve in increase, depress or cause fluctuations in the market price of the securities. The prohibition of unfair trade practices are presented below:

(a) No person should engage in any act which appears as a fraud in connection with the purchase or sale of any securities.
(b) No person should indulge in the falsification of his books or account and records for the purpose of market manipulation.
(c) No person should delay the transfer of securities.

The SEBI has the right to investigate the affairs of the suspected persons. The board can inspect the books of accounts, records and documents of any person who buys or sells the securities. The SEBI has the authority to investigate into the complaints received from the investors/intermediaries/or any other person on any matter. The board has also the power to investigate *suo moto*. The SEBI sends a notice to an investigation under regulation 6 to the concerned person. Sometimes, according to the situation, the SEBI is empowered to investigate the affairs of a person without any complaint or notice in the interest of the public. The concerned person should obey the rules and regulations imposed by the Act. The person should submit all the required documents to the inspecting officer for verification. The inspecting person is empowered to examine or record the statements of any member, director, partner and employee of the concerned person. The inspecting officer should submit a report to the board after the verification of the records and facts. On receipt of the report from the inspecting officer, the board takes measures as it may deem fit including issuing directions in the interest of the securities market. The SEBI is empowered to give the directions in the following situations.

(a) The SEBI can direct the person not to deal in the securities in any manner.
(b) It can direct the person to call up any of its officers, employees or representatives to refrain from dealing the securities.
(c) It can prohibit the person from disposing off any of the securities acquired in violation of the regulations.
(d) It can take the disciplinary action against the person/intermediary holding a certificate of registration under Section 12 of the SEBI Act.

Procedure for Action in case of default

The SEBI is empowered to take the action in case of default by any person/intermediary. The procedure for the action in case of default is presented below:

(a) If any person/intermediary violates the provisions, then he is liable to suspension or cancellation of registration/imposition of civil penalty.
(b) The penalty should be imposed after the end of a detailed investigation.
(c) For the purpose of holding an enquiry under Section 13, the board may appoint an enquiry officer.
(d) The enquiry officer should issue a notice to the person at the registered office or at the principal place of the business of the person.
(e) The person should furnish a reply to the enquiry officer within **30 days** from the date of receipt of such notice.
(f) The person should appear in person or through any authorised person before the enquiry officer.
(g) During the period of enquiry, the officer should have the power to summon any person relevant to the subject matter of the enquiry.
(h) If any person neglects or refuses the enquiry, the officer may proceed the enquiry in the absence of such person.
(i) The enquiry officer will give a chance to appoint a presenting officer on behalf of the board.
(j) The enquiry officer should recommend the penalty to be awarded.
(k) On receipt of the report from the enquiry officer, the board

can issue a show-cause notice to the person.

(l) The concerned person should submit a reply to the board on receipt of the notice within **21 days**.

(m) On receipt of the reply from the concerned person, the board should take the action as early as possible but not later than **30 days** from the receipt of the reply. The order copy should be sent to the concerned person.

The board has the power to take initiate criminal proceedings before the court of competent jurisdiction. **The Metropolitan Magistrate or Judicial Magistrate** of the first class is empowered to punish the concerned person under the regulations of the Act. According to **Section 24** of the act, if any person gives a false explanation in an enquiry, a **penalty** should be imposed under this regulation. If any person is aggrieved by an order of the board, he may appeal to the Central Government.

SEBI Guidelines to Stock broker/Sub-Brokers

The entry into the stock market is not open to the pubic. The buying and selling of shares and securities is done through the members of the stock exchanges. The financial assets such as **Equity, Preference Shares, Bonds, Debentures** are issued by the companies. Bonds, securities issued by the Government are traded on capital markets. The buyer and seller of the financial asset do not meet directly meet in an organised stock market. The transactions take place through the brokers. They work as agents only. They charge a commission on each transaction. The stock-brokers play an active role and support the stock exchanges by performing the following useful economic services:

(a) ready marketability and price stability for the securities.

(b) contributes to the growth of savings.

(c) contributes to the growth of industrial sector development.

The brokers meet in the stock exchange at specified hours for executing the transactions of their clients. All the transactions done on the stock exchange will be entered in the slips. The transactions will be settled through bids and offer. The broker is responsible for the delivery of the share certificates to the buyers. The sale or purchase of shares' procedure is presented below:

(a) Orders are placed with the brokers for buying or selling of shares at best rates.

(b) The order price may inclusive of a broker's commission or market price *i.e.* excluding broker commission. It is to be added.

(c) The transactions will be settled through the system of clearing transactions.

(d) The clearing house acts as the coordinator of all the activities among the members of the stock exchange.

(e) The Competition among the bidders for buying and selling of securities may stabilise the securities prices in the market.

(f) The settlement period is generally a week and the transactions made during this period are settled either by payment or by delivery on the specified days of the clearing programme.

(g) After the closing hours of the market, every member should submit his **Sanda Sheets** to the computer centre which effect the purchase and sale of shares on that day. All the activities of the brokers will be checked by the computer itself. All the adjustments are made in the Computer during the settlement period. A statement of all the sender thus adjusted is printed out. A **balance sheet** for the member in total receivable or payable is also printed out. The sum of the total shares to be delivered should be equal to the sum of the total shares to be received for each security. Every member will be provided with a statement showing the details of deliveries to be effected by him to others and *vice versa*. The total transaction report should be prepared after adjusting all the transactions. The details of the unmatched transactions should be printed out.

(h) In case of the specified shares, the settlement transactions are settled through **Three options**. The broker has to terminate his contract of sale or purchase by a cross contract or squaring up to complete the contract by delivery or payment or to carry over the contract to the next settlement.

(i) The settlement system offers greater liquidity to the authorities in the secondary market.

Registration of Stock-Broker

The interested person should make an application for the grant of certificate in **Form A** through the stock exchange. It may forward the application to the SEBI within **30 days** from the date of its receipt. After receiving the application from the concerned stock exchange, the SEBI will scrutinise it. The SEBI may ask for further information or clarification regarding the dealings in the securities in order to grant the certificate. The applicant or its principal officer, if necessary should appear before the board for personal representation. The SEBI on being satisfied, the person is eligible as a stock broker. It grants the certificate in **Form D** to the stock broker and sends an intimation to that effect to the stock exchange. The person who holds the stock broker certificate should at all times abide by the code of conduct as per the Act. Sometimes, the SEBI may reject the application of an interested person for registration. Then the person should follow the following process for the grant of the certificate:

(a) The SEBI may reject the application on the following grounds:
   1. If the broker has no eligibility.
   2. If he does not have the necessary infrastructure facilities.
   3. If he does not have any past experience in dealing the securities in the market.

(b) The refusal of grant of certificate should be communicated by the SEBI within **30 days** of such refusal to the applicant and concerned stock exchange.

(c) On receipt of the communication from the SEBI, the applicant should apply again within a period of **30 days** from the date of receipt of such intimation for reconsideration of its decision.

(d) Finally the SEBI may communicate its decision in writing to the applicant and to the concerned stock exchange.

(e) A stockbroker whose application for the grant of certificate has been refused by the board should not deal in the securities as a stock broker.

Every applicant who is eligible for the grant of a certificate should pay such fee as specified in the Act from time to time. At some moments, the board may give for the payment of the fee before the expiry of **6 months** from the date on which such fee becomes due. If a stock-broker fails to pay the fee as prescribed, the board may suspend the registration certificate.

Registration of Sub-brokers

The stock sub-brokers should apply to the SEBI in **Form B** for the grant of a certificate. The application for registration should contain a recommendation letter from the stock-broker in **Form C** along with the recommendation from his banker also. The application form should be submitted to the concerned Stock exchange. The Concerned stock exchange on receipt of the application should verify the information contained. It should also certify that the applicant is eligible for the registration as per the Act. The eligibility criteria for the registration as a sub-broker is as follows:

- **(a)** for Individuals
- **(b)** for Partnership firms/body corporate

In the case of registration for individuals the following norms should be fulfilled by the applicant.

1. The applicant should be 21 years of age.
2. The applicant should not be convicted of any offence involving in **fraud or dishonesty**.
3. The applicant should have the minimum educational qualification *i.e.* **10+2** or its equivalent examination recognised by the government.

In the case of registration for firm/corporates the above regulations should be fulfilled. If the board satisfies with the eligibility of the stock sub-broker, then it grants a certificate in **Form E** to the sub-broker and an intimation to the concerned stock exchange. The sub-broker should pay the fee as specified in the Act and abide by the code of conduct. The sub-broker should enter into an agreement with the **stock-broker** for specifying the scope of his authority and responsibility.

Code of Conduct of the StockBroker

The stock-broking is a highly specialised skillful work. It needs talent, knowledge, sincerity, a thorough understanding about the economy, a clear idea about the government policies, etc. He must fully acquaint with the latest developments in the national programmes. He should be decent. He must be a dynamic personality and have his own style of functioning. The broker must be in a good position to maintain relations with all the parties as below:

(a) **General Relations**
(b) **Investors Relations**
(c) **Relationship with other Brokers**

(a) Relations with General Public

The stock-broker should maintain high standards of integrity, promptness and transparency while conducting his business affairs. A stock-broker should act with due skill, care and deligence to conduct his business affairs. He should not involve in manipulative, fraudulent deceptive or spread rumours to make personal gains. He should not create false market or indulge in any act detrimental to the investors. He should not involve himself in **excessive** speculative business in the market. He should abide by all the provisions of the Act, rules and regulations issued by the government, the SEBI and the stock exchange from time to time.

(b) Relations with the Investors

The stock brokers should maintain better relations with the investors. The **Customer** is the king in the market. The broker should be sincere to his investors. He should deal with his clients faithfully in executing the orders for buying and selling the securities at the best available market price. He should not refuse to deal with a small investor merely on the ground of the volume of the business. He should promptly inform his client about the **execution** or **non-execution** of an order. He should make prompt payment in respect of the securities sold. He should also arrange for the prompt delivery of the securities purchased by the investors. The broker should issue a contract note to his client without any delay in the prescribed form. He should maintain a high confidentiality about the transactions. He should not disclose any information to any other person. He should not encourage his clients for the sale or purchase of the securities with the object of generating brokerage or commission. He should not furnish false or misleading quotations/advice/information to the clients to earn commission or brokerage. He should not deal or transact with other brokers for a defaulted client. He should not make a recommendation to any client or investor. He should have adequately trained skillful and talented staff. He should arrange to render fair, competent and prompt services to his clients.

(c) Relations with other Brokers

The stock-broking is a highly talented skillful job. It requires a careful handling of the assignments. The stock-broker should maintain healthy relations with the other brokers. He should be in a cooperative manner with the other contracting parties while comparing the unmatched transactions. He should be careful in the delivery of shares. He should cooperate with others in finding **bad delivery**. He should cooperate with other brokers in protecting the interests of his clients for their rights to **bonus, rights and dividends** related to securities. He should cooperate with other stock brokers for the smooth settlement of transactions. He should advertise only with the permission from the concerned stock exchange. He should submit a correct and accurate required returns to the SEBI and to the concerned stock exchange.

General Obligations and Responsibilities

The following obligations have to be fulfilled by every registered broker in India. He should normally keep the following books of accounts, records and documents. All these books should be maintained by all the brokers.

- **(a)** Sanda book (Register of transactions).
- **(b)** Clients ledger.
- **(c)** General ledger.
- **(d)** Journal.
- **(e)** Cash book.
- **(f)** Bank passbook.
- **(g)** Documents register.
- **(h)** Members contract books.
- **(i)** Margin deposit book.
- **(j)** Register of the accounts of the sub-brokers.
- **(k)** Duplicate of the Contract notes issued to the clients.
- **(l)** An agreement with the sub-broker.

The stock-brokers who register with the SEBI should intimate to the officials about the place of keeping the books. Every stock-broker should submit the accounting information after closing the books of accounts within **6 months** from the closure of the financial year to the SEBI. Every registered broker should preserve the books of accounts and other records for a minimum period of **5 years**.

The Procedure for Inspection

The SEBI has the full authority over the financial intermediaries. It controls, regulates, monitors, evaluates and directs the markets. It can inspect any stock broker's premises who registers with the SEBI. The Board may appoint one or more persons as the inspecting authority to inspect the books of accounts, records, documents of the stock-broker for any purpose. Basically the SEBI undertakes the inspection for the following purposes:

- **(a)** to check the maintainance of the books of accounts as per the Act.
- **(b)** to observe whether the registered broker has fulfilled all the legal formalities or not.
- **(c)** to investigate into the complaints received from the investors and other stock brokers.
- **(d)** To investigate the ***suo motu*** in the interest of securities business or investors interest into the affairs of the stock-broker.
- **(e)** the board should give a reasonable notice to the broker before undertaking the inspection.
- **(f)** if the board feels necessary to inspect the registered stock-broker it can commence the inspection without sending any notice to the broker in the interest of the investors.
- **(g)** the stock-broker should be bound to discharge his obligations.
- **(h)** during the tenure of the inspection, it is the duty of every director, partner, officer and employee of the broker to produce the records.
- **(i)** the inspecting authority should submit the inspection report to the board after the completion of the inspection.
- **(j)** on receipt of the inspection report, the board should communicate the findings to the broker. Before taking an action, the board may give him an opportunity of being heard his version.

(k) the board may appoint a qualified auditor to investigate into the books of account or affairs of the broker.

Procedure in Case of Default

The SEBI has the right to take the action in case of default by a registered stock-broker in India. If the stock-broker fails to comply with any of the conditions for which the registration has been granted, then he is liable for taking an action. A broker who contravenes any of the provisions of the Act, rules and regulations, there is a liability to take an action against such broker. He should strictly follow the rules and regulations of the stock exchange and the Securities Contract Act. If he fails to comply with the norms, he is liable to pay the **penalties** as specified in the Act. The penalty in case of default may be either suspension or cancellation of registration. The suspension may be imposed on the following grounds. If:

(a) the broker violates the provisions, acts, rules and regulations.
(b) the broker does not follow the code of conduct.
(c) the broker fails to pay the fee.
(d) the broker violates the conditions of the registration.
(e) the broker fails to resolve the complaints of the investors.
(f) the broker indulges in the manipulation of the share prices.
(g) the broker has an improper/unbusiness/unprofessional conduct.
(h) the membership of the broker is suspended by the stock exchange.
(i) he fails to respond the board communication.
(j) the broker involves in price rigging/cornering activities in the market.
(k) the financial position deteriorates the broker.
(l) the broker fails to furnish any information to the board.
(m) the broker furnishes wrong or false information.
(n) the broker does not submit the periodical return.
(o) the broker does not corporate during the enquiry period.

The stock broker's registration can be cancelled by the SEBI, if

(a) the broker violates the takeover provisions or any provisions of the insider trading regulations.
(b) the membership of the broker is cancelled by the stock exchange.
(c) the broker is convicted of a criminal offence.

(d) the broker is guilty of fraud.

Any broker being aggrieved by an order of the board may appeal to the Central Government under the provisions of the Act.

SEBI Investor's Protection

The Investors are the most important persons in the capital market. They come under the perview of the Consumer Act. Generally in India, they face many problems like **Non-receipt of refund, allotment order, delay and non-receipt of interest and dividend.** These problems arise due to the negligence of the **corporate bodies and financial intermediaries**. These problems are solved by the regulatory authorities like the SEBI and the stock exchange. The basic redresal of grievances is done by the stock exchanges and corporate sectors. All the exchanges in India have the Investors services cell to resolve the grievances. But there have been inordinate delays in resolving such grievances. The guidelines include the aspects like Insider trading, Inspection of stock exchanges and their records, scrutiny of prospectus for adequate disclosures, credit rating for financial instruments like debentures, deposits. The stock-brokers are required to disclose the statutory requirements. They should bring transparency in the clients transactions. The SEBI has issued guidelines to the companies and stock exchanges for the following aspects:

1. Inspection of books of brokers.
2. Transparency in prices and volume of trade in the stock exchange.
3. Enforcing the margin norms strictly.
4. Amendments to the bye-laws of the exchanges with regard to capital adequacy.
5. Indicating the brokerage and security price separately in the contract note.
6. Reviewing and redressing the investor grievances promptly.
7. Amendment to the relevant bye-laws for the issue of contract note by the brokers to the client mandatory.

The Joint Parliament Committee has expressed its opinion for providing protection to the small investors. The Committee recommended an effective system to handle the complaints and taking of the follow-up action within the specified time frame. The SEBI has been vested with adequate powers through the ordinance to protect and safeguard the interests of the investors. The following elements cover the investors' protection and grievances.

(a) Investor protection—SEBI plus Investors' associations.
(b) Provisions of the Companies Act.
(c) Provisions of the **SCR Act**.
(d) Listing Guidelines on the investor protection.
(e) Investor guidance series.
(f) Computerised process of redressal of investors' grievances.
(g) Company Law Amendment.
(h) Companies Act analomies.

(a) Investor Protection

The SEBI has the full authority to monitor the stock market activities. It has decided to intensify the efforts to redress the complaints of the investors in collaboration with the recognised investor associations. The recognised investors association is empowered to facilitate the filing of class action **suits** in the consumer courts against the concerned compaies. In India, the sharing of information is first done with the **Consumer Education Research Centre** (CERC) Ahmedabad. Section 12 of the Consumer Protection Act 1986 enables the Consumer Associations to file the suits in the district forums. The suit by the investor associations in the district is based on the information of investors complaints. It implies saving the legal cost apart from benefitting a large number of complaints through a single suit. The SEBI publishes the names of the **Top Twenty** defaulting companies every fort-night. The SEBI has the power to issue the **show cause notices and award penalty points** under the SEBI guidelines. It has the power to issue the **No Objection Certificate** to the Companies for releasing their **1 per cent** deposit with the stock exchange. It emerged as a major check point for complaints. It has the power to recommend a suitable legal action against the defaulters to the Department of Company Affairs and for suspension of trading of their shares to various stock exchanges from time to time.

(b) Provisions of the Companies Act

The Government of India has been flodded with a number of complaints from time to time. The Complaints have been made by the shareholders, investors, debenture holders regarding the delay in the transfer of shares, delay in the issue of allotment letters or share/debenture certificates or refund of share/debenture application money to non-allottees to the applicants of public issue.

The following provisions of the Companies Act imposes various penalties depending upon the severity of the defaults :

- **(a)** **Section 113** of the act indicates that every company should within **3 months** after the allotment of shares/debenture has any default in compliance of the provision of law, it is punishable.
- **(b)** If any company fails to register the share after transferring such share within 2 months, then it is liable to the punishment.
- **(c)** The Companies Act, 1956 has issued the listing guidelines in this regard:
    1. According to the listing guidelines, the companies must issue the allotment letters or share certificates to the allottee immediately after the allotment of shares. But it should not be later than **2 months** from the closure of the subscription list.
    2. The company should issue letters of regret along with the refund orders to the non-allottes.
    3. The listed company must issue the share certificate within **1 month** from the date of lodgement of transfer of shares.
    4. If a company refuses to register any transfer of shares to the transferee within 2 months, **Section III** of the Act permits to file an appeal before the **Company Law Board.**
    5. After closing the Public Issue Process, **Section 73** of the Companies Act imposes conditions for the despatch of allotment letters/certificates as to shares and debentures within the stipulated period of time.
    6. Companies entering the capital market are required to pay the unsuccessful applicants and liable to pay the **interest** for the delayed period from the date of closure of the subscription list.
    7. **Section 621 of the Companies Act, 1956**, authorises a share-holder to file the prosecution against the company

and its officers. The concerned companies are advised to ensure that they should strictly follow the provisions of the Companies Act, otherwise they would be punished.

(c) Provisions of the Securities Contract Regulation Act, 1956

Section 22A of the Securities Contract (Regulation) Act, 1956 deals with the registration and transfer of shares. A company cannot register the transfer of shares on one or more of the following situations:

(a) If the transfer of the security is in contravention with any law.

(b) If the transfer of the security is prohibited by any order of any Court or tribunal.

(c) If the financial instrument of the transfer is not in proper method.

(d) However, the company should make a reference to the **Company Law Board** on the above grounds within **60 days** of the lodgement of the instrument of transfer.

(d) Listing Guidelines on Investors Protection

The listing guidelines for the investors protection has been issued by the **Department of Economic Affairs**. The shareholders can take up the matters with the concerned Registrar of Companies in regard to non-compliance of the guidelines. A reference can be made to the concerned stock exchange.

(e) Investor's Guidance Series

The Investor's guidance series is issued by the SEBI in the interest of the public to educate the investors on the basic features of various investments. They are required to make precautions before choosing an investment or dealing with the intermediary. The Indian investors simply depend on the advise but not on their own assessment. They simply handover the cheques to the brokers. They do not know how to select a scrip. They do not know the product which is manufactured by the selected company. Even they do not know some basic financial parametres like **EPS, PE ratio, Debt Equity Ratio, Leverage** and about the company's market share, company's expansion or diversification, products' life cycle etc. Therefore they motivate the investors to develop the Capital Market. The SEBI creates an awareness about the investor's rights and remedies. The investors should take their investment decisions in the light of their individual circumstances. The SEBI has issued the following series of guidance to enlight the investors.

(i) **Investors Guidance (Debenture holders)**
(ii) **Investors Guidance (Transfer of Securities)**
(iii) **Investors Guidance (Stock Investment Scheme)**

(i) Investors Guidance (Debenture holders)

In India, some companies are unable to service the Debenture holder. The Companies are unable to pay the redemption amount because of financial difficulties. Some other companies delay the interest on debentures or may not redeem the debentures on schedule. They are issued by the companies, secured against the assets. The assets are mortgaged on the names of the trustees which are mostly **Financial Institutions.** A trust deed is executed between the company and the trustee. The trust deed contains all the conditions and movements of the two parties. According to the guidelines issued by the Ministry of Finance, the trustees are more powerful in protecting the interests of the debenture holders. The trustees should observe the affairs and the activities regarding to the debentures aspect. They should verify whether a debenture redemption reserve is created or not. They have the responsibility in monitoring the activities regarding the creation of security for the debentures and debenture redemption reserves. The India Trust Act indicates that a trustee may do all the acts which are reasonable and proper while protecting a beneficiary. The following steps are involved in case of complaints:

(a) **Section 113 of the Companies Act** deals with the issue of debenture certificate to the debenture holder within the specified period. Every company must within **3 months** after the allotment of debentures deliver the certificate.
(b) The company should transfer the registration within **2 months** after applying for the transfer of registration.
(c) The Companies Act specifies the above schedule for the delivery of certificate and transfer process. The extension of time will be granted by the Company Law Board. Any default

in Compliance with the provisions is **punishable** with fine under Section 113(2) of the Act.

(d) An aggrieved debenture holder may apply to the **CLB** to direct the company to deliver the debenture certificate.

(e) The investor can also file a complaint before the **Magistrate Court** forward his complaint to the stock exchange division of the Department of Economic Affairs.

(f) **The Companies Act Section 118** permits the debenture holder to obtain the copies and inspect the Trust Deeds and other documents.

(g) According to **Section 56** of the **Indian Trust Act**, he has the right to ask the trustee for the enforcement of the security created in case of default in the payment of interest and principal.

(h) The investor has the right to bring the matter to the notice of the SEBI, stock exchange and also financial institutions for the redressal of the grievance.

(i) The debenture holder can compel the trustees to perform any particular act or duty.

(j) The debenture holder can also approach the civil court for the recovery of the due amounts. When a Company is unable to pay its debts he can file a winding up petition under Section 433 of the Companies Act to a **High Court**.

(k) The debenture holder has the right to approach the Consumer Disputes Redressal Forum (District Forum), a State Commission, a National Commission for claims at various levels stipulated by the Act.

(ii) Investors Guidance (Transfer of Securities)

This is another set of series issued by the SEBI in the public interest to enlight the investors on the basic features of the Investor's rights, and remedies. The major problem faced by the investors is delay in the transfer of securities. The following are the steps involved in the settlement of the investors' problems:

1. **Transfer of securities**
2. **Registration of securities**

Transfer of Securities are the obligations to the corporate sector.

They are to be delivered through registered post or personally. **The Companies Act Section 43** reveals that every Company has to compulsorily apply for the registration of securities to the buyer party within **2 months** from the date of application. The Company Law Board has the power to extend the time for not more than **9 months** within the stipulated period to deliver the certificates. A Company is required to send the share certificates duly endorsed within **one month** of the lodgement of the transfer deed.

Registration of transfer can be refused by a Company. It should send a notice to the buyer and seller giving the reasons for such refusal. Section 111 of the Companies Act provides that a company can refuse the transfer of registration on some grounds. Besides this the **Securities Contract (Regulation) Act** provides the following grounds for the refusal of registration of transfer of securities. They are:

- **(a)** that the financial instrument transfer is improper.
- **(b)** that the transfer of financial asset is in contravention with any law.
- **(c)** that the transfer of security is harmful to the existing investors.
- **(d)** that the transfer of financial instrument is prohibited by any Court/Tribunal.

The Company should inform to the applicant whether his application is transferred or refused within **2 months** from the date on which the instrument of transfer is lodged. If the Company has no interest to transfer the shares, it should intimate to the investor with a reference to the **CLB**. On the other hand, if the Company has no interest to transfer the securities to such registration, it should intimate to the buyer and seller in a prescribed form. A reference has to be made within **2 months** to the CLB and also to the concerned parties.

(iii) Investor Guidance (Stock Investment Scheme)

The Stock Investment Scheme has been recognised by the **RBI, the Department of Company Affairs and the Government of India**. It has been treated as one of the tools by which the application money for subscription to shares and debentures may be paid. The RBI has issued instructions to all the scheduled commercial banks to make the stock invest scheme a friendly investor. The stock invest may be described as a postal order. It can be used for the payment of money instead of cash. Three persons involve in the appraisal of the stock invest scheme.

(a) Issuing banks
(b) Investors
(c) Registrars

(a) Issuing banks

At present all the scheduled commercial banks are issuing the stock invest instrument to the investors. While issuing this instrument, the issuing bank has to observe carefully.

1. Before issuing the instrument it should be properly dated and issued under the signature of the authorised signatory.
2. Every issuing instrument should contain the particulars as to the name and code number of the branch.
3. It should be marked as non-negotiable/transfer crossed and payable to the banker.
4. It should contain the name and full address of the purchaser on its reverse.
5. The issuing bank should have branches or make necessary arrangements to facilitate the payment against the stock invest.
6. The Registrars to the issue are required to return the stock invest duly cancelled to the unsuccessful applicants.

(b) Investors

The following steps are needed to participate in the Primary Market through the stock invest instrument.

1. The Investor can approach any scheduled commercial bank for the issue of stock invest in desired denominations for the payment of money while applying for shares in the primary market.
2. The Investor should not withdraw the money from the account until the payment has been made on this instrument.
3. The investors should take care about the use of the stock invest. Because it should be used within **10 days** from the date of issue.

4. The Investor should indicate all the particulars about the stock invest instrument in the specified place of the application form.
5. The Investor should use only one stock invest along with each application for subscription.
6. The Investor should not make available the stock invest to the third party. It should be used by the account holder only.
7. After the allotment, it will be sent to the issuing bank through the controlling branch.
8. The enquiries relating to the stock invest should be addressed to the Registrar only.
9. After closing the public issue, the controlling branches of the collecting banks will forward to the Registrar with a clear seggregation of the information.

(c) Registrars

To complete the process of a public issue, the following steps involve:

1. The Registrars should receive the applications for subscriptions accompanied by the stock invest from the controlling branches.
2. On receipt from the controlling branches, the Registrar should give the house number on the back side of the stock invest. The stock invest should be detached from the application and kept in the safe custody.
3. The Registrar should process the applications. He should work for the allotment and despatch of the certificates to the allottees.
4. The Registrar should report to the non-allottees and cancel their stock invest. Then he should return them to the applicants.
5. The Registrar should deposit the stock invest, duly filled in the bankwise and branchwise. Thus the process should be completed.
6. The Registrar should reject the multiple applications received with a single stock invest.
7. The Registrar should maintain a proper record of applications which are received with the stock invest.

(f) Computerised process of redressal of investors grievances

The problems of the investors lie with the companies and financial intermediaries. In view of a large number of complaints, the Department of Company Affairs has set up a machinery for handling these complaints..It has also decided to take strict action against the default companies. The procedure of handling the complaints is by introducing a fully Computerised system of processing. The information should be furnished by the companies regarding the action taken on each complaint within a stipulated period of time. The senior officials have been carefully observing the progress of action taken on the investor's complaints. The Department of Company Affairs has succeeded in settling the investors' grievances. **The senior officers** will hold the meetings of the companies against whom a large number of complaints register. Therefore, the Companies may concentrate in solving the problems of the investors because of the pressure from the senior officials. If the Company and the Registrar show negligence towards the investor's complaints, they can directly report to the SEBI for an appropriate action against such Registrars. The Computer System in the investors protection cell will solve the problem by designing the status system of complaints.

(g) Company Law Amendment

The Company Law Amendments are made for the benefit of the Investors:

(a) The Companies Act has permitted the companies to hold shareholders meetings on **Sundays** to attract more gathering.
(b) The shareholders, debenture holders and fixed deposit holders can now enjoy the nomination facility.
(c) Credit Rating is made mandatory.
(d) Auditing Standards would be enhanced to the extent of international standards.
(e) The Defaulted Companies are prohibited from raising further loans from the market.
(f) The directors of the Companies are made more accountable.
(g) The debenture holders can enforce the CLB for the payment of their principal and interest.
(h) The unpaid dividends are transferred to the Investors Protection Fund.
(i) Enforcement of fee transferability of shares and debentures.

The advantages of the Companies Act Amendment are presented below:

(a) There is no need to disclose the information regarding the large remuneration drawing employees along with the director's report.
(b) The Companies can now file all the returns and records through floppy discs to the Department of Company Affairs.
(c) The share premium amounts will be included in the free reserves.
(d) The Companies have freedom to convert the loans/debentures into equities without the approval of the government.
(e) The Companies can now issue non-voting shares under certain limitations and regulations.
(f) The Companies will be happy because they can buy back their shares and can retain the control of the Company.
(g) The Companies have the freedom to maintain the records is loose-leaf form.
(h) The Companies need not submit the full list of shareholders particulars along with the annual returns.
(i) If the shareholders accept the amendment of the objective clause there is no need to get the approval from the CLB.
(j) The Companies can now get the quick approvals for Mergers and Acquisitions from the Government.
(k) The directors of the Companies can now have the tax-free payments from the Company and their relatives can be accommodated in the board.
(l) The limit for the managerial remuneration of directors is increased.
(m) The concept of the deemed public company is removed from the Act.
(n) Inter corporate funding are increased to a certain level of the specified amount.

(h) Companies Act Anomalies

According to the Companies Act, 1956, **Sections 73 and 113** deals with the allotment process of the share capital offered to the public. Every company should approach the public for the issue of share capital and to get its shares listed within **10 weeks** from the date of closure of the subscription list. The Company should despatch the share certificates within **3 months** from the date of allotment. Therefore the time-gap between the legal formalities logically pushes the share prices up. After the despatch of share certificates, the investors may increase the supply position in the market. Then automatically the supply of shares in the market becomes more and more, it leads to the decline of the prices in the market. The situation will be encashed by the well-experienced market men to book profits by covering their position. These people will never lose money in such deals.

SUMMARY

Financial Markets

Each and every business unit must operate within the financial system. The financial system consists of a number of organisations, institutions and markets. The demand for **capital** will be influenced by the business expectations regarding the future state of the economy. The financial markets are usually determined by the supply and demand of funds. The financial markets are classified as organised and unorganised, formal and informal, official and parallel, domestic and foreign. The **Money market** is a market for the short-term funds. The RBI is the watch dog of the monetary system. It refers to lending and borrowing activities of banking, financial institutions and individuals. The central bank acts as a promotional and development banker in the money market. The main borrowers of the short-term funds in the money market are: **commercial banks, Central Government, state government, corporate sector and local bodies**. Money market is a coordinator between borrowers and lenders of the short-term funds. The objective of the investor in the money market is about the safety and liquidity of the principal amount. They also expect some return along with their principal amount. The money market is dominated by the RBI. **Capital market** is the market for long-term funds. It consists of shares, stocks debentures and bonds. The Indian Capital Market has been broadening slowly. There is a steady improvement in the volume of savings and Investments. Many steps have been taken to protect the interests of the investors. Capital market consists of gilt edged market and the industrial securities market considerable deregulation of financial markets whose taken place in India favouring the unbridled growth of financial services companies. The capital market consists of a number of individuals and institutions. The Indian financial system is both developed and integrated today. The **development banks** in the Indian financial system have witnessed vast changes in the planning periods. The development of the capital market is highly influenced by such as; economic development, technology advances, regulatory frame work, corporate performance, government policies etc. **New Issue market** is known as primary market. The NIM creates financial claims. It deals with the securities which have been made available to the public for the **first time.** The methods of public issue in the market are: **public issue, offer for sale and private placement**. The sale of shares and debentures through prospectus is known as public issue. It is one of the method of flotation of shares and debentures. The sale of shares is made indirectly by an issuing house is known as **offer for sale**. Private placement refers to the direct sale of newly issued securities by the issuer to a limited number of big investors. It is an indirect method of sale of shares. Public issue process contains pre and post issue activities. The secondary market is an important component of the capital market. The stock exchanges are known as **secondary markets**. They play an important role in the securities. The stock exchange is a medium of transfer of resources for the securities. The stock exchange is established for the purpose of providing a market place. The stock exchange is an organised place where the securities are purchased and sold. The stock markets are highly specialised institutions in India. India has excellent technical skills in the information technology. With the help of the IT, India can become a 24 hours stock market. India can teach lessons to the western markets. India has an excellent potential and manpower to construct the **technology bourses**. The stock exchanges in India should work within the framework of the act. The stock exchanges involve in accordance with the laws of the Companies Act, 1956, Income Tax Act, 1961 and FEMA. The stock exchanges are self regulatory organisations supervised by the **Ministry of Finance**. Stock exchanges regulations cover the entire operations. Bombay stock exchange is the largest stock exchange in India. It was established as a voluntary and Non-profit organisation. It is the Premier stock exchange in India. The membership fee in 1857 was Just **Rupee one** only. Now it commands more than **Rs. 2 crore**. BSE introduced **on line** system trading on January 1995. The BSE started publishing an index numbers of equity prices is known as BSE sensex. The SEBI was established as an *interim body* under the administrative Control of the Finance Ministry. The SEBI is the most powerful organisation in the stock market. It is the watchdog of the market. The SEBI has emerged as an important constituent of the Indian financial system. The powers of the Indian financial system delegated to the SEBI.

NOTES

1. Van Horne. *Fundamentals of Financial Management,* p. 23. Prentice Hall of India.
2. M.N. Mishra, *Money Banking and International Trade*, p. 340, S.Chand and Co.
3. I.M. Pandey, *Financial Management*, Vikas Publishing House, 1999, p. 964.
4. James C. Vanhorne, *Fundamentals of Financial Management*, Prentice Hall of India, p. 526.
5. Arun K. Datta, *Government Finance and Capital Market*, P.G. Book Depot, Calcutta, p. 18.
6. F. Liuingston, *The English Capital Market*, Methus London, 1929.
7. James C. Van Horne, *Fundamentals of Financial Management*, p. 527, Prentice Hall of India, 1999.
8. *Economic Times*, dated 1-10-2001, p. 13.
9. Van C. Horne, *Fundamentals of Financial Management*, p. 537, Prentice Hall of India, 1997.
10. For a detailed discussion—Manual of SEBI, Nabhi Publications, New Delhi
11. Roshnini Jayakar, BSE Then and Now; *Business Today* Anniversary Issue 2002, p. 63.
12. *ibid.*
13. The Sensex, Roshini Jayakar, *Business Today* Anniversary Issue, 2002, p. 69.
14. Van Horne, *Fundamentals of Financial Management*, p. 641.
15. N. Gopalaswamy, *Inside Capital Market*, Deccan Publications, p. Va 125.

PART - III

- ❖ Financial Institutions

1

FINANCIAL INSTITUTIONS

Introduction

Financial institutions are the active players in the capital market. These organisations provide long-term loans on easy installments to the corporate sector. They help in promoting new business enterprises for expansion and diversification of the existing companies. In underdeveloped countries, there is a strong need for the establishment of the financial institutions because of a large number of industrial organisations exist. A number of financial institutions have been set up all over India and at regional levels for acceleration the growth of industries.

They involve in the mobilisation of funds and in chennelising the savings towards the productive way. These institutions provide credit to the commercial enterprises. They provide a wide range of services to the public. They deal with the financial assets like deposits, banks and securities. They mobilise the savings either directly or indirectly from the financial markets. They deal with the financial market. The financial institutions are a part of the financial market. They always rotate in a business environment. The peace of the industrialisation of a country depends upon the disbursements of loans by these institutions. They play an important role in the development of a nation for the following reasons:

1. Lack of organised capital market
2. Low rate of savings
3. Low capital formation
4. Lack of entrepreneurial spirit
5. Low rate of the GDP
6. Attitude of the investors
7. Lack of the financial facilities to the mega projects

The financial institutions do not directly add to the volume of the real capital formation. They are only the intermediaries between the savers and the user. They encourage savings. They are classified into the following categories:

1. **Regulatory**
2. **Intermediaries**
3. **Non-Intermediaries**
4. **Others**

The financial institutions may be categorised as **Banking and Non-Banking**. They completely involve in money and finance aspects of the entire nation. Banking institutions are based on service basis. They can create money or finance. They are the creators of wonderful sculptors of a new economy. They create the wealth of a nation. They comprise of **Commercial banks and Cooperative banks.** The Non-banking institutions involve in the indirect finance of the corporate sector. They actively participate in the capital market. However, the Non-baking financial institutions have a financial muscle and vast resources at their disposal. They will fulfill the needs and objectives of the socio-economic and political aspects in a mixed economy. The examples of the Non-banking institutions are LIC, UTI, IDBI etc. All the insurance companies were nationalised and renamed as LIC in 1956. The Unit Trust of India was started in 1964. The IDBI was established in 1964 as a subsidiary to the RBI.

The financial institutions are further classified as **Intermediaries and Non-Intermediaries**. The intermediaries involve in the mobilisation of the deposits from the customers to dispose the funds at interest for various purposes. They provide deposits, grants, loans to the needy sector. They disburse the loans in the form of **short, medium and long-term loans**. All banking institutions belong to the intermediaries. The **Non-Intermediary Institutions** lend the money from their own resources. All the non-banking Institutions act the Non-banking financial intermediaries. IDBI, IFCI are the best examples. These institutions are established to provide the financial assistance for the specified purposes, sectors and regions. They are established by the Government of India by introducing an act in the Parliament. The structure of the intermediaries is presented below:

Intermediaries

- **Banking**
  - RBI
  - Commercial Banks
  - Cooperative Banks
  - Urban Co-op. Banks
  - Post Office Saving Banks
- **Non-Banking**
  - Provident Funds
  - Small Savings Organisation
  - LIC
  - GIC
  - UTI
  - Mutual Funds
  - Investments Trust
  - Housing Dev. Finance
  - Investment Companies
  - Manufacturing Companies
  - Finance Companies
  - Venture Capital
  - Leasing Companies
  - NHB
  - Hire Purchase Companies
  - HUDCO
  - Chits, Nidhis

REVERSE BANK OF INDIA

Introduction

The Central Bank plays an important role in the monetary and banking structure of nation. It supervises, controls and regulates the activities of the banking sector. It has been assigned to handle and control the currency and credit of a country. In older days, the central banks were empowered to issue the currency notes and bankers to the Union governments. The first central bank in the world was Riks Bank of Sweden which was established in 1656. The Bank of England was established in 1694 for advancing money to the government. It led to the development of the Central Banks in other parts of the world. The Bank of France was established in 1800. The Bank of Netherlands was established in 1814. The National Bank of Austria was instituted in 1817. The Bank of Norway was established in 1817. The National Bank of Denmark was set up in 1818. The National Bank of Belgium was formed in 1850. The Bank of Spain was set up in 1829. All these ones were the landmarks in the history of the Central Banking. The Bank of Russia was established in 1860. The Reichs Bank of Germany was instituted in 1875. The Bank of Japan was established in 1882.

Definition

The Central Bank has the responsibility of managing all the economic and monetary affairs of the nation. The Central Bank looks after the welfare of the population. The Central Bank has been defined by **R.P. Kent** "as on institution charged with the responsibility of managing the expansion and contraction of the volume of money in the interest of the general public welfare".

According to **De Cock** the Central Bank has been defined as "A central bank being generally recognised as a bank which constitutes the apex of the monetary and banking structure of its country and which performs as best as it can. In the national economic interest, it performs the following functions:

1. The regulation of the currency in accordance with the requirements of business and the general public, for the purpose of which it is granted either the sole right of note issue or atleast a partial monopoly there of.

2. The performance of general banking and agency services for the state.
3. The custody of the cash resources of the commercial banks.
4. The custody and management of the nations reserves of international currency.
5. The granting of accommodation in the form of rediscounts or colleteral advances to the commercial banks, bill brokers, dealers or other financial institutions; and the general acceptance of the responsibility as the lenders of the last resort.
6. The settlement of clearance balances among the banks.
7. The control of credit in accordance with the needs of business and with a view to carry out the broad monetary policy adopted by the state.

A further requisite of a real central bank is that, it should not to any extent perform such banking transactions as accepting the deposits from the general public and accommodating regular commercial customers with discounts or advances.

The central banks are not profit making enterprises. But they earn much profits through its functioning. The central bank monitors the operations of commercial banks, industrial banks, agricultural banks and investment banks. The central bank is controlled by the Central Government. The bank has certain relationship with the commercial banks. An independent act is formulated to regulate the activities of the central bank. It has no authority to accept the deposits from the public. The central banking system has been playing an important role in the economy. It plays a more positive and dynamic role in the development of a country. The financial muscle of a nation depends upon the soundness of the policies of the central banking. The objectives of the central banking system are presented below:

1. The central bank should work for the national interest of the country.
2. The central bank must aim for the stabilisation of the mixed economy.
3. It aims at the stabilisation of the price level at average prices.
4. Stabilisation of the exchange rate is also essential.
5. It should aim for the promotion of economic activities.

The central bank is the nucleus of the Indian financial system. It is the apex institution. Since the inception of the economy, it has been guiding, regulating, controlling and monitoring the Indian financial system. It is the oldest among the other developed countries banks. The functions of the Central bank as mentioned by **De Cock'** are as follows:

1. Bank of Issue
2. Banker to the government
3. Bankers' bank
4. Lender of the last resort
5. The Controller of credit

The regulatory frame work of the financial sector in India is formulated by the Ministry of Finance and the GoI. The Ministry of Finance administers **The Companies Act, 1956; The Securities Contract Regulation Act, 1956; The RBI and the SEBI, the IRDA, the Stock Exchanges and the Apex Financial Institutions**. The RBI and the SEBI have a special role and responsibility. At first, let us discuss about the RBI.

The Reserve Bank of India (RBI) is the Central bank of the country. It has been occupying an important role in the Indian financial system. It started its functioning from April 1, 1935. It was set up under the RBI Act 1934. The RBI till January 1949, under the management of private shareholders. The private institution became a state-owned institution under the RBI Act, 1948. The Act empowers the Central Government to issue the directions in the interest of the public. The Central Government has the authority to guide, regulate, and monitor the activities of the RBI. It has the authority to appoint **the Governor and the Deputy-Governor** of the RBI. The RBI is managed by a Board of Directors. It consists of the governor, 4 deputy-governors and 15 directors nominated by the Central Government. The Board of Directors consists of 4 local boards of directors and a committee. The local boards are set up for giving advices to the central board on specific matters. It is also required to perform the duties delegated to them. The board has the supreme authority to control the activities of the bank. The internal organisation of the bank structure may change from time to time depending on the volume of work. It has been working on the basis of the **Functional Specialisation** with adequate coordination for the smooth functioning of the RBI. It has been divided into **20 departments** and three training establishments besides banking and issue departments.

Functions

The RBI functions are based on the mixed economy. The RBI should maintain a close and continuous relationship with the Union Government while implementing the policies. If any differences arise, the government's decision will be final. The main functions of the RBI are presented below:

1. Welfare of the public.
2. To maintain the financial stability of the country.
3. To execute the financial transactions safely and effectively.
4. To develop the financial infrastructure of the country.
5. To allocate the funds effectively without any partiality.
6. To regulate the overall credit volume for price stability.

Authorities

The RBI has the full authority in the following aspects:

1. Currency issuing authority.
2. Monitoring authority.
3. Banker to the Union Government.
4. Foreign exchange control authority.
5. Promoting authority.

1. Currency Issuing Authority

The RBI has the sole authority to issue the currency notes and coins. It is the fundamental right of the RBI. The coins and one rupee notes are issued by the Government of India and they are circulated through the RBI. The notes issued by the RBI will have legal identity everywhere in India. The RBI issues the notes in the denominations of **Rs. 500, 100, 50, 20 and 10**. The RBI has the authority to circulate and withdraw the currency from circulation. It has also the authority to exchange notes and coins from one denomination to other denominations as per the requirement of the public. The note issues and exchange of denominations are handled by the **Issue Department**. The currency notes may be distributed throughout the country through its 15 full pledged offices, 2 branch offices, and more than 4000 currency chests. The currency chests are maintained by different banks in various locations. The RBI issues currency notes, based on the availability of balances of gold, bullion, foreign securities, rupees, coins, GoI securities and permitted bills. The RBI notes are backed by 100 per cent asset security. At present, the RBI is following a minimum value of gold coin, bullion and foreign securities as a part of the total approved assets.

2. Monitoring Authority

The RBI has the full authority to control all the aspects of the banking system in India. The RBI is known as the **Banker's Bank**. The Banking system in India works according to the guidelines issued by the RBI. The RBI is the premier banking institute among the commercial banks. All the commercial banks, foreign banks and cooperative urban banks in India should obey the rules and regulations which are issued by the RBI from time to time. The RBI controls the deposits of the commercial banks through the CRR and the SLRs. Every bank should deposit a certain amount in the RBI. The commercial banks have the power to borrow the money from the RBI when they are in need of finance. Hence it is known as **the lender of the last resort**. The RBI has the authority to control the credit supply in the economy or monetary systems of the nation. The RBI has the following powers with regard to the banking system.

- **(a)** It has the power to grant the licences for the establishment of the new banks in India.
- **(b)** It has the power to grant the lincences for the branch expansion of the commercial banks.
- **(c)** It has the power to inspect the commercial banks and its branches in India and abroad.
- **(d)** It has the authority to fix the norms regarding the paid up capital, reserves, transfer of reserve funds, maintenance of cash reserves and other liquid assets.
- **(e)** It can check the commercial banks organisational set up, branch-expansion, mobilisation of funds, credit portfolio management, region-wise performance, profit planning training, appraisal etc.
- **(f)** It has the authority to conduct the enquiry, investigations against complaints, irregulations and frauds in the banks.
- **(g)** It has the authority of mergers and acquisitions among the banks.

(h) It has the authority to appoint the CEO's of the private banks. Reappointment and termination of the chairman also lies with it.

(i) It also controls the methods of operations of the banks.

The Narasimham Committee (1991) recommended that for the supervision of the commercial banks, a separate department should be created. On the basis of the recommendations, the Government of India created a separate Department of supervision on 22 November 1993. The RBI had set up a particular department on the eve of the Securities scam for monitoring the activities of the financial sector. The Board of Financial Supervision was formed on 16th November 1994. The Department of Supervision took the responsibility of conducting the inspection. From 1995, it also supervises All India Financial Institutions and NBFCs. The Board of Financial Supervision has a full-time Vice-chairman and 6 other members. The RBI Governor is the Chairman. The wing has the powers to supervise and inspect banks, financial institutions, NBFCs. A five members Advisory Council has been formed for rendering the services. The Department of Supervision assists the Board of Financial Supervision. However all these bodies failed to curb the rising number of frauds and irregularities in the financial sector. Therefore, the Department of Supervision should have the full powers in detecting the frauds and irregularities in the banking sector.

3. Banker to the Union Government

Generally in any country all over the world the Central bank dominates the banking sector. It advises the government on monetary policies. The RBI is the bankers to the Union Government and also to the state governments in the country. It provides a wide range of banking services to the government. It also transfers the funds, collects the receipts and makes the payment on behalf of the Government. It also manages the public debts. The Government will not pay any remuneration or brokerage to the RBI for rendering the financial services. Any deficit or surplus in the Central Government account with the RBI will be adjusted by creation or cancellation of the treasury bills. The treasury bills are known as the **Adhoc Treasury bills**.

The RBI has the authority to maintain the **ways and means advances** to both the central government and state governments. The ways and means is a device to the governments for borrowing the money from the RBI. The RBI will make temporary advances to bridge the gap between the receipts and payments of the State and Central Government affairs. The maximum maturity period of these advances is three months. The Central Government will issue the Adhoc treasury bills for adjusting the deficit in the ways and means account. The ways and means advances to the state governments are subjected to certain conditions. They are:

(a) Clean advance.
(b) Secured advance.
(c) Special advance.

The clean advance means the advances are made by the RBI to various state governments without any collateral security. **The secured advance** is made by the RBI to the state governments against the pledge of the Central Government securities. **The special advance** is a facility granted by the RBI to the state governments. These advances are offered by the RBI to various state governments on interest basis which will change from time to time.

The RBI sanctions not only the ways and means advances but also overdrafts to various state governments. The over drafts are the excess limits of the ways and means. On the overdrafts, the RBI may charge interest above the bank rate. Almost all the states have been utilising this facility. The major function of the RBI is to issue the management and administration of the public debt. To render these services the RBI charges a commission from the Central and State Governments.

4. Foreign Exchange Regulation Authority

The RBI's another major function is to control the foreign exchange reserves position from time to time. It maintains the stability of the external value of the rupee through its domestic policies and forex market. The RBI has the full authority to regulate the market as presented below:

(a) to monitor the foreign exchange control.
(b) to prescribe the exchange rate system.
(c) to maintain a better relation between rupee and other currencies.
(d) to interact with the foreign counterparts.

(e) to manage the foreign exchange reserves.

It administers the FERA, 1973. It is replaced by the FEMA (Foreign Exchange Management Act) which would be consistent with full capital account convertibility with the policies of the Central Government.

The RBI administers the control through the authorised forex dealers. The RBI is the custodian of the country's foreign exchange reserves. The foreign exchange is prescious and it takes the responsibility of the better utilisation.

5. Promoting Authority

The RBI's function is to look after the welfare of the financial system. It renders the promotion services to strengthen the country's banking and financial structure. It helps in mobilising the savings and diverting them towards the productive channel. Thus the economic development can be achieved. After the nationalisation of the commercial banks, the RBI has taken a number of series of actions in the following sectors to develop the economy of the nation.

(a) Agriculture Sector
(b) Industrial Sector
(c) Lead Bank Scheme
(d) Cooperative Sector

The **Agriculture Sector** has been facing the financial problems. It occupies an important role in the Indian Economy. The RBI has been rendering the services to the agriculture sector by providing the credit flow. The RBI Act also emphasises the need to support the agriculture sector for the better output of the commodities.

The RBI appoint a Deputy Governor especially for providing the rural credit. The RBI has conducted an indepth analysis on the problems of the rural credit. It had conducted an All India Rural Credit Survey in 1954. It was followed by studies of the All India Rural Credit Review Committee in 1968. In 1978, another Committee was formed as the Committee to review the arrangements for the Institutional Credit for Agriculture and Rural Development. As a part of its efforts, the Agricultural Credit Review Committee was formed in 1986. The RBI fully involves in providing short term finance at a concessional rate for seasonal agricultural operations and marketing of crops. It contributes to the Debenture of Land Development Banks. It helps the Agricultural sector through the Cooperative institutions for the long and short-term finances in the form of the **National Agricultural Credit Fund (long-term) and the National Agriculture Stabilisation Fund**. It established especially for the Agriculture sector in July 1963, a separate entity known as the **NABARD.** The **NABARD** was established for providing the medium and long-term finance for the agriculture sector. The Agricultural Finance Corporation was established by the RBI to look after the welfare of the farmers.

The RBI has been playing an important role in the **Industrial Sector**. The RBI has established all the special development institutions to undertake the welfare of the Industrial sector at Central and State levels. It has been rendering the services for promoting several financial institutions. The RBI took initiative steps for the establishment of the Unit Trust of India. A number of Institutions have been established and also they have been rendering services such as guarantees, technical consultancy etc. only because of the efforts of the RBI.

The **Lead Bank Schemes** were proposed and implemented by the RBI. It has been acting as a leader in sponsoring the scheme. The RBI has the statutory authority to grant the licences. Therefore it has been expanding the branches with an appropriate geographical distributions of bank branches. The RBI has taken a step in 1962 to ensure the security of deposits with the banks. Hence it took an initiative in the setting up of the **Deposit Insurance Corporation**.

Monetary Policy of the RBI

Every nation's Government objective is to stabilise the economy by framing the policy matters. The RBI treats the monetary policy as a weapon. The aim of the planning is growth, social justice and stability. Stability is the most important factor in a planned economy. The objective of the monetary policy is to accelerate the economic development of a country. It has been encouraging the sectoral and overall development of the social justice. It is concerned with the control of credit and money supply with reference to the seasonal requirements for credit. The credit expansion process will be undertaken by the light of price variations without considering the industrial output. The monetary policy is able to avoid the waste resources and it creates an environment for the better employment opportunities. The policy also helps to eradicate poverty and regional imbalances. It strives for the self-sufficiency.

Monetary policy aims to boost the exports. The policy has done a programme of food procurement operations. The steps have been taken to deregulate the interest rates. The policy concentrates for introducing flexibility, encouraging diversification, promoting more competitive environment and imparting greater discipline.

Techniques of the Monetary Control

The Monetary Policy is basically concerned with the regulation of money supply and interest rates. The policy describes various control techniques to stabilise the Indian economy. The techniques are presented below:

1. **Open Market Operations**
2. **Refinance and rediscounting**
3. **Bank rate**
4. **Credit planning**
5. **Regulation of interest rates**
6. **Credit norms**
7. **Credit authorisation scheme**
8. **Selective credit controls**
9. **Credit rationing**
10. **Cash Reserve Ratio**
11. **Statutory Liquidity Ratio**

The above techniques were not used equally and actively in the past. Some of the important techniques are evaluated here.

1. Open Market Operations

Open market operations are actively used in USA, UK and many other countries. Open market operations deal with the purchase and sales of government securities. The RBI has the authority to monitor the reserve positions of the banks, yields on government securities and cost of bank credit. This technique is a powerful weapon in the hands of the RBI. The RBI may not restrict the quantity or maturity of the government securities in buying and selling or to hold it. The bank has the authority to conduct the open market operations in treasury bills,

Central Government securities and state government securities. But actually the transactions are carried out in the name of Central Government securities. It does not purchase them against cash. It purchases and sells the government securities from time to time with surplus funds of the IDBI, NABARD and EXIM Bank. The open market operations are performed according to the objectives of monetary and fiscal policy. The objectives of the policy are presented below:

- **(a)** To control the reserves of the banks.
- **(b)** To maintain stability in the government securities market.
- **(c)** To make bank rate more effective.
- **(d)** To facilitate the government borrowing programme.
- **(e)** To provide smooth flow of credit regional requirement basis.

The open market operations are carried out by the RBI for the purpose of Debt Management. But the government securities market is not well organised. The RBI has recognised the open market operations as one of the important monetary policy tools in stabilising the Indian economy. The RBI has taken a large number of measures to develop the open market operations. Therefore the coupon rates of the government securities have been raised and thus made the market more competitive. The open market operations have helped in regulating the flow of bank credit to the private sector more effectively.

2. Refinance and Bank Rate

The RBI is the premier bank in India and it provides the financial accommodation to the banking sector, the industrial finance sector and cooperative banks sector. It provides the finance provision in the form of rediscounting bills, promissory notes, loans and advances etc. The bank rate is the most important factor in refinancing and rediscounting the facilities. The bank rate is defined by the RBI Act, Section 49, "as the standard rate at which the bank is prepared to buy or rediscount bills of exchange or other commercial paper. In the olden days the financial accommodation was made by the RBI to the banking sector at the bank rate. The bank rate is charged by the RBI for various sectors at different rates. The bank rate and cost of refinance are used to regulate the volume of resources of the banks and other financial institutions. The refinance policy has to be kept in mind about the seasonal requirement of funds for various sectors. The major changes will arise in the refinance policy of the RBI from time to time.

3. Cash Reserve Ratio (CRR)

The commercial banks should follow the guidelines issued by the RBI from time to time on various aspects. As per the norms, every bank should keep a fraction of their deposit liabilities in the form of liquid cash. The system is known as the **"Functional reserve banking system"**. The RBI utilises the CRR as a weapon to ensure the safety and liquidity of deposits of the banking sector. The CRR has become an important tool for regulating the lending capacity of the banks. The RBI uses the two important financial weapons for controlling the credit in the country. These two financial weapons are known as **"Cash Reserve Ratio and Statutory Liquidity Ratio".** The Cash Reserve Ratio means, the cash which banks have to maintain with the RBI, as a certain percentage of their demand and time liabilities. The RBI has the authority to change the CRR from time to time according to the market situations. The CRR is also applicable to various **NRI deposits** account. The RBI has the power to impose penalty interest rates if any bank fails to the requirement of the prescribed CRR. The RBI disallows the refinance and rediscount of bills for the defaulted banks in the CRR.

4. Statutory Liquidity Ratio

Another financial weapon to control the credit flow in an economy is **Statutory Liquidity Ratio**. The RBI frequently uses this ratio to monitor and control the banks. The SLR is the ratio that every bank keeps cash in hand, balance in current account with the SBI, The balances with other counter parts and the RBI. It also includes gold and approved securities. The SLR is the most important ratio in the banking sector. The SLR is also applicable to the co-operative banks, non scheduled banks, and regional rural banks. The norms are applicable to **Foreign Currency Accounts (Non-Resident) and Non-Resident Rupee Account (external)** deposits. The RBI has the authority to change the SLR according the market movements. An increase in the SLR is possible only through the expenditure of the private sector. The SLR involves in distribution of the bank resources in favour of the government sector.

5. Credit Planning

The credit plan was introduced by the RBI in 1967-68. It is an innovative tool for the management. It is made as a product of economic planning. It is aimed to work as a tool in the macro credit management of the economy. It works in a specified environment. It is a unique tool of credit management. The objective of the credit planning are presented below:

- **(a)** To facilitate the flow of funds to a desired level.
- **(b)** To facilitate the flow of funds to desired sectors, specified areas, purposes, uses.
- **(c)** The quantum and qualitative aspects of a fund flow.

The credit plan is an input for the national monetary plan, fiscal plan and economic plan. The credit plan will be prepared at national level, and district level. The process of credit plan involves at the bank level. Every bank is required to prepare the realistic annual credit budget incorporating the estimates of volume and growth of deposits and demands for credit. The budgets are revised in the light of changes in the credit policy and banking trends. All the banks, their budgets are submitted to the RBI for its finalisation. The credit budget will be finalised in every May/June of the year. The RBI makes continuous monitoring and controlling of these budget aspects.

6. Regulation of Interest Rates

The RBI has the authority to directly regulate the interest rates on bank deposits and credit. The bank rate technique has been very weak till 1999. Basically a change in the bank rate is reflected in all market rates of interest and helps to achieve the objects of the monetary Policy. The bank rate has lost its significance. It used to solve the situation by regulating the market rates of interest directly. The RBI has been fixing all the deposit rates of the commercial banks and their lending rates. The co-operative banks, deposits rates have come under the regulation in 1974. The 1991 policy has changed the entire picture of the market with the introduction of the deregulation of interest rates.

7. Credit Norms

The RBI has undertaken the responsibility for the direct administration of the interest rates in the economy, when the bank rate technique, weakened. The monetary policy's objective is to quantify the control of credit or credit ceiling. The credit technique was introduced in November 1973 by the RBI. The RBI has been stipulating certain targets for the credit distribution to various sectors.

8. Credit Authorisation Scheme

The RBI had introduced credit authorisation scheme in November 1965. The scheme was promoted to regulate the heavy amount of borrowers. The scheme is aimed to sanction the financial assistance for the short-term needs of the corporate sector. The objectives of the scheme have been presented below:

- **(a)** to regulate the credit to control the inflation.
- **(b)** to impose the financial discipline on the commercial borrowers.
- **(c)** to provide the credit for the productive ways.
- **(d)** to ensure that the credit is supplied in accordance with the planning.
- **(e)** to curb the monopolistic ways for the credit sanctions.

The scheme is applicable to the commercial banks, public sector banks, cooperative banks and private sectors. It is also applied to the large and short-term loans. It operates for more than 20 years and the RBI decided to withdraw after the review of its working. It is replaced by a new scheme known as **credit monetary arrangement**. According to this scheme, a credit proposal for Rs. 5 crores and above should be submitted to the RBI, as a working capital more than Rs. 2 crores should also be submitted to the RBI for the term loans as a credit proposal.

9. Selective Credit Control

The selective credit control is a popular technique. It is widely used in our economy. The seasonal nature of our environment and the inflation pressure have made it useful in our context. The selective credit control technique changes the composition of the credit. These controls are used to reduce the supply of credit and prevent the speculative holdings in sensitive commodities. The commodities such as paddy, pulses, oil-seeds, vanaspati, cotton and sugar influence the speculation on motives. These credit controls are applied to the credit given for trading in shares. These credit controls are now applied both to commercial and cooperative banks. These techniques are applied to the private sector trading. But the public sector trading is not covered by these control techniques. The RBI applies these control in three forms.

(*a*) Fixation of margin requirements.
(*b*) Fixation of separate minimum lending rates.
(*c*) The fixation of ceiling on flow of credit.

The Assets and Liabilities of the RBI are presented below:

(Rs. in crore)

Assets and Liabilities	1990-91	1999-2000	2000-01	2001-02
1. Issue department	53,807	1,92,532	2,12,937	2,37,515
2. Banking department	66,884	1,60,654	1,72,028	1,72,956
	1,20,691	**3,53,188**	**3,84,965**	**4,10,461**

The break up values of other particulars are presented in the preceeding pages.

Assets and Liabilities of the RBI (Issue Dept.)

(Rs. in crore

Liabilities	1990-91	1999-2000	2000-01	2001-02 upto Jan.
1. Notes in circulation	53,784	1,92,483	2,12,858	2,37,484
2. Notes hold in banking department	23	51	79	31
Total Liabilities	**53,807**	**1,92,534**	**2,12,937**	**2,37,515**

(Rs. in crore)

Assets	1990-91	1999-2000	2000-01	2001-02 upto Jan.
1. Gold coin and bullion	6,654	10,598	10,324	11,242
2. Foreign securities	200	72,700	91,700	1,23,700
3. Rupee coin	29	102	78	107
4. Government of India	46,924	1,09,134	1,10,835	1,02,466
	53,807	**1,92,534**	**2,12,937**	**2,37,515**

Sources: RBI Bulletin February 2002, p. 5108.

Assets and Liabilities of the RBI (Banking)

(Rs. in crores)

	Liabilities	1990-91	1990-2000	2000-01	2001-02
1.	Deposits	38,542	86,551	87,828	70,618
2.	Central Government	61	500	100	101
3.	State Governments	33	41	41	41
4.	Scheduled Banks	33,484	77,781	76,939	60,854
5.	Scheduled state cooperative banks	244	816	978	1,099
6.	Non-scheduled cooperative banks	13	45	61	42
7.	Other banks	88	246	918	1,276
8.	Others	4,619	7,122	8,791	7,206
9.	Other liabilities	28,342	74,102	84,199	1,02,338
		66,884	**1,60,654**	**1,72,028**	**1,72,956**

	Assets	1990-91	1990-2000	2000-01	2001-02
1.	Notes and coins	23	52	80	31
2.	Balances held at abroad	4,008	52,313	92,600	99,161
3.	**Loans and Advances**				
	(a) Central Govt.	—	982	—	9,221
	(b) State Govt.	916	7,519	4,395	8,035
	(c) Scheduled banks	8,169	9,513	5,980	1,927
	(d) Scheduled co-op. bank	38	15	27	25
	(e) IDBI	3,705	1,740	1,440	1,110
	(f) NABARD	3,328	5884	6,580	5,855
	(g) EXIM bank	745	697	617	532
	(h) others	1,616	11,541	9,104	4,201
4.	Bills discounted	41,670	62,660	43,127	36,682
5.	Other assets	2,666	7,738	8,078	6,176
		66,884	**1,60,654**	**1,72,028**	**1,72,956**

BANKING INSTITUTIONS

Introduction

Banks deal mainly with money and credit. They are manufacturers of money. Industrial and economic evolution would not have occurred in the absence of banks. They play significant role in the shaping and in the advancing of modern societies. They have contributed a lot in advancing the developed countries. They are the architecture of the digital economy. They serves the country in a number of ways. They helps in the proper use of surplus funds. They encourage trade and industry. They provide the habit of thrift, create credit and capital. They distribute the funds equitably, reduce cyclical fluctuations. The industrial development will not be possible without the help of the banks. They purchase and sell money and credit. Creation of credit is a special function of banks.

Banks are the oldest, biggest and fastest growing financial mediators in India. They provide various types of financial services to customers. Their objective is to make profits. They deal in other people's money. They are working for the principles of profit maximisation and liquidity management. They predominantly follow the liquidation approach. Their business is subject to seasonal variations.

Banks have been defined by several authors. Some of the definitions are given below:

According to Section 5(b) of Indian Banking Act, 1949 "Banking means the accepting, for the purpose of lending or investment, of deposits of money from the public repayable on demand or otherwise, and withdrawal by cheque, draft order or otherwise."

Sayer has defined the bank "Bankers are not merely traders in money, but also important manufacturers of money."[1]

According to **Prof. Hart** "A banker is one, who in the ordinary course of his business, receives money which he repays by honouring cheques of persons from whom or on whose account he receives it."[2]

According to **Section 5(c)** of Indian Banking Act 1949 "Banking Company means any company which transacts the business of Banking."

Characteristics

The bankers accept deposits from the public and grants loans. The main **characteristics** of bankers are given below:

(*a*) Banks accept deposits of the savers.
(*b*) The deposits are advanced in the form of loans.
(*c*) The money will be disbursed through credit instruments or in other modes.
(*d*) They render utility services to the customers.
(*e*) They must have a geographical place to carry their business.

Functions

The functions of banks are classified as:

1. Basic functions,
2. Other functions,
3. Agents functions.

1. Basic Functions

The functions are the main income sources of money. Every bank must follow these functions. The basic functions of a bank (*i*) **Accepting of Deposits**, (*ii*) **Advancing of Loans**.

(i) Accepting of Deposits

Deposits are the most important element in the banking sector. They collect surplus money from the public. The deposits will be mobilised by banks. The money collected from the public are preserved by banks and interest will be paid by the banks. The depositors are benefitted and their amount of money is safe at the banks. In this situation the banks can earn a sum of money on the amount collected by them. The banks create credit on the basis of deposits. The level of creation of credit is depend upon the amount of deposits. The banks have introduced different types of deposits to suit the various requirements of the depositors. The types of deposit schemes are briefly discussed below:

(a) Fixed Deposits
(b) Current Account
(c) Savings Bank Account
(d) Money Multiplier Account
(e) Other accounts

(a) Fixed Deposits

Under this scheme the banks mobilises the deposits which are repayable after the expiry of **Three months to five years**. The banks are free to use the deposits for a certain period. They grant loans at higher rate of interest on these deposits. They can use the deposit money for a certain period of time for more remunerative purposes. The small savers will get more benefits from this scheme. The small customers are unable to make investments in the industrial securities market. They do not want to take risk from the securities market. A large number of savers prefer this mode of investment. The fixed deposit has become more lucrative as rate of interest has increased up to 10 per cent. At this present situation they offer only 5 per cent rate of interest. The customers can earn more by combining the Fixed Deposit account with recurring deposit account. The interest on FDR will be credited to the recurring deposit account.

The amount of fixed deposit cannot generally be with drawn before the expiry of the period of deposits. However banks can advance money of the security of fixed deposits if the depositors are not willing to withdrawn the amounts deposited. Recently some banks have introduced various types of other deposits, which are a slight modification of the fixed deposit. The rate of interest is higher than that of other deposits in case of **"whole life deposits"**.

The Fixed Deposits are also known as **Term Deposit**. Fixed deposits have grown in importance and popularity in India during recent years. These deposits constitute more than half of the total bank deposits. The rates of interest and other terms and conditions are regulated by the RBI. The RBI revised the rates of Interest on fixed deposits several times. The main object of the step was to make bank deposits more attractive as compared to other savings instruments.

(b) Current Account

Current account is more beneficial to those who withdraw several times from the account of deposits. No interest is paid on this account. Cheques are generally used for withdrawing a certain amount from the deposits. Current Accounts are more useful to the businessmen. They can produce this account as an evidence of revenue for the assessment of Income Tax. The businessmen are not required to keep with them a large amount of money. He will make payments by issuing cheques to the parties. The cheques can be transferred to any person for the settlement of dues. The current account is opened subject to the conditions. Generally no interest is paid on the amount of deposit balances and no charges are required for maintaining such account. Current Accounts are more useful to the businessmen, firms, companies and individuals.

(c) Savings Bank Account

Savings bank account is useful to middle and low income groups. They can save certain amount during a certain period. It is a flexible account. In this account, the depositor can withdraw money about thrice a week. The account holder can deposit money at any time. The interest is calculated on the minimum balance maintained each month. A person wishing to open saving bank account will have to fill up a form. He has to furnish his specimen signature. A passbook will be issued to the account holder. If the depositor wants to withdraw money he must fill up a withdrawal form and must present his book for payment. Now some banks extended the cheques facility to the savings bank customers.

(d) Money Multiplier Account

The persons who are interested to deposit money for more money at short period of time. Under this scheme the amount of interest is also redeposited. The rate of interest is highest on this deposit. The depositor can withdraw the accumulated money after stipulated period. The depositor can withdraw the whole amount either in lump-sum or in instalments. If the depositor opted for instalments higher amount is returned to the person. This is most suitable for old age provision.

(e) Other Accounts

There are so many saving deposit accounts like Recurring deposit account, private savings account and special saving account. **Recurring deposit accounts** are more popular in India. A fixed amount is deposited at a regular interval and it attracts accumulated at compound rate of interest. Under this scheme the interest and the principal amount is returned to the depositor after the fixed period. The rate of interest is higher than of Saving Bank A/c and lower than of fixed deposit account. It is a great source of stimulating short deposits. These schemes are designed to meet the requirements of **education and marriage**.

(ii) Advancing of Loans

Bank deals with money of other persons. Bank does not lend its own money. It is the other's money in which it deals. The advances of bank may be granted in the form of loans, overdraft, cash credit, credit discounting bills of exchange. The bank advances loan more than the amount of deposits, because all the loans are not withdrawn immediately. Therefore the loan creates deposits. The bank, creates loans and loans create deposits, while advancing loans, the bank gives priority to safety and next profitability. In advancing loans the principles of investment safety, liquidity and profitability, diversification and social objectives are considered. Generally the bank advances in the following ways:

(a) Loans
(b) Cash credit
(c) Overdraft
(d) Discounting of Bills

(a) Loans

Loans are important element of the profitability of the banks. They are made by debiting the customers loan account and by crediting his current account. The customer is allowed to withdraw the loan amount by instalments. The regular customers are permitted loans by crediting to their accounts, proper care is taken while granting the loans. All of the loans require a proper security or mortgage. Sometimes only the personal security is required for advancing the loan. The interest is charged on the loan amount. Loans involve low operating cost than any other kind of loans. Loans are given against the securing of movable and immovable assets.

(b) Cash Credit

Cash credit is the another method of advances made by banks. In this method the banker grants his customer to borrow money upto a certain sanctioned limit. The bank requires security of certain bonds, promissory notes, shares, other commodities. Sometimes commodities are kept in the possession of the bank in its godowns. The borrower is charged interest on the amount of advance. Generally the cash credit system provides adequate amount for meeting essential expenditures of the business. The large amount of credit is granted through credit system because the whole amount of credit is not required to be withdrawn at once. It is the best method to suit the requirements of the business community. Generally raw materials are purchased on the basis of this credit. This type of loans are mostly short-term credit. The borrowers can withdraw the sanctioned loan according to their convenient. The interest will be charged on the dates of withdrawals of the amount.

(c) Overdraft

Bank overdraft is allowed to current account holders. The current account holders may be allowed to overdraw. The overdraft facility is more advantagous to the customers because interest is charged only on the amount withdrawn. There is no need to provide collateral security for the facility of overdraft. It can be used at any time of requirement. It is used for long-term purposes. It is the most useful form of loans to commercial and industrial units to avail from time to time. The overdraft will be granted by the bank with the mutual agreement with the customer and bank. This form of advances has undoubtedly more benefits.

(d) Discounting of Bills

It is one of the method of advances made by the banks. The banks involves in discounting of bills. They discount only clear and reputed bills. Discounting of bills is one of the method of advances made by the banks. The banks involve is discounting of bills. They discount only clear and reputed bills. The working capital of the corporate sector are mainly provided by banks through cash credit, overdrafts, and discounting of the commercial bills. The bills are used for financing a deal in goods that takes same time to complete. The bill of exchange reveals that the liability to make the payment on a fixed date when the goods are bought on mercantile basis. The bills of exchange will be treated as negotiable instrument. The bills are drawn by the seller (drawer) on the buyer (drawee) for the value of the goods delivered by him. These bills are called as trade bills. If the trade bills are accepted by the commercial banks are known as commercial bills. If the seller provide some time for the payment of the bill payable at a future date is known as usance bill. If the seller party is in need of finance, he may approach the bank for discount of the bill. The commercial banks generally finance the business community through bill discounting method. The banks can rediscount the bills in the discount market. A bill is always drawn by the creditor on the debtor. A bill may be payable at sight or after the expiry of a certain specified time. There will be 3 days of grace period for a bill. The discount amount on the trade bill becomes income to the commercial banks. It is an income generating activity for the banks. The RBI introduced a bill market scheme in 1952. According to the scheme, the banks are required to select the borrowers after careful examination of their credit worthiness and reputation.

2. Other Functions

It involves a number of miscellaneous functions. They act as a catalyst, under writers, mediators of their customers. In business, knowing of the financial position of the parties are very common. Whenever any person is willing to know about the financial position of a business unit, the concerned bank can furnish necessary information. Bank act also as underwriters of shares and securities of their customers. Banks collect various informations and statistics of the nation. Banks protect the valuable ornaments, jewels, documents deeds for safe custody. They protect the articles from theft and fire. Banks issue letters of credit for their customers. The banks also helps in foreign exchange market.

The Role of Banks in Financial System

The role of the banks would be easily assessed from the progress and development of the globe. The industrial and economic evaluation would have occurred with the presence of banks. Banks played an important role in the shaping and designing of modern societies. Banks have contributed a lot in advancing the developed countries. Banks serves the country in different ways. They encourage industry and trade create credit and capital, provide funds equitably and reduce cyclical fluctuations. The industrial development will not be possible without the existence of banks. We cannot imagine the existence of the present society without banks seller of goods and is accepted by the purchaser. Therefore the purchaser accepts the credit conditions and pays the amount of dues after due period. In this situation if the seller is willing to discount the bill, he can do so from his bank and obtain the amount of discount. Sometimes bills of exchange can be made by Railway receipt or bill of lading. This form of loans is becoming very popular in India. The commercial banks can rediscount these bills of exchange from the RBI. The bills of exchange can be transferred from one person to another and from one bank to another. There is no need of collateral security in discounting the bills of exchange. The bill market is increasing gradually as the industrial activities are increasing.

3. Agents Functions

The banks are the agents of their regular customers. They act as trustees, attorneys and administrators of their customers. The banks collect and pay their cheques on behalf of the customer. They purchase and sell on behalf of their customers. They collect subscriptions, rents, income tax, insurance premium of their customers. A nominal commission is charged for these services. They act as broker for purchasing and selling of securities on behalf of their customers. They get commission for this purpose. They also collect the interest and dividend of their customers.

The banks play an important role in the construction of a modern community. The following factors will help us about the importance of the banks:

- **(a)** Increases productivity
- **(b)** Helpful to industry and trade
- **(c)** Better use of funds
- **(d)** Expansion of business
- **(e)** Reduces regional disparities
- **(f)** Cultivate savings habits
- **(g)** Creates credit
- **(h)** Capital formation
- **(i)** Economic development

The natural resources of a nation will be fully utilised with the help of banks. The bank helps the society to produce wealth by lending money to producers. They provide adequate supply of funds to acquire raw materials, machines for maximising the production. Banks may divert the idle funds for productive purposes.

The banks are always **helpful to industry and trade** by providing loans and advances. They arrange the required credit as demanded by the corporate sector. The cheques, hundies, promissory notes and bills have provided adequate funds for better functioning of industry. These credit instruments are properly handled by banks. The business community will get the funds from the banks when their funds are locked up and not in a position to settle the transactions. The finished goods and raw materials can be used as securities for obtaining loans. The banks provide adequate amount for short-term and long-term requirements of Industries. The banks help in promoting the new business enterprises. The new enterprises are facing the financial problems to obtain raw materials and labour etc. Some sectors are given priorities in securing loans. The industries depend mostly banks for their developments.

The surplus funds of the community are channelised towards productive purposes by the banks. They invite various types of saving schemes. The surplus cash balances are pooled by banks, capital is circulated to the community. The financial circulation of funds provide the industry more flexible to reduce their financial costs. The demand for the funds depends upon the seasons. The banks will grant the loans according to the seasonal situations to different units. The funds of the society flow from one individual to another one geographical area to another according to the needs of the persons of the society.

The banks provide sufficient funds to the business community. Therefore the trade and industry will expand their activities with the help of banks. Banks provide more funds to purchase the raw material and to pay other expenses. If the expansion of credit creates the full employment, it leads to inflation. If the credit supply reduces, the business and economic activities decline. The increase of financial resources, the corporate sector is able to acquire more raw material, semi-finished goods or finished goods. Therefore, the business community can sell more goods than then can originally sell from their resources. There is a relationship between bank credit and economic activities. The banks can accelerate with a faster speed of the business activities. In the absence of the banking system it would have been slower in the business activities. The accelerated trade-cycle leads to higher profit to the corporate sector.

The banks will provide the financial assistance to the corporate sector irrespective of their location of industries. The banks provides assistance to all areas. The regional disparity is abridged. The disparity will be minimised by operating the new branches and advancing loans. The surplus funds of developed centre is flown to the centres of deficit. The less and ignored developed areas get the opportunities of development. The banks will distribute the funds equitably to all areas. The funds are transferred to where it can be more utilised and effectively deployed. The balanced development of a nation is possible only with the support of banks.

The banks can cultivate the habit of savings among the public. They are more powerful in attracting the small savings by a wide network of the branches. The small amounts from millions of account holders will make crores of rupees. These amounts of funds are available at the disposal of the banks. The persons who are unable to utilise their funds in a proper way, can get higher returns by depositing in the banks. The banks provide safety, liquidity and profit to their funds. They are just parking place for **idle funds** of the community. The idle funds are properly utilised by banks. The depositors are encouraged for savings by paying a higher rate of interest for their savings.

They create credit on the availability of their deposits and loans. The creation of credit level depend upon the level of deposits with them. They invite more deposits by allowing higher rate of interest. They can create credit not only on the basis of deposits, but also on the volume of loans. Because the total advances are not granted in cash at a time. The loan amount will be credited to the individual accounts and they are permitted to withdraw the money at the borrower's flexibility. The loan-deposits are created in exchange of debts. The banks are more powerful in creation of credit.

Banks are the financial nervous of the business community. They utilise the funds of other persons for granting loans to another. They invite the deposits from the savers and lend the money to the needy persons. They invest the accumulated funds of the society in a productive way. The bank credit provides more financial muscle to industries and business community. They invite saving at remunerative way. The idle funds are mobilised and inactive capital of the society is perished. The unused resources are cannalised for more productive purposes. The capability of production of the society is enhanced. The financial and economic development of the nation is accelerated. The financial resources are properly utilised. The banks generally provide assistance to the new enterprises by way of capital formation. The capital formation is the most important element in the economic development of a country.

A developing country definitely get maximum assistance by the banks. The unutilised resources are fully utilised with the help of the bank credit. Regional disparities are minimised. Production and employment activities are carried on by a accelerated peace. Economic activities are reached to the peak level to boost the development of industries. The banks can open branches even in remote areas. Rural and semi-urban areas are developed. The expansion of the banking facilities are influence the total structure of the nation. The new entrepreneurs get the chances of establishing new productive units.

Kinds of Banks

A single bank is unable to serve all the needs of the country. Therefore the various types of banks have formed for serving different needs of the society. The specialisation has also been required by the banking industry. Specialised banks have been established to fulfill the needs of persons. Some banks serve the various purposes of the community. Some banks have been specialised in short-term loans, some are specialised in long-term loans, others are interested in foreign trade and other are related to agriculture or industry. There are different kinds of banks which are discussed below:

1. **Commercial banks**
2. **Industrial banks**
3. **Agricultural banks**
4. **Exchange banks**
5. **Central banks**
6. **Savings bank**
7. **Miscellaneous banks**

1. Commercial Banks

Commercial banks are engaged in performing the basic banking business. They accept the deposits of public and grants loans and advances. They are mainly grant the short-term loans only. They are unable to grant the long-term loans because the depositors may call their money at any moment. Their aim is to protect the interest of the depositors. The commercial banks also known as public banks. The common man deal with them for their deposits and short-term borrowings. The commercial banks are the most important kind of banks and collect the idle funds of the public. They fulfill the needs of the commercial class. At present the time deposits have been encouraged by offering attractive rates of interest. Therefore, they were able to grant long-term loans. The long-term loans creates the possibility of bad debts. Therefore they discourage the long-term finance to avoid the bad debts. The banks are competent in providing of short-term loans. The traders and businessmen can get short-term loans to purchase the raw material and machines. The regular financial requirements are fulfilled by the commercial banks.

The commercial banks accept the deposits and granting the loans. The commercial banks have played an important role in the development of a country. They will fulfill the objectives of achievement of balanced growth. Balanced growth will be achieved by through reducing the regional disparities. The functions of commercial banks will be different according to the needs of the country. The commercial banks are free to grant loans and advances to the agriculture sector after nationalisation of commercial banks. But they have to maintain proper balance between safety and profitability. They should think about the redemption while investing bank funds in a particular sector. The political and economic climate of the country determine the direction of role of the functions.

The commercial banks always invest fund in non-speculative activities. In some situations the commercial banks permit loans for those activities which may provide more profits. Hence they should avoid those activities which may provide more profits. Hence they should avoid these activities, because the confidence of public may be lost. The credibility is the most important factor in the banking industry. If public looses its credibility in a particular commercial bank, it will suffer heavily. Therefore the consequences are declining deposits and lending capacity of a bank will go down. The bank will be collapsed. The commercial banks can create credit. They issue credit instruments, which will be treated on par with currency by masses. They are known as bank money. They create credit on the basis of term deposits. They manufacture credit money. They will settle the transactions without payment of the cash but with the help of cheques. All the cheques are not paid at the bank counter. They are multified and settled on the basis of book-keeping entries. They are able to provide more credit than the amount of deposits held by them.

2. Industrial Banks

The Industrial banks are also known as development banks. These banks meet the requirement of different industries. They deploy the funds in long-term loans. Commercial banks are unable to grant the long-term loans. Therefore these development banks have been established for this purpose. These banks have got long-term deposits and can deploy the funds on long-term basis. They provide the financial resources to the industrial community. They have financial experts to study about the investment proposal and renders the advisory services to the banks. They can understand the intricacies of the long-term investments to the industries. These banks are appointing the experts as the nominee director in the board of directors of the industries to which loans are permitted. The banks help the industries by permitting loans directly to them by underwriting their shares and debentures. Therefore, the capital and loans are provided by the Industrial banks. These banks are funded with their own share capital, and issues debentures and bonds. They also get the financial support from the Government of India and International Financial Institutions. They have mutual agreements with other financial institutions at the time of disposal of loans. These banks are playing an important role in rapid industrialisation of the country. The peace of industrialisation depends upon the speedy disposal of these banks. They evaluate the projects, appraises the projects and giving suggestions to the industrialists. They will submit the feasibility reports for consideration of financial assistance to the board of directors. The banks inquire and investigate the future of the industry bounders of financial investment and utilities of the projects. The Industrial Units also approaches these banks for underwriting of their issue of shares. If the shares and debentures are not fully subscribed by the public within a limited period, these banks will come into the picture and take up the residual amount of shares and debentures. The new industrial organisations are benefitted through underwriting of securities and direct financial aids. They advise the industries in financial and non-financial areas because they are experts in those matters. They assist financial support as well as they suggest various types of sources for raising funds. They can explain where the funds are available? At what rate of interest? At what time to refund the debt? The functions of these banks can be divided into three kinds.

- **(a)** Accepting of long-term deposits.
- **(b)** Deployment of funds on long-term basis.
- **(c)** Advices and consultancy.

The fundamental function of any type of bank is to accept the term deposits. The term deposits are the **oxygen** to banks. These deposits are attracted by paying higher rate of interest. The deposits of the public and other financial institutions are often invited. They are mainly established for providing financial assistance to the industrial sector. They grant direct financial aids to the industries. They are established for granting long-term loans generally on the mortgage of land, machine and other fixed assets. But in some situations they also grant the loans for short-term credit. These short-term loans will be utilised for purchase of raw material and fulfilling short-term commitments. They have first hand information about the financial and economic climate of the nation at macro and micro level. They are well competent to give advises in the financial and non-financial areas of the corporate sector. These banks are more popular in **USA, Germany and Japan**. These banks also contributed a lot to the economic development of the country. For example **IDBI, ICICI, IFCI, SFCs** etc.

3. Agricultural Banks

The commercial banks are unable to cater the needs of agriculture. The commercial banks only to concentrate on the financial needs of the business community. Therefore there is a need to concentrate towards agriculture sector. Agricultural banks have been set up to assist the agriculturists. The cultivation of land is full of **risk**. The investment in agriculture does not always yield better returns. Hence there should be certain specialised institutions which may endeavour to meet the financial requirements of agriculture. In agriculture, there is a need of short-term and long-term loans. The agricultural machinery equipments like tractors, pump sets are long-term investments. These assets will be purchased through long-term loans only.

The land development, and buying more land requires long-term investments. The short-term credit is required to meet general requirements like buying of seeds and payment of labour expenses. The **cooperative banks** and land mortgage banks were established. These banks are assisting agriculture sector to a considerable extent. The agriculture banks caters the financial requirements of the entire agriculture sector in India. The agriculture sector needs are fulfilled by the following banks:

(a) Cooperative banks
(b) Land mortgage banks

Cooperative banks are established to fulfill the needs of agriculture sector. The short-term needs are catered by the co-operative banks. In India, there are three forms of cooperative banks exists, they are presented in below:

(i) State co-operative banks.
(ii) Central cooperative banks.
(iii) Primary credit societies.

The above banks are functioning at state, district and village levels respectively. In past, the financing of agriculture sector were made by the money lenders and indigenous bankers. But there were a number of defects in such financing. No other institution came for assistance to provide short-term finance to the farmers. The agriculture finance involves inherent risk. Therefore, the co-operative banks came to the rescue of the formers from the clutches of the moneylenders and indigenous bankers. The cooperative societies are the association of the borrowers. They pool their resources and can borrow from the mobilised funds on the personal securities. The cooperative society gets the power to raise the fund from the open market. Basically the primary societies borrow from the central cooperative banks. Therefore the central cooperative bank borrow the money from the **state co-operative bank**. The primary cooperative societies get sufficient funds to cater the needs of their members. But the societies are not in a position to continue forever and they should have an independent powers and authorities. The **central co-operative banks** are in such a position to help the members and non-members according to the situation. These banks are useful in other ways. They mobilise the deposits from rural areas. They encourage to savings and train them for self development. The role of central cooperative banks have been expanded and diversified. They can borrow the funds from **commercial banks, state co-operative bank, central bank** at a lower rate of interest. Therefore, they accumulate adequate funds for advancing to the agriculture sectors. At present the cooperative banks are sanctioning the loans to **small scale industries and export institutions**. The cooperative banks are emerging as a financial nervous of the digital economy.

The Land development bank is also known as development bank. The bank grant primarily loans on the mortgage of land for the purchase of land and development of land. The bank acquires funds from the government and public by issuing shares and debentures. The debentures issued by the bank backed by the securities. The bank sanctions the loans for productive purpose only. The financial experts of the bank evaluate the project thoroughly and reasonably. The bank will charge a reasonable rate of interest from the farmers. The other banks and financial institutions do not take the liabilities of granting loans at the mortgage of land, real estate, houses etc. These assets involves a complicated formalities and legal hurdles in the evaluation and transfer of these assets. These hurdles are taken up by the development banks. These banks are very useful in agriculture societies.

4. Exchange Banks

Exchange banks deal mainly with the Foreign exchange. These banks helpful in international trade. They will undertake the responsibility of settlement of foreign exchanges and make the foreign business. They involve in foreign exchange bills and manage it. They have opened the branches throughout the globe on important locations to purchase foreign exchange. The commercial banks and other financial institutions are not able to conduct this business transactions. These exchange banks do know the intricacies of the forex market. They do perform the functions of commercial banks and also tactfully handle the foreign exchange business. The foreign exchange banks do arrange shipment, insurance and settlement of transactions. They are highly specialised to handle the international transactions very smoothly. These banks purchase bills from the export oriented units and sell them to the importers. The transactions between exporters and importers will be realised in the form of bills. These bills are discounted by the exchange banks. The exporters will get the whole proceeds excluding the discounting commission from the exchange banks. The exporters need not to wait till maturity of the bills. These banks carry on their business through their branch offices which are located throughout the globe. The transactions of the banks are made easy with the assistance of their branches. The importance of these banks are very crucial in minimising the fluctuations in exchange rates. The commercial banks are also now undertaking the business of forex markets. They also opened branches or representatives in foreign countries to increase the business volume and smooth functioning of the transactions. Foreign banks were dominating the business of forex markets in India. The forex market now dominated by the **State Bank of India** and other commercial banks.

5. Central Banks

The central banks are the most important bank to govern national economy. They are fully involved to direct guide, take steps, measure the economy of a nation. The economy of a nation depends upon the efficiency of the central bank in that country. The central bank was established to discharge functions of issue of notes and coins. They also involved in framing the monetary policies of the Central Government. The Union Government will implement its policies through the central banks. The central banks were primarily responsible for the issue of currency notes and coins. They were assigned the names of banks of issue or National banks. The **Bank of England** was the first bank to act as a central bank. The central banks got momentum following the recommendations of the Brassels Conference in 1920. The central banks act as bankers to the Central Government. They work as financial advisers to the government. These central banks have vested the responsibilities of achieving full employment and the economic development of the nation. They are guiding force of the national economy and they are responsible for the development of the money and capital market in the country. The central banks are required to strengthen the liquidity, solvency and proper functioning of the banking system in the country.

6. Savings Banks

Savings banks deal with public deposits. They mobilises small savings from the community. They cultivate the habit of savings among the public. They encourage to increase the savings of the public. They are not permitted to grant the short-term loans like commercial banks. They need not to maintain certain portion of their assets in liquid forms. They are usually invest their funds in the government securities. Every citizen is allowed to deposit their small savings in the savings bank. The depositors are provided a passbook. The passbook contains each and every transactions made by the customer. The account holders are not permitted to withdraw their amounts. They allow withdrawal twice a week. If the depositor to withdraw more than a specified amount the branch manager permission is required. The depositors are allowed a nominal rate of interest. The savings banks are the commercial banks in our country which allow with the facilities of time deposits. **Post Offices** also doing the same business in India. They cover rural and remote areas also.

7. Miscellaneous Banks

There are various other banks which renders the specialised services to the public. The miscellaneous banks are categorised as follows:

(a) **Investment banks**
(b) **Acceptance houses**
(c) **Merchant banks**
(d) **Discount houses**

Investment banks deal with the controlling and distribution of capital. They were established in USA. They became very popular in western countries. **The Acceptance houses** are highly specialised institutions. They were established in U.K. The acceptance houses fully involved in discounting of bills. They accept the bills and provide finance to the business community. **The Merchant banks** are involved into look after the welfare of the businessman. The merchants are selling goods in foreign countries. The international trade requires a highly specialised skills to handle the transaction very smoothly. The trade involves high risk and complications are arised at each stage. All of these hurdles are easily met by these banks. The general business man do not know these intricacies of the foreign trade. **The Discount houses** are another specialised agencies. They are engaged in discounting the commercial bills. The discount houses discounts the commercial bills for very nominal commission and provide immense services to the business community. They are fully involved in bills of exchange of different businessman of several countries. They issue shares and debentures to get adequate fund for smooth functioning of the business. They enjoy some times the arbitrage of discounting rates. They do their business throughout the globe through their branch officers and their business representatives.

Types of Commercial Bank

Commercial banks have been categorised into various categories of the banking system. They are classified into different ways. One of the classification of banks are presented below:

- **(a) Branch banking.**
- **(b) Unit banking.**

Another classification of banks are:

- **(a) Group banking.**
- **(b) Chain banking.**

They are also classified on the basis of merits:

- **(a) Deposit banks.**
- **(b) Investment banks/mixed banks.**

(a) Branch banking

Branch banking means a number of branch offices scattered throughout the country to look after the banking business. It refers to that banking system assumes each bank as a single entity having one board of directors and one group of share holders in the whole of the branches. In someone situations the branches may extend beyond the territories of the country and may spread over to different countries. The policies and instructions are laid down by the head office and the branches are instrumental to implement the instructions. The branches undertake the business and perform the functions. In this banking system a single bank is able to transact the banking business in a broader way. At present the branch banking has become very popular. USA and European nations have developed branch banking system. In India it has also become very popular. All of the major commercial banks have opened their branches in rural and remote areas. The branch banking system has the following advantages:

1. They are involved in extensive coverage of business.
2. They are doing the business more efficiently with talented skills.

3. They do the business in large scale.
4. Rationalisation and scientific management is possible.
5. Investments can be made in diversified areas.
6. The personal bias and favouratism is avoided in this system.
7. The diversification of investments reduces the risk.
8. Non-performing assets may be reduced substantially.
9. The economies and operations are available in this system.
10. The financial stringencies is possible with the system.

Disadvantages

The branch banking system suffers from certain disadvantages which are presented below:

1. This system ignores the needs of people.
2. The head office sometimes unable to understand the local position.
3. The regional disparities will be increased.
4. Partiality will be shown while granting the loans.
5. The small customers may be ignored.
6. There is no proper control on branches.
7. Head office is holding all the powers.
8. The redtapism and delay of decisions.
9. It leads to concentration of economic power in few hands.
10. Speculative activities may develop and favouritism may be exercised.

(b) Unit banking

Unit banking refers that the business operations are carried on through a single office and at one place. The units are working within a limited area. The banking business are not carried on through the wide net work of branches. Unit banking was very popular in **U.S.A.** Branch banking operates through only one office. Unit banks are separate entities and have their own capital, board of directors and shareholders. The area of the operation is very smaller. The unit banks understand the needs of the local people. These banks give first priority to the local requirements and then invest in government securities. The local funds are used for local developments and the funds are not transferable to any other areas. The unit banks know the pulse of the local customers and know better to cater the needs of the local business community. The local industries agriculture get the opportunities for their development. Individual entrepreneurs are given personal attachment by the unit banks. The unit bank is very small and does not exist any problem relating to the management and control of the business. In unit banking there is no chances for frauds and irregularities. It also suffers from limited resources. They cannot expand their business. The banks are unable to earn maximum profits because of the scarcity of resources. They are liable to work in a limited area. The possibilities of survival are least. The cyclical fluctuations of business may severely hit the business. The economies of large scale are not available in this system. They are unable to achieve balanced growth. The Unit banking system neglects the backward people where the financial assistance is much required to develop the nation. These banks suffers from the local influence, to patronage the unworthy of the credit are granted. It suffers from numerical disadvantages.

(a) Group Banking

The commercial banks may be known as group banking. The group banking have some special distinctive features. These banks are the direct outcome of the defects of the unit banking. In this system two or more banks are brought directly or indirectly under the control of holding company. The holding company will coordinate all the things of the affairs. Group banks are very common in the USA. The group banking system have been emerged with the combination of the advantages of branch banking and unit banking. Each member bank maintains its identity and functions economically without losing the confidence of people. Each bank has its own board of directors and officers. The member bank can enjoy the experience and technical expertism of the holding company. The business can be expanded and profitability can be increased. The holding company provides the advertisement support and standardises the accounting pattern. The member bank can avail of the services of the holding company. The member banks will get instructions from the holding company to carry out the business very smoothly and effectively. Therefore, there are some intricacies in the group banking system. It operates on the principles of centralisation. Every decision will be taken by the holding company and there may not be no freedom to member bank. The member bank is only an instrumental to implement the policies of holding company. The holding control does not impact on the functioning of the member bank. In the group banking there will be possibilities of manipulation and speculation are higher. The failure of the member bank will adversely affect on other banks.

(b) Chain Banking

The chain bank were emerged in America and was very popular upto 1920. In this banking system the individual banks are incorporated and brought under common control. There is no existence of holding company. Some persons are directors of two or more banking companies. The ownership is common. In India the managing agents were playing an important role and they were utilised the resources of the chain members. The chain banking system enjoys the advantages on par with the group banking. It also suffer from the problems as in the case of group banking.

Deposit Banking

The another classification of commercial banks are three kinds. They are categorised on the basis of deposit and investment. They are presented below:

- (a) Deposit banking
- (b) Investment banking
- (c) Mixed banking

Deposit banking is the another type of banking where the deposits are mobilised from the public. These banks are known as deposit banks. They sanction the loans for the short-term loans. These loans are sanctioned to meet the needs of working capital of the industry. These banks have grown in England. These banks connot freeze their funds in long-term investments. They were sanctioning the loans for only short-term basis. They were not grant the loans for long-term capital investments. These banks were to provide working capital for cúrrent and seasonal requirements.

The deposit banks are acting as trustees of the depositors. The depositors are the main customers of the banks. The business of the bank depends upon the credibility. The depositors hard earned money should be preserved. The depositors may demand their money at any time. Therefore, the bank should maintain the liquidity position. Hence these banks are interested towards short-term finance to the corporate sector. These banks providing finance to the industrial sector and to small or medium type industries.

Investment banking is mainly interested for proving long-term finance to the corporate sector. The investment banks are also known as "Industrial banks". These banks are advancing loans on long-term basis. The commercial banks are unable to provide long-term finance to the industries. The Investment banks are very popular in German. These banks were established to promote industrial development. These banks did not accept the deposits initially. But later on, they mobilised the resources from the public. Several banks were formed as consortium or syndicate. They took the responsibility of financing to industrial units. These banks were closely related with the industries. The investment banks enjoyed the mutual cooperations of the industries. The promotion of new industries and development of established industries were developed by the mutual assistance of the banks and other related industries. The banks were expertised in the mobilisation of resources and sanctioning loans to the industries. The ***Mixed Banking*** involves in mobilisation of deposits and grant term loans to the corporate sector. It developed in **U.K.** after World War I. Industrialisation, competition, mass production encouraged the mixed banking system. They functioned as investment banking. In India the mixed banking system was emerged on the recommendations of Central Banking Enquiry Committee (1931). The **Shroff Committee** also recommended indirect participation of banks in Industrial finance. The demand of industrial financing through commercial banks have been increasing tremendously. The IDBI was established in 1964. It took initiatives to finance the industry. The RBI also encourages the commercial banks to enter this segment. At present the term lending of commercial banks has been increasing. The term lending was very popular in USA and is taking important position in India. There are several industrial financial institutions have been established to look after the welfare of industrial sector. These institutions were established in the Parliament by making an Act. They are **IFCI, ICICI, IDBI, IRCI etc.** The term lending finance have extended from industries to **agriculture** after nationalisation of banks in 1969. The commercial banks in India are turning to mixed banking.

Commercial Banking in India

The nature and significance of the emerging trends in Indian banking system can be studied since the early 1950s. The evaluation of Indian banking system can be divided into 3 phases:

(a) **From 1951 to 1964 (Ist phase)**
(b) **From 1965 to 1990 (IInd phase)**
(c) **From 1990 onwards, (IIIrd phase)**

Ist Phase

The first phase of the banking sector is, to consolidate its position on the eve of Independence. The banking structure at the initial stage was faced by a number of problems like unsound and uneconomic, frauds, and malpractices etc. The system failed to attract the public confidence. It had lost its credibility. The failures were a frequent occurrence. There is a strong need for the promotion of sound banking. The evaluation of the banking system in the **Ist phase** can be studied on the following elements:

(a) **Structure of the system**
(b) **Credibility**
(c) **Banking policies**

(a) Structure of the System

The banking structure should be stable and strong to meet the growth of the economic development of a nation. The structure should be able to prevent the frauds, failures and to restore the public confidence. The Banking Regulation Act, 1949 expressed for the promotion of sound banking. The Act was replaced with Banking Companies Act. The objectives of the legislation was to weed out.

(i) **Non-viable units**
(ii) **Small banking units**

The Act is also tone up the administration by eradicating unsound practices and great protection to depositors. The RBI was taken a decision to amalgamate the small and non-viable banking units with strong units. Therefore the banks were reduced to **108 in March 1966** from 566 in 1951. The RBI had taken a strong measure to strengthen the system.

(b) Credibiity

The Government of India took a decision to provide public confidence on the banking system. With the aim of restoring public confidence, the deposit insurance was introduced in 1962. The protection for the small depositors have been provided under the **"Deposit Insurance Corporation Act 1961"**. The Deposit Insurance Corporation was set up in January 1962 to provide protection to depositors. Under this Act, the insurance cover was upto Rs. 1500 at initial period. Later it was raised to deposits upto Rs. 5000 in January 1968, and Rs. 10,000 in April 1970. The insurance covers was raised at present upto Rs. 1,00,000.

(c) Banking Policies

The changes in policies and practices of Indian banks have been related to:

- **(i) Credit**
- **(ii) Diversification**
- **(iii) Priorities sectors**
- **(iv) Regulation of bank credit**

(i) Credit

The Ist phase of the evaluation of the banking structure is consolidation and changes in the banking policies and practices. There is a strong need to integrate the banking operations and policies. The RBI had modified the monetary and credit policies in the form of instruments. The instruments such as credit control and macro type control to encourage the banks to finance the industry. Prior to this, the banks were mainly grants the loans to trade and commerce. After the commencement of second Five Year Plan, there is a rapid industrialisation occurred in the country. The industrialisation leads to increase in the bank financing of industry. The bank credit to the industry have been increased tremendously. The credit rose by an average of about **Rs. 14 crore** per year during the First Plan period

(1951-55), Rs. 68 crore per year during the second plan period (1956-61) and Rs. 164 crore per year during the third plan period (1962-66). The upsurge in the bank credit to industry during this period shows the raising importance of credit as a main source of finance to the corporate enterprises.

(ii) Diversification

The commercial banks in India were encouraged to enter the new mode of financing based on two factors:

1. **Term lending**
2. **Underwriting**

The term loans are occupying an important portfolio in their loans and disbursement programmes of the commercial banks. Prior to this period the banks were restricted to provide short-term loans only. The commercial banks traditional role have been changed and they are actively participating in the development of the industrial growth. During the second five year plan there were modifications in the existing pattern of financing to industry. There was a strong need for expansion of institutional credit facilities for the small and medium sized enterprises. Therefore, the Government encouraged the commercial banks to involve in term lending to the industry and designed a specific scheme for this purpose in 1958. According to this scheme the **Refinance Corporation of Industry Ltd.**, had been created for the purpose of refinancing facility. The new scheme reveals that the commercial banks which were lending the term loans to the industry, will have refinancing facility against approved term loans from the **RCI**. The RCI was merged with the **IDBI** on 1-9-1964. The flow of bank credit was encouraged as being in confirmity with the policy of industrialisation in the country.

Underwriting is the another innovation during this phase. The entry of commercial banks in the area of underwriting of new issues have been created a new dimension in this sector. The entry of commercial banks towards underwriting activity had been suggested by the Indian central banking enquiry committee on 1931. The same activity was also recommended by the **Shroff Committee** in 1953. The committee also recommended the formation of Joint underwriting consortium of banks and insurance companies. The commercial banks not only sanctioning of term loans, involving underwriting activity but also entered into financial services sector. They are actively involved in providing finance to the corporate sector partly through direct subscription to the shares and debentures. A seminar was organised by the Reserve Bank of India at Hyderabad in 1959. The RBI had taken initiative steps to provide finance to the neglected sector of SSI.

Secondly, in pursuance of the problems focussed by the seminar, the Government of India formulated a **'credit guarantee scheme'**. The scheme was finalised in consultation with the Reserve Bank in July 1960. According to the scheme, the Central Bank will guarantee the major part of the advances given by banks to the SSI. The credit guarantee scheme was administered by the RBI. The guarantee was given by the Central Government. The RBI had appointed a working group to examine the provisions of this scheme in detail. The working group has also suggested some modifications in the scheme which effect from 1-2-1970. The aim of the scheme was to provide financial assistance to all eligible advances on an automatic basis. Every eligible institution have to be entered into an agreement with the credit guarantee organisation. The approved institutions were provided bank finance and the guarantee cover was upto **75 per cent** of the amount defaulted or the amount guaranteed whichever was lower. The CGS covers all credit facilities allowed to small units. The maximum amount recoverable from the CGS was **Rs. 7.50** lakhs for working capital advances and a further sum of Rs. 2.50 lakh in respect of the term loans per borrower. The CGS helped the banks in taking more responsibilities in the financing of small scale enterprises.

The commercial banks are helping the corporate sector by subscribing shares and by underwriting the public issues. Therefore the growth of corporate sector depended upon the commercial banks.

(iii) Priorities Sector

Some of the sectors of the Indian economy have been neglected by the authorities. These sectors were identified during this phase and the commercial banks were directed to channelise their resources towards neglected areas. These neglected areas were identified the **small scale industries, exports and agriculture**. These sectors received very little credit from the banks previously. The policy and institutional measures to stimulate bank credit to the following sectors are described below:

1. **Small scale industries**
2. **Exports**
3. **Agriculture**
4. **Institutional sector**

1. Small Scale Industries

The small scale industries is one of the most neglected sector in the Indian economy. The government taken a policy to provide financial assistance to this sector. The provision of finance to this sector depends upon three steps.

(a) Systematic study of problems.
(b) Credit guarantee scheme.
(c) Credit policy.

At the first step, a systematic study of SSIs problems involved was studied indepthly. The small scale industrialists and bankers were brought together to sort out the problems for replying the solution to the financing of small scale industries.

Finally the credit policy contains the facilities to stimulate bank credit of the small scale sector. The RBI introduced in 1962, a policy of granting additional rights to the banks to borrow from it, at concessional rates if they sanctions excess quantity of amount. These concessions were provided to the commercial banks by the RBI in different forms. The RBI arranges the refinance at bank rate, the rediscounting of bills under the new bill market scheme. As a consequences of these measures there was a tremendous rise in the quantum of credit expanded to the small sectors by the banking industry.

2. Exports

The export sector is another one of the negleted sector in the Indian economy. The Government of India have taken an important measure to provide finance for exports. For this purpose the Central Government had established the **"Export Risk Insurance Corporation"** in 1957. It was promoted to offer insurance to exporters against exchange controls. There is no clear information was available regarding the creditworthiness of Importers. The Export Risk Insurance Corporation was remained as the **"Export Credit and Guarantee Corporation Ltd.** It extended guarantees to the Commercial banks providing financial assistance to the exporters and also it covers the insurance to the exporters. The ECGC providing concessional rate of interest were fixed for export credit by the banks.

3. Agricultural Finance

The agricultural sector was totally ignored by the banking sector. To improve the credit facilities to these sectors the **Agricultural Refinance Corporation Ltd.** had been established. It was set up as a subsidiary to the Reserve Bank of India. It was established in 1963 for providing long-term finance to eligible banking and financial institutions. These institutions will be provided refinance facility for promoting the development of agriculture and allied activities. The ARCL financed to agricultural development projects. These agricultural projects could not be financed by the any other existing credit agencies.

4. Institutional Credit

The RBI introduced this scheme in November 1965 to regulate the bank credit to institutional borrowers. According to this scheme, the commercial banks were directed to secure the RBI for granting the cash credit limit more than one crore to any single party. Every commercial bank shall get the permission of the RBI to grant the cash credit to Institutional borrowers. But actually there is no need to get approval from RBI for sanctioning the cash credit facility. The scheme is popularly known as **"Credit Authorisation Scheme"**. The objective was to control the institutional borrowers as well as to align the credit facilities of the bank. The CAS was modified to suit the needs of customers by the banks. The CAS was now replaced by credit monitoring arrangement.

(iv) Regulation of Bank Credit

The banking sector faced a remarkable changes during the First Phase. The banking operations have been modified to suit the needs of the five year plans. The banking policies have been influenced the monetary policies of the Reserve Bank. The government has modified the credit policies in the form of selective credit control moral suasion, and other such macro type controls. The banks are engaged to serve the needs of trade and commerce only. The commercial banks have neglected all the sectors, prior to the Ist phase. The second five year plan has concentrated on rapid industrialisation. This was reflected in the total advances made by the banks.

IInd Phase (1965-90)

The second phase of banking (1965-90) may be described as the innovative banking. The period after 1964 there was a radical changes in the country. During this period there was an increasing concern about the problem of concentration of economic power in few hands. This period had also witnessed a widening economic disparities. These problems have been studied by several officials and the following developments deserve to be presented in this context.

(*a*) The Mahalanobis Committee, 1964
(*b*) The Monopolies Inquiry Commissions, 1965
(*c*) R.K. Hazari Committee, 1966
(*d*) The Patel Committee, 1966
(*e*) The R.K. Hazari Committee, 1967 (Licensing policy)
(*f*) The Dutt Committee, 1969

The **Mahalanobis Committee** had been appointed for studying about the distribution of Income levels of living. The **Monopolies Inquiry Commission** have been set up for study about the concentration of economic power in few hands. In 1966 a committee was formed to study about the concentration of private corporate sector and its ownership and control. The committee was headed by a well known expert Sri R.K. Hazari. In the same year another committee have been established for inquiring about the affairs of managing agency system. The **Hazari Committee** had been appointed to look into the matters of industrial licensing policy. The **Dutt Committee** was made inquiries regarding industrial licensing policy in 1969. These committees have framed the guidelines to change the Indian banking system. The main objectives of the committee is to look after the equitable distribution of bank credit to all classes of borrowers. It was found that the large scale industries, institutional borrowers, big corporate houses had almost enjoyed the bank credit. It was also found that the commercial banks have been entirely neglected the sectors such as **small scale industries, agriculture, and exports.** No bank credit had been available to these sectors. These committees had been provided a broad setting for the radical changes in the structural operations and policies of the Indian commercial banking system during this phase. The main features of second phase were presented below:

(a) Community control.
(b) Organisational changes.

During this second phase, the RBI had been enforced the rigorous control to strengthen the banking system. The banking system have been continued to suffer in terms of credit coverage. The large net work of branches covered only to small segment of the community. The bank credit have been enjoyed by a portion of the population, mostly in the big cities, almost completely excluding the rural areas and the smaller towns. However there were substantial credit gaps to such sectors agriculture, and small scale industries. It was found that some steps have to be taken to provide finance to the **artisans, retail traders, self-employed persons.** All of these community members did not enjoy the facility of institutional credit. The banking system have been controlled by the big industrial houses in order to look after their welfare. It was the most important weak element in the banking system. Therefore the Government of India was introduced the scheme of social control at the end of 1967. The bank credit was an important element for achieving socio-economic objectives of the state policy. The socio-economic objective is to achieve a wider spread of bank credit to all priority sectors, preventing its misuse, directing large volume of credit flow to developmental activities of the country. The government had been decided to remove the control of big business houses over banks without removing their ownership. Therefore, it was sought to be achieved by bringing reforms to the banking sector. The concepts and goals of the banking system have been changed dramatically. The elements of community control were:

(*a*) Structural Changes,
(*b*) National Credit Council
(*c*) Agriculture Finance Corporation Ltd.

(a) Structural Changes

Structural changes is the basic step under the scheme of community control. According to the structural changes, the changes in the Board of directors of bank have been made accordingly. The board was reconstituted by introducing the persons with specialised knowledge or practical experience in **agriculture and rural economy; Cooperation, SSIs and banking**. The bank chairman was replaced by an expert of banking, finance, business administration or economics. Therefore the entire structure of the banking system had been changed to meet the socio-economic objective of the state economy.

(b) National Credit Council

National Credit Council have been established in February, 1968. The creation of NCC is to achieve the objectives of providing bank credit to priorities sectors on all India basis. The basic functions of the credit council were presented below:

- **(a)** to estimate the demand for bank credit to the various sectors of the economy.
- **(b)** to determine the priority sector for providing financial assistance.
- **(c)** to assure the optimum utilisation of resources by coordinating the lending and investing policies of the banks.

(c) Agriculture Finance Corporation Ltd.

The Agriculture Finance Corporation was established for the purpose of financing agricultural projects. It was set up as a Joint venture by the leading commercial banks. This corporation was set up to help the banks to participate actively in developing the agriculture sector in our country.

The commercial banks were advised by the corporation to adopt the specific areas/projects in consultation with the concerned state governments. The aim of the programme was to expand the agricultural credit in order to maximise the benefits to the sector. The benefits which were available to this sector such as supply of inputs, marketing processing, procurement operations, storage and transportation.

The objective of the socio-economic system is to provide equitable allocation of bank credit to all the priorities sectors. Therefore the **National Credit Council** appointed two committees in October, 1968.

The first committee was headed by **Prof. D.R. Gadgil** to study about the organisational frame work for the implementation of social control objectives. The committee probed into the credit gaps. The another committee was appointed to study on the extent to which credit needs of industry and trade are likely to be inflated and how such trends can be checked. The committee was headed by **Sri V.T. Dehejia** to examine the problem of an unduly large proportion of bank credit by big industrial houses.

The first Committee's report addressed the task of identifying the credit gaps and made suggestions to provide adequate institutional credit could be made available to the neglected sectors of the economy. The Committee was also found that bank credit was unevenly distributed among different states of the country. The Committee provided a solution an **Area approach** for branch expansion. The individual banks would select particular areas for intensive development and in the process expand the deposit mobilisation to finance the agriculture and small scale industries. Therefore, the lead bank scheme was finalised by the RBI at the end of 1969. According to this scheme the 336 districts in India with the exception of Metro's were allotted among the major scheduled banks to provide finance in their concerned territory. The allotments were made on the basis of size of bank, the size of the resources, cluster area, regional orientation of the bank, the requirement of each state etc.

Nationalisation

The banking system had taken several measures for achieving the social economic objectives. The Government of India had been changed the ownership of commercial banks to satisfy the socio-economic objective. Therefore, the Government of India nationalised 14 major banks with individual deposits exceeding **Rs. 50 crore** on 19-7-1969. The aims of the nationalisation were:

- **(a)** to control the heights of the economy.
- **(b)** to serve better the needs of development of the country.
- **(c)** to provide a great impetus to new orientation to the banking system.

The post-nationalisation period made significant changes in the operational policies and practices of the banks. There were more and more committees had been appointed to study the various problems of the banking sector. The committees such as **Narasimham Committee, Tandon Committee, Chore Committee, Maratha Committee** have been appointed.

IIIrd Phase

The Liberalisation, Privatisation and Globalisation policies have been changed the banking sector tremendously. The post era 1991 of Indian banking is essentially a phase of profitable banking/viable/prudential. The Narasimham Committee have been established to look after the financial sector. The Narasimham Committee (II) had been appointed to look after affairs of the banking sector reforms 1998. The banking system in India has grown tremendously in this IIIrd phase. In this phase the implementation and recommendations of the Narasimham Committee played an important role in the transformation of traditional banking into modern banking in the **digital economy**.

The following financial institutions provide finance for the development of industries in the country:

1. Industrial Finance Corporation of India.
2. Industrial Development Bank of India.
3. Industrial Credit and Investment Corporation of India.
4. Export and Import Bank of India.
5. National Bank for Agricultural and Rural Development.
6. Shipping Credit and Investment Corporation of India.
7. Tourism Finance Corporation of India.
8. Risk Capital and Technology Finance Corporation.
9. Industrial Reconstruction Bank of India.
10. Insurance Regulatory Authority.
11. Stock Holding Corporation of India.
12. Discount and Finance House of India.
13. Technology Development and Information Company.
14. Custodians.
15. Depository system.
16. State Finance Corporations.
17. Merchant Banking.
18. Credit Rating.

All of the above financial institutions are covered in this book for an indepth understanding of the Indian financial system.

1. INDUSTRIAL FINANCE CORPORATION OF INDIA

Introduction

The Industrial Finance Corporation of India was established in 1948. This financial institution provides funds for the development of industries in the country. It is the premier institution in the industrial sector to enhance the productivity of the corporate sector. The objective of the corporation is to provide term loans to the industries. It provides the financial assistance to the public limited companies, Cooperative Societies. It renders the services to the following sectors:

(*a*) Manufacturing of goods
(*b*) Processing of goods
(*c*) Shipping business
(*d*) Power generation and distribution sector
(*e*) Hotel industry
(*f*) Mining industry

Share Capital

The IFCI was established with an authorised capital of Rs. 10 crores. The Face value of the share is Rs. 5,000 and issued 20,000 shares. The authorised capital has been raised to the extent of Rs. 339.1 crores. The 50 per cent of paid up capital held by the IDBI and the rest is held by the scheduled banks, LIC, trusts, and Cooperative banks. It has an excellent financial support from the Central Government in the form of loans. It has large financial resources other than share capital, in the form of retained earnings and sale of investments etc. It also raises funds in foreign currency. It mobilises the funds by issuing bonds, accepting the public sector.

Management

The institution is managed by the board of directors. The board of directors consists of a whole time chairman and 12 directors. The chairman will be appointed by the Central Government. Two directors are nominated by the Central Government. Four by the IDBI and the remaining 6 directors are elected by the other shareholders.

Functions

The IFCI was established for the purpose of financial assistance to the corporate sector. The functions of the IFCI may be categorised into

1. Financial Assistance.
2. Promotional Assistance.

1. Financial Assistance

The IFCI has full freedom for granting of loans, recovery of loans, terms and conditions etc. It is authorised to provide financial assistance in the following forms:

(*a*) It can grant loans to the industrial concerns which can be repayable within 25 years.
(*b*) It can subscribe debentures to a business concern.
(*c*) It can make advances to commercial enterprises.
(*d*) It can involve in the underwriting business.
(*e*) It may act as an agent of the Central Government.
(*f*) It may act as an agent to the world bank in respect of loans sanctions to the Indian companies.
(*g*) It can give guarantee to the industrial concerns for the loans sanctioned by the scheduled commercial banks, co-operative banks.
(*h*) It can give guarantee to loans that are raised for the purchase of capital goods from abroad or within India.
(*i*) It also provides financial assistance for establishing a new undertaking.
(*j*) It provides finance for the expansion or diversification of the existing business concerns.
(*k*) It provides financial assistance to the eligible industrial enterprises irrespective of their size.

The IFCI grants loans to the projects which exceeds Rs. 2 crores project cost. Generally the project which are below Rs. 2 crore will be handled by SFCs, scheduled commercial banks and others. The IFCI grants loans, only after thorough scrutiny of the project. It gives more importance to the feasibility of the project, its importance to the nation, location of the industry, social and economic environment etc.

2. Promotional Assistance

The IFCI has been playing an important role in the development of a nation. It actively involves in financing the eligible industrial concerns. It encourages the new enterprises by providing the financial assistance. It also helps to develop small and medium scale entrepreneurs by providing excellent services in the identification of projects, assessment of future profits and in implementation of the projects. It sanctions loans to all the industrial concerns by reducing the regional imbalances and income disparities.

2. INDUSTRIAL DEVELOPMENT BANK OF INDIA

The Industrial Development Bank of India was established in July, 1964. It was registered as a subsidiary to the RBI. It was formed under the IDBI Act of 1964. It is wholly owned by the RBI. In 1976, the ownership of this corporation has been transferred to the Central Government, in terms of the Public Financial Institutions Laws (Amendments) Act of 1975. The IDBI has been assigning the role of the principal financial institutions to promote the industrial growth in the country. It has been enacting a special role in the industrialisation of the nation. It is actively involving in planning, promoting and developing industries to fill the gaps in industrial structures.

Objectives

The following are the main objectives behind the establishment of the IDBI:

(*a*) To provide excellent services to the new enterprises.
(*b*) To build an excellent Industrial structure in the country.
(*c*) To provide technical and administrative assistance for the formation of companies or expansion of Industries.
(*d*) To conduct market and investment research and also surveys in connection with the development of industry.
(*e*) To coordinate, guide and monitor the entire range of credit facilities offered by the other institutions, to the small and cottage sector.

It actively involves in financing all types of industrial concerns engaged in the field of,

(*a*) Manufacturing.
(*b*) Processing or preserving of goods.
(*c*) Mining.
(*d*) Shipping.
(*e*) Transport.
(*f*) Hotel industry.
(*g*) Generation/distribution of power.
(*h*) Fishing/providing shore facilities for fishing.
(*i*) Testing or servicing of machinery or vehicles/vessels.

(*j*) Exporting of engineering goods.
(*k*) For the establishment of R&D for promotional growth of industries.

Capital and Financial Resources

The IDBI has been formed with an authorised capital of Rs. 50 crore. It was enhanced to Rs. 2000 crore in October 1994 by the Central Government. The main sources of financial resources other than its share capital are retained earnings, loan collections, borrowings from Government and RBI, acceptance of public deposits, issue of bonds, debenture and other financial products etc.

Management

The IDBI has been turning as India's premier banking institute which actively involve for the peace of industrialisation in the country. It has been run by 22 persons including a full-time chairman and the Managing Director and the Board of Directors. The Chairman will be appointed by the RBI. The Board of Directors comprises of the following representatives.

(*a*) A representative from the RBI.
(*b*) A representatives from all India financial institutions.
(*c*) Two members from the Central Government.
(*d*) Three members from the public sector banks and the SFCs.
(*e*) Five members from industry who have a special knowledge.

The Board also constitutes an executive committee of ten members.

Functions

The main functions of the IDBI are follows:

(*a*) To grant direct loans and advances to industries concerns.
(*b*) To render co-ordinative activities for term loans.
(*c*) To provide refinance facility to the financial institutions.
(*d*) To provide refinance to the cooperative banks and scheduled banks.

(*e*) To provide excellent technical and administrative assistance for promotion, management and growth of industry.
(*f*) To undertake market surveys and techno economic studies for the development of industry.
(*g*) To provide technical guidance for establishment of R&D wings for promotion of industries.
(*h*) To provide medium and long-term loans to the Industry.
(*i*) Acts as Export and Import Bank of India.

The IDBI is empowered to finance all types of industrial concerns The bank also assist in establishing new industries and in providing technical expertism. The bank's day to day operations are carried on by the Chairman and Managing Director. He is assisted by the executive directors. The bank has its Head Office in Mumbai and Regional Offices are located in Ahmedabad, Kolkata, Chennai, Gawhati and New Delhi. It also has regional committees to advise and guide its Regional Offices, besides, it has Branch Offices in semi-metropolitan cities.

Features

The salient features of various schemes operated by the bank are presented below:

(*a*) Term loans
(*b*) Specified sector loans
(*c*) Refinance of loans.
(*d*) Technical development fund scheme.
(*e*) Bills re-discounting scheme.
(*f*) Seed capital assistance scheme.
(*g*) Development assistance fund.

(a) Term Loans

The IDBI provides financial support in the form of term loans. Financial assistance is usually sanctioned to the new projects as well as for the expansion, modernisation and renovation of the existing units. It also subscribes the issue of shares or debentures. It undertakes the underwriting for the issue of share. It extends financial assistance to medium and large scale projects undertaken by public limited companies. It pays special attention towards mega projects and sophisticated technology promoted by the technocrat, located in the backward areas and exploring the new technology units. It also provides foreign currency loans to the projects for the purchase of fixed assets.

(b) Specified Sector Loans

The IDBI sanctions loans to the units in the specified industry groups *i.e.*, sugar, textiles and jute. It extends the loans for modernisation, replacement of machinery and renovation of plant to enhance the higher levels of production and improve their competitiveness. This facility is operated with other financial institutions, IFCI and ICICI with overall responsibility lying with it. The IFCI is specialised in lending the money to jute and sugar industries. The ICICI concentrates the engineering units. The IDBI focuses on cotton textiles and cement industries.

The loans under this scheme are extended in concessional terms in the form of rate of interest. The scheme depends upon the promoter's contribution, Debt equity ratio, initial moratorium and repayment period.

(c) Refinance of Loans

Under this scheme, the refinance facility can be availed to the small and medium size units. The IDBI sanctions refinance assistance through the eligible institutions only *i.e.* SFCs, commercial banks, rural banks, state cooperative banks, State Industrial Development Corporation etc. It has extended the flow of credit to village and cottage industries. Refinance is provided at concessional rate of interest for loans to (*a*) SSI, (*b*) units in backward areas, (*c*) single truck operators.

The IDBI provides refinance scheme by not only offering the interests at lower rates but also it gives, some other relaxations like central subsidy, interest free, exemption of sales tax, to SSIs and projects in backward areas. It also sanctions the refinance facility to SC/ST entrepreneurs at lower rate interest irrespective of their units.

(d) Technical Development Fund Scheme

It provides loans to the industrial concerns to utilise import licences under this scheme. The scheme changes from time to time in force.

(e) Bills Re-Discounting Scheme

The IDBI rediscounts bills of a commercial enterprise. The bill or promissory notes aroused in the sale of machinery by the manufacturers, are discounted by them with the concerned bankers. The banker in turn rediscounts the same with the IDBI. The scheme is more useful to the commercial enterprises to purchase machinery and equipment on deferred payment basis. This scheme is applicable to approved design engineering concerns, selling agents and distributors of the machinery manufacturers etc. The scheme is also applicable to SSIs, State Road Transport organisations, and state electricity boards in the country.

(f) Seed Capital Assistance Scheme

According to this scheme, the IDBI assists those entrepreneurs who have skills but lack of finance to run their establishment. It operates two schemes under this assistance programme.

1. SFCs sponsored schemes.
2. IDBI's own schemes.

Under the SFCs sponsored schemes, the concerned SFCs and State Governments will provide financial assistance to the SSIs projects which in turn are contributed by the IDBI. In this type of finance facility, the IDBI will render its contribution indirectly to the SSIs projects through the SFCs. According to the IDBI's own scheme, it is operated through State Industrial Development Corporations for sanctioning the seed capital to the medium size projects. Financial assistance under the schemes is interest free with a minimum service charge, the scheme is more useful to the SSIs and medium term projects.

(g) Development Assistance Fund

Under this financial assistance programme, the IDBI will sanction the requisite amount of fund to the needy projects. The fund is available to the projects where the financial institutions and commercial banks are unable to provide financial assistance in the ordinary course of business.

3. INDUSTRIAL CREDIT AND INVESTMENT CORPORATION OF INDIA (ICICI)

The Industrial Credit and Investment Corporation of India was established on 5-1-1955. It's Headquarters was in Mumbai. It has been set up to encourage and provide assistance to the corporate sector in India. It provides various kinds of financial assistance schemes to purchase land, building and machinery.

Objectives and Functions

The corporation has been established for rendering the financial assistance to the private sector by:

(*i*) Providing assistance in the creation, expansion and modernisation of industrial concern.
(*ii*) Promoting and encouraging private ownership.
(*iii*) Rendering financial assistance in the form of long or medium term loans.
(*iv*) Providing excellent services to the corporate sector, *i.e.* technical, management services.
(*v*) Sanctioning loans to import the machinery.
(*vi*) Providing underwriting services to issue sharer and debentures.
(*vii*) Expansion of investment markets.

Capital and Sources of Funds

Industrial Credit and Investment Corporation has been established with an authorised capital outlay of Rs. 50 crores. At the end of March 1996 paid up capital of the corporation amounted to Rs. 376.3 crores. The major shareholder in the corporation are LIC, GIC, UTI and Banks. The share capital has been contributed by the Government of India, the world bank and all financial institutions. The financial resources of the corporation have been further augmented by issuing debentures in India, bonds and Euro dollars in abroad.

Management

The ICICI is managed by a Board of Directors. The Board of Directors consists of 15 members including the chairman. Two directors are elected by the UK shareholders. The remaining directors are nominated by the Government of India and USA.

Types of Financial Assistance

The main aim of establishing the ICICI is to provide the financial assistance to the industrial projects for foreign currency. It encourages and promotes industries in private sector. It has diversified into a number of other activities and offers a complete package of financial services directly or through its subsidiaries. It has been managing the US Agency for International development and World Bank funds through its technological financing programmes. It also provides financial packages for R&D, commercialisation of technology, pollution control, environmental protection and venture capital. To fulfill its objectives for promoting the industrial development, it provides the following facilities to the corporate section.

(*a*) It provides the underwriting facilities to the issue of shares and debentures etc.
(*b*) It contributes direct subscription to securities issued by the companies.
(*c*) It provides services like evaluation of projects, monitoring and subsequent following.
(*d*) It arranges consortium financing services (IDBI, IFCI, LIC, UTI, GIC etc.).
(*e*) It provides assistance to projects in backward areas.
(*f*) It provides merchant banking facilities to the corporate sector.
(*g*) It encourages and promotes industries which are incorporated in rural areas.

Importance of Financial Institutions

After the second world war many countries felt that there was a strong need for establishment of financial institutions. In undeveloped countries, it is necessary to establish the financial institutions to boost the activities of industrialization like our nation. In 1918 the Industrial commission has recommended the establishment of financial institutions in India. After independence a number of financial institutions has formed on All India basis. These institutions are rendering specialised services not only finance but also rendering technical services and guidance. The following table may reveal the importance of All India Financial Institutions in our economy.

Industry-wise Assistance Sanctioned and Disbursed by All India Financial Institutions

Sector	All India Financial Institutions (Rs. in crores)														
	Sanctions					Disbursements					Utilisation (%)				
	1994-95	95-96	96-97	97-98	98-99	94-95	95-96	96-97	97-98	98-99	94-95	95-96	96-97	97-98	98-99
1. Food Products	2151	2100	1091	1688	2027	1459	1500	1232	1230	1391	68	71	113	73	69
2. Textiles	7531	4624	3576	5206	5208	4385	4296	3286	3934	4723	59	93	92	76	91
3. Paper Products	676	1754	1052	909	1139	471	935	1058	942	916	70	53	101	104	80
4. Rubber	286	364	462	1067	694	162	293	346	278	427	57	81	75	26	61
5. Chemicals	6462	7548	6342	5631	5767	4588	4681	5149	4913	5297	71	62	81	87	92
6. Crude oil	477	100	9	1	8	49	57	28	31	4	10	57	327	2354	49
7. Refineries	3522	2483	1348	4037	7782	1265	510	892	4391	4796	36	21	66	109	62
8. Fertilisers	983	2676	1824	1997	2753	663	907	1559	1740	2060	68	34	85	87	75
9. Cement	1986	2710	1710	1968	1754	1363	1256	2485	1857	1440	69	46	145	94	82
10. Basic metal															
(a) Iron & Steel	4607	3868	3877	7343	4434	2748	2732	3103	5492	3563	60	71	80	75	80
(b) Non-ferrous	358	267	966	571	1047	189	158	347	586	593	53	59	36	103	57
11. Metal products	864	2239	2063	1422	1289	709	1527	1486	996	1049	84	68	72	70	81
12. Machinery	1464	1662	1904	1460	2004	907	1276	1958	1301	1398	62	77	103	89	70
13. Electrical equipment	713	972	1209	1467	1299	395	377	732	815	1102	55	39	61	55	85
14. Electronic equipment	1721	2686	1427	2616	2166	1090	1725	1295	1899	1635	63	64	91	73	76
15. Transport equipment	1304	1996	2696	2189	2669	755	1067	1797	1518	1947	58	53	67	69	73

(*Contd.*)

(*Contd.*)

All India Financial Institutions (Rs. in crores)

Sector	Sanctions					Disbursements					Utilisation (%)				
	1994-95	95-96	96-97	97-98	98-99	94-95	95-96	96-97	97-98	98-99	94-95	95-96	96-97	97-98	98-99
16. Infrastructure															
(a) Power generation	5517	5705	5024	12534	17768	1994	2600	3447	4465	4038	36	46	69	36	23
(b) Telecommunication	1021	1029	797	4752	4151	165	619	294	1170	1030	16	60	37	25	25
(c) Roads/ports/bridges	354	162	490	2260	3186	9	45	39	1775	2276	3	28	8	79	71
17. Services	4865	5263	5150	9180	9788	3279	4675	4534	6540	7166	68	88	88	71	73
18. Other industries	7183	4732	3021	4650	8054	4046	3584	3336	4461	6143	56	76	42	96	76
Grand Total	**54026**	**54942**	**46050**	**72849**	**84986**	**30691**	**34821**	**38454**	**50331**	**52992**	**57**	**64**	**84**	**69**	**62**

Source: *The Economic Times*, dated: 7-4-2000.

The All India Financial Institutions have been helping the corporates to mobilise the resources. They have been playing a vital role. They provide a variety of customised financial products and services. The investment activity abide reflected in the disbursement of funds as a percentage of sanctions had shown a downtrend since 1996-97. The latest annual report on the development banking published by the IDBI revealed this fact. The under utilisation of funds was partially responsible for the sluggish market conditions and cost cutting exercise adopted by the corporates, whose profits have been dwindling.

The All India Financial Institutions constitutes the following institutions:

(*a*) Industrial Development Bank of India (IDBI).
(*b*) Industrial Finance Corporation of India (IFCI).
(*c*) Industrial Credit and Investment Corporation of India (ICICI).
(*d*) Small Industries Development Bank of India (SIDBI).
(*e*) Industrial Investment Bank of India (IIBI).

Specialised Financial Institutions

1. Risk Capital and Technology Finance Corporation (RCTC).
2. ICICI venture.
3. Tourism Finance Corporation of India (TFCI).

Investment Institutions

(*a*) Life Insurance Corporation (LIC)
(*b*) Unit Trust of India (UTI)
(*c*) General Insurance Corporation (GIC)

During 1998-99, the sanctions and disbursements of these institutions increased from 18.9 per cent and 8.4 per cent to Rs. 89,877 crore and Rs. 56,204 crore respectively.

With the sanctions and disbursements of All India development banks, they increased to 20.5 per cent and 7.7 per cent respectively to Rs. 79,483 crore and Rs. 46,332 crore respectively. The sanctions and disbursements of the specialised financial institutions decreased to 32 per cent and 28.4 per cent respectively to Rs. 243 crore and Rs. 161 crore respectively during 1998-99.

The investment institutions recorded an increase of 8.9 per cent and 12.9 per cent in sanctions and disbursements to Rs. 10,151 crore and Rs. 9,721 crore respectively during the year under review. .

The disbursements as a percentage of sanctions by All India financial institutions which was at the peak of 82.21 per cent in 1996-97 plunged to 68.58 per cent in 1997-98 and further to 62.63 per cent in 1998-99. The fall in this ratio was mainly attributed to the slow pace of growth of funds disbursed as against sanctions by the leading financial institutions like IFCI, ICICI and specialised financial institutions like RCIC.

4. EXPORT AND IMPORT BANK OF INDIA (EXIM) BANK

The Export and Import Bank of India was established on 1-1-1982 for promoting the foreign trade. It renders the financial assistance to the corporate sector in export and import business. It also coordinates the working of other financial institutions which engage in foreign trade. It functions as an apex body by assisting and developing the Export business sector. It undertakes the promotion activities and provides counselling services to the persons and institutions. The bank renders financial assistance to different types of schemes. The bank rediscounts the export bills of banks for a period of 180 days only. It is an indirect finance to boost the export business. It also arranges the refinance in respect of post-shipment credit facilities. The bank grants the finance in the form of term loans. The financial assistance should be for exports of plants, equipments, machinery etc. The bank also contributes the equity investment to the Indian Promoters in Joint Ventures abroad. The bank participates with the commercial banks to the guarantees issued in foreign currencies on behalf of the Indian exporters and importers. The bank offers the credit directly to the buyers for importing the capital goods. It also offers advisory services to the exporters.

During the year 1993-94 bank offered new and varied services to the exporters. It has been approved only as an agency in India to facilitate the forfeiting transactions. Thus it offers the Indian exporters as alternative trade financing mechanism. The banks relationship with the European Commission is strengthened through the sponsorship of the joint venture projects in India.

5. NATIONAL BANK FOR AGRICULTURE AND RURAL DEVELOPMENT (NABARD)

The National Bank for Agriculture and Rural Development was established on 12-7-1982. It was established for the purpose of financing the agriculture sector. The major functions of the agriculture credit department of the RBI were taken over by the NABARD. All the assets and liabilities of the National Agricultural Credit Fund were transferred to the NABARD. The entire work of the agriculture sector of the RBI is taken over by the NABARD. The NABARD has the full authority to refinance and inspect the Regional Rural Banks. It has also the authority to look after the developmental functions of the **Regional Rural Banks**. It is the premier institution in the sphere of the rural credit. It has emerged as an Apex National Institution. It fully involves in refinance, loans and advances to the **State Cooperative Banks**, Land Development Banks, RRBs and other approved institutions. It looks after the financing function of production, marketing and investment activities relating to the rural development, small scale industries, village industries and handicrafts.

The NABARD has a share capital of **Rs. 100 crores**. It was subscribed equally by the RBI and the Government of India. It also borrows from the RBI and the Central Government. The lending rates and deposit rates changes from time to time. The interest chargeable to the ultimate beneficiaries is very less for farmers and small farmers. It also sanctions the loans to the agriculture sector on medium and long-term basis. It charges different rates of interest for different purposes. However the less rate of interest will be charged for agricultural purposes.

6. SHIPPING CREDIT AND INVESTMENT CORPORATION OF INDIA (SCICI)

The Shipping Credit and Investment Corporation of India was set up in 1973. It is the youngest and highly performing financial institution. It plays a vital role in financing the infrastructure development. The aim of the Institution is to finance the green field and export inducing projects and infrastructure financing. It commits to provide the finance to the major Power Projects. They include the Enron Project, Torrent Project in Gujarat, Valley Project in Orissa and two projects in Andhra Pradesh. Most of the projects are being funded in a consortium basis and the maximum lending will be facilitated.

The SCICI has been encouraging the entrepreneurs to invest in funding the National Highways. However the return on the investment would be poor. Privatisation in the transport segment should take off initially with small projects. It thinks about the viability of funding the national highways by diverting the funds from other financial institutions.

It has been riding on a wave of success with its operations and performance. It becomes the envoy of other financial institutions. It has completed the assignments for restructuring the plan for the ONGC. The funds will be mobilised from the market.

7. TOURISM FINANCE CORPORATION OF INDIA

Introduction

The Tourism Finance Corporation of India was incorporated as a Public Limited Company in **1989**. It has an authorised share capital of **Rs. 500 crores** of which **Rs. 67.42 crores** is paid up. The institutions hold nearly **75 per cent** of the equity. The Nationalised banks hold **15.04 per cent**.

It provides the financial assistance to the enterprises for setting up and developing the tourism related activities, facilities and services. Such assistance is extended for setting up new projects as well as for expansion, diversification and modernisation of the projects. It extends rupee loans, guarantees for deferred payments and credits raised in India and abroad, equipment finance, equipment leasing, suppliers credit and advisory services. It also coordinates and formulates the guidelines and policies relating to finance such projects.

It provides the surplus amount to the Government of India. During the financial year that on March 31, 2001, it had earned a profit of **Rs. 137.53 crores** from the operations of business. During the year that ended on March 31, 2000, it earned a net profit of Rs. 141.32 crores.

8. RISK CAPITAL AND TECHNOLOGY FINANCE CORPORATION (RCTFC)

The Risk Capital Fund was sponsored by the IFCI. The corporation was established in 1975. It was set up to provide an assistance to the entrepreneurs. It encourages the medium sized industrial projects. It provides assistance to the entrepreneurs in the form of equity capital. It is popularly known as the **RCTFC**. It is aimed to encourage the high technology profitable ventures which involves innovative products. It also encourages venture capital firms. It floated a venture capital firm in July 1991. It also entered in **Non Fund** based activities. It also acts as a financial intermediary to its assisted units. It obtained the membership from the O.T.C. The company perceives itself the role of sponsor. Primarily for the units assisted by it.

The RCTFC manages a venture capital scheme known as the **VECAUS-III** venture capital unit scheme III was floated by the UTI. The VC firm has been established by the IFCI and the UTI. The world bank also supports the RCTFC. The financial assistance will be facilitated by the world bank through the IFCI.

The RCTFC concentrates to focus on the projects which involves in newer technologies or innovative services. It assisted in manufacturing of automotive press forgings, fully machanised crank shafts, high tension ignition resitive codes, speciality tissue papers and allied products, densified cattle feed, based on wheat/rice straw and sugar cane leaves, telecommunication and pagers etc.

9. INDUSTRIAL RECONSTRUCTION BANK OF INDIA (IRBI)

The Industrial Reconstruction Bank of India was set up in 1985. It was established as a statutory body under the IRBI Act. It was empowered to reconstruct the sick industrial units. Its main objective is to revive the sick industrial units. Its objectives can be fulfilled by assisting them in their expansion, modernisation, diversification, reorganisation and rationalisation.

Functions

The functions of the IRBI are presented below:

1. Provides loans and advances to the corporate sector.
2. Contributes/subscribes to equity/debentures of the companies.
3. Provides hire purchase facilities.
4. Provides consultancy services.
5. Provides merchant banking facilities.
6. Provides legal, technical and financial assistance to the mergers and amalgamations units.
7. Provides infrastructure facilities.

The RBI has the right to takeover the management of the assisted companies. It acts as a coordinator in securing the assistance from the banks and financial institutions. It is aimed to solve the labour problems immediately when the assisted firm approaches. It also offers advices on product mix and allied matters. The IRBI involves in corporate and financial restructuring. **The Corporate** restructuring made it as a Government Company. Its name was changed as **Industrial Investment Bank of India**. Financial restructuring involves its conversion of dues transferred to the **IIBI Ltd.**

10. INSURANCE REGULATION AUTHORITY

Introduction

Insurance organisations are the repositories of the public trust. Before the nationalisation of life and general insurance, LIC and GIC dominated the market. These institutions were regulated under the provisions of the Insurance Act 1938. The Act was administered by the **Controller of Insurance.** The Insurance Regulatory Authority is set up as a statutory body. It is similar to the SEBI. It should have a full time chairperson, two full time and some part time members. The chairman and board members should be familiar. They should have integrity, ability, rich experience in finance, insurance, law, administration and other relevant disciplines. One of the board members should have a strong background in general insurance and another must be in **life insurance**. The IRA should discharge its functions in a free and transparency manner.

Functions

The functions of the IRA are as follows:

(*a*) The IRA should observe the provisions of law about capital adequacy, solvency margins and other norms.
(*b*) It has the authority to grant the certificate of registration.
(*c*) It should look after the interest of the consumers.
(*d*) It has the authority to modify the rates, terms and conditions.
(*e*) To monitor the performance and quality of **reinsurance**.
(*f*) To ensure high standards of accounting and transparency.
(*g*) It has the power to detect badly managed, unhealthy or failing insurers.
(*h*) It has the power for consumers grievances.
(*i*) It has the power to prepare the annual report on the state of the insurance industry.
(*j*) It has the power to ensure a variety of insurance products in a transparent manner.
(*k*) It has the power to design the new products to meet the needs of the rural population.

The authority has the right to levy **0.5 percent** of the premium income of insurance companies, which they are collected from policy holders. The Controller of Insurance was replaced by the **IRA** on September 6, 1995. The Ministry of Finance has taken over the overall control in the insurance sector. It has been entrusted with the task of assigning the responsibilities.

Salient Features

The salient features of the IRA are presented below:

1. The chairman of the IRA is appointed by the Government of India.
2. It has the authority to think about the introduction of privatisation in the insurance industry wholly or partially.
3. It has the power to regulate, promote and control the activities of the insurance industry.
4. The chairman of the IRA has the status of an **Additional Secretary** to the Government.
5. The board should consist of seven members.
6. 3 board members should be full time nominated by the Central Government.
7. The board may continue until the pleasure of the Central Government.
8. The government should provide adequate grants for financing the expenses incurred by the IRA.
9. It would deal with all the matters relating to the promotion and growth of the insurance industry.
10. It has its own procedure and powers.
11. It has the powers to call for records, returns, notes, memorandum, data or any other information relevant to its working from official and non-official bodies.
12. It has the responsibility to submit a periodical report to the Government of India on various aspects of insurance industry.
13. It is also responsible for the submission of specific matters as desired by the government from time to time.

11. THE STOCKHOLDING CORPORATION OF INDIA

Introduction

The Stock Holding Corporation of India was established in July 1986. It was incorporated under the Companies Act 1956. It was promoted by the All India Financial Institutions. The promoters involve in the formation of the Corporation. They are **IDBI, ICICI, IFCI, UTI, GIC and IRBI.**

It was established to eliminate the paper work in relation to the transactions in shares, debentures and securities by introducing the book entry system for the transfer of scrips. Transferring the scrips through immobilisation and dematerialisation of securities. It facilitates the elimination of frauds and errors. It creates greater liquidity of investments in scrips. The main objective of its formation is to provide comprehensive custodial services. It facilitates fully automated infrastructural facilities for trade, clearances, settlement and depository services for the securities. It offers its services to the institutional investors. It work out the clearance function of the NSE for their whole sale debt market segment. The Secondary market trading in India has been creating waves in the market with the help of Information Technology. The information technology makes India to reach the world standard in trading methods. It has recently formulated the framework for a National Clearing and Depository System. It will act as the founder of developed secondary market trading in India. National Clearance and Depository System comprises of **National Trading Report System, National Clearing System, National Depository System**. The NTRS creates the terms and conditions of a contract after the execution of a trade in the market. The NCS takes place nationally on a standard basis. The NDS makes the transfer of scrips with the physical movement of scrip.

12. THE DISCOUNT AND FINANCE HOUSE OF INDIA (DFHI)

The Discount and Finance House of India was incorporated in **April 1988**. It was promoted on the basis of the recommendations of **Sri N. Vaghul** Committee. The paid up capital of **Rs. 100 crores** was contributed by the RBI **(51%)**, public sector banks **(33%)** and financial institutions **(16%)**. The basic aim of the corporation is to provide liquidity to the money market instruments in the market. It deals with the short-term instruments. The sources of the finances of the corporation are **paid up capital, Refinance with RBI, and credit limits to PSBs for Rs. 200 crores.**

Functions

The functions of the corporation are presented below:

(*a*) It involves in buying or discounting of 91 days and 364 days treasury bills.
(*b*) It actively participates in the inter bank call money market.
(*c*) It discounts and rediscounts the short-term commercial bills for the financial institutions and banks.

It develops the Money Market Mutual Fund. It actively involves in the call money market. The RBI had allowed the entry of any mutual fund and any entity during 1991. The DFHI operates the money market. It is a vehicle for operations of the RBI in the money market. It also involves in purchasing and selling of commercial bills, commercial papers and certificate of deposits. It also quotes bid and offer notes for the response. *i.e.* buy back transactions. Its presence in the money market stimulates the secondary market. There has also been a significant improvement in the number of participants. The DFHI was converted into a Primary Dealer in 1995. The setting up of the Primary Dealers and Satellite Dealers made the money market more liquid. The Primary Dealer adds the liquidity and the Satellite Dealer makes the market broads.

13. TECHNOLOGY DEVELOPMENT AND INFORMATION COMPANY OF INDIA LTD. (TDICI)

Introduction

The Technology Development and Information Company of India Ltd. was established in January 1988. It was promoted by the ICICI and the UTI. It started India's first venture fund, the VECAUS **Venture Capital Unit Scheme** with a corpus fund of Rs. 20 crores. It has been rendering the services to 37 small and medium enterprises. It also provides financial assistance to the software companies.

It works now as a venture capital institution and provides technical services to the information technology companies. It provides marketing services to the export oriented units. At present, it concentrates on **high tech and low tech** industries for financing the projects. Investment decisions always depends upon the courage of the entrepreneur. It takes interest to fund the high risk investment projects.

The high risk projects generally generate high returns and lead to a high rejection rate as much as **90 per cent** of all proposals. It gives top priority to the close ended companies. They provide finance to those companies which have no access to the public issue and to the unknown ones. It will nominate a member as the board of director in the assisted companies.

It provides financial assistance to the companies ranging from software, foods, power generation and art, painting etc. A large number of firms are located in Mumbai, Pune, Nashik and Chennai.

14. CUSTODIANS

The evolution of the stock market lead to so many innovations. The custodial services is one of the emerging elements in the stock market. It plays a crucial role in the secondary market. The **SEBI** has defined its framework and made it as the SEBI custodian of Securities Regulations, 1996 for the proper conduct of safe guarding of the securities of a client. The client enters into an agreement to avail the services. The custodians offer their services to the clients on the following aspects:

(a) They provide services to maintain the accounts of the securities of a client.
(b) They collect the accruals of the benefits of the client on behalf of him.
(c) They will equip the client about the actions taken by the issuers of securities.
(d) They reconcile the records of the clients transactions.

Registration

The SEBI is the most powerful organisation in the stock market to monitor, regulate and guide the situation. Every custodian should register with the SEBI. The custodian should apply for the registration to the SEBI with an application fee of **Rs. 10,000**. On receipt of the application from the custodian, the SEBI would grant the registration if it satisfies with the particulars submitted by the custodian. The SEBI will examine whether the applicant,

(a) Fulfils the net worth of **Rs. 50 crores** (paid up capital + free reserves).
(b) Has the adequate infrastructure.
(c) Has the best talented manpower.
(d) Has the arms length relationship to be maintained in his other business affairs.
(e) The registration is in the interest of the investors.
(f) The applicant is a body corporate.
(g) His associates/employees are involved in litigation connected with offence.

The custodian who has been granted the registration should pay a registration fee of **Rs. 15,00,000**. The SEBI after scruitinising, the application may grant the registration under certain conditions.

(a) Every custodian should fulfill the capital requirement of **Rs. 50 crores.**
(b) Every custodian has to obey the rules and regulations of the SEBI.
(c) Every custodian has to make a valid agreement with his clients for rendering such services.
(d) The custodian has to pay the annual fee of **Rs. 5,00,000**.

Any wrong information/false in any particular content should be informed to the custodian by the SEBI in writing.

Obligations

The custodian is an important person in the stock trading mechanism. The SEBI is the mandatory organisation to look after the interest of the general investors. The rules and regulations have been framed by the SEBI and every custodian should fulfill the obligations as follows:

(a) Code of Conduct
(b) Uniform norms

The custodian functions relate to the service sector. He should abide by the code of conduct. Now-a-days it became a profession. The custodian should maintain a high standard of integrity, transparency and maintain a professionalism manner. He must have a staff with high skills, talents and dynamism. He should be prompt in the collection of dividends from the issuers company and interest on behalf of his client. He is responsible for the movement of securities in the custody account. He should maintain the transactions of deposits and withdrawal of cash from the clients. He should be in a position to provide everything within a short span of time.

He should provide best infrastructural facilities to his clients. The operating procedures and systems should be in a systematic manner. He should maintain the confidentiality of the affairs of his clients. He should record the transactions in an electronically stored manner. He should take all the precautions to keep the information in storage and is not lost. He should obtain the duplicate documents to be provided in the event of loss of the original document. He should be cooperative with counterparts, depositories and clearing organisations. He should maintain an arms length relationship with other associates. He should take precautionary measures while administrating the assets of his clients. He should not manage all the activities of the business. He should make demarcation of all his activities. The staff and his officers should not engage custodial services or any other allied activities. The custodian functions cannot be delegated to any other person except to the custodian. The custodian should be in a position to monitor, review and evaluate the procedures and systems. The activities should be inspected by an expert and the report should be submitted to the SEBI within 3 months. The custodian should implement the internal control system in his organisation to avoid manipulations of records and malpractices. The custodian should maintain the records for at least five years. The SEBI has the authority to conduct the inspection under the supervision of an auditor to check the books of accounts and records. The SEBI should ensure that the accounts are being maintained properly. The SEBI has the power to investigate the complaints made by the investors. On completion of the inspection, a report should be submitted to the SEBI. On the basis of the report received by the SEBI it can call up on the custodian to take such measures as it deems fit. The registration of the custodian is liable to be suspended by the SEBI for the following reasons:

1. Any violation of the rules and regulations of the SEBI.
2. Failure to pay the annual fee.
3. Any breach of code of conduct.
4. Fails to attend the complaints of clients.
5. Fails to submit the periodical returns to the SEBI.
6. Non-cooperation during the inspection of the SEBI.
7. Fails to follow the guidelines of the SEBI.
8. Furnishes false information to the SEBI.

The SEBI has the ultimate final authority to punish the custodian if he fails to obey the rules and regulations of the Act. It can cancel the registration of the custodian if he involves in an offence of moral turpitude or he is guilty of repeated defaults.

Uniform Norms

The SEBI controls the activities of the custodians by preparing uniform norms. They are presented below:

(*a*) Custodians should work as an integral part of the system.
(*b*) It advises all its clients to settle their transactions through the corporation.
(*c*) Participates in clearing and settlement process through them for all the securities.

15. DEPOSITORY SYSTEM

Introduction

The liberalised, deregulated and globalised economic environment led to the evolution of the Indian financing system. Gradually transformation shifted from the financial institutions to the capital market and related institutions. The gross inadequancies of the market infrastructure were revealed by the entry of the FIIs and capital markets growth. This was to support the volumes of securities trading in India. The existing traditional methods are time consuming. The modern techniques and the state of art are to be replaced in the place of traditional methods such as **trading, clearing, settlement, transfer, registration, maintenance of records**. The latest technology may be helpful for smooth functioning of the stock market. More exposure of the markets occur with the rapid changes in the investors' habits. The sensex movement reflects the investor's perception. It is highly influenced by the GDP. A mathematical basis for the future expectation of the market is provided by the past behaviour of **the Sensex** and its link with the **GDP**. In 1995-96 the Sensex grew **27 per cent** touching **3598.37** and the GDP at **Rs. 10,73,300 crores** grew **7.3 per cent**. In 1995-96 the market capitalisation of the BSE was 43 per cent of the GDP. The year also witnessed record investments of **$3.05 billion** by the FIIs. All these factors increased the systematic risks like credit risk, bad-deliveries, long-delayed deliveries, counterfeit scrips, forged certificates, wrong signatures and stealing of shares. A new modern infrastructure has been created to overcome the problems in computer recording of transactions, paperless trading and depositories. The technological revolution has created waves in trading methods. Now-a-days trading can be done by clicking the mouse. Trading became a highly sophisticated execution in transactions. There is no need of physical presence in the stock exchange. The scenario of trading has changed with the entry of **bulk buyers/FIIs**. The stock market reforms cleared the way for introducing depository/custody in the securities. The system of trading is based on physical transfer and efficient functioning of the markets, especially in the context of high volume transactions.

Problems

The investors face many problems regarding the buying and selling of shares in the stock market. The problems faced by the individual investors/institutional investors/foreign institutional investors are presented below:

1. Delay in the transfer of securities.
2. Delay in getting the duplicate share certificate.
3. Delay in getting the duplicate debenture/Bond certificate.
4. Delay in the receipt of securities allotment order for the allottees.
5. Delay in the non-receipt of refund orders to the non-allottees.
6. The return of share certificate is common in the following situations such as **bad deliveries**.
   (*a*) in case of forged transfer deeds.
   (*b*) in case of false certificate.
   (*c*) on account of forged signature.
   (*d*) on account of mis-match of signature.
7. Lack of infrastructure facilities to handle a bulk volume of transactions—inadequate banking and postal facilities.

The Government of India took an initiative to introduce the scripless trading to revamp all the problems. Through the book-entry method, steps have been taken to bring the auctions in the securities without the physical delivery. The ingredient of the scripless trading is the **dematerialisation** of the share certificates through the depositories. All the certificates are surrendered to the issuer company in this method. The issuer company can cancel the share certificate after receiving them through the depository. The names of the depositories should be entered in the Company Register. The name of the beneficial owner whose name is recorded with the depository should be **deleted**. In September 1995, the Government has introduced an ordinance for the **Depositories**. This ordinance was converted into Depositories Act 1996. The Depository system operates within the framework of the Depositories Act 1996 and the SEBI regulations.

1. Depositories Act 1996

The objective of the Depositories Act is to provide the regulation of depositories in the Securities Market. The Depository Act discloses the following procedure:

(a) **Certificate of Commencement of Business**
(b) **Obligations of depositories.**
(c) **Enquiry and inspection.**
(d) **Powers of the SEBI.**
(e) **Bye-laws**
(f) **Amendments**

A certificate from the SEBI is essential for any individual/company to act as a Depository. Every company should get a registration certificate from the SEBI. Without the SEBI's permission, no company is allowed to act as a depository. The SEBI is empowered to grant the certificates to the concerned parties, when they apply to the SEBI for registration. In the scrutiny, it must satisfy that the depository has adequate infrastructure. He should have the technical capabilities to prevent the manipulation of records. He should also have the excellent facilities for the smooth functioning of the trading activities.

The Obligation of the Depository is to make an agreement with the **Depository Participant (D.P.).** The services such as recording of allotment or transfer of securities can be used by any investor. A **D.P.** should record all the transactions in a depository by surrendering the certificate to the issuer company in a prescribed manner. After receiving the certificate from the D.P., the issuer company cancels the certificate and substitutes in its records the name of the depository as a registered owner. The depository inturn records the name of the person as the beneficial owner. Generally while subscribing the shares, the investors indicate either to receive the certificate or hold with the depository. The full information about the allotment process and the names to be recorded as the beneficial owners of the financial instruments are transmitted to the depository through the Public Issue Company. The securities which are at the disposal of the depository would be in dematerial position. On behalf of the beneficial owner, the depository has the full authority to transfer the ownership. But he does not have voting rights in respect of the securities held. Regarding the financial instrument, the beneficial owner has the rights and benefits. He is also responsible for the liabilities effected from that financial instrument. The Companies Act indicates that every depository should maintain a register and an index of the beneficial owners. He has the right to pledge/hypothecation with the prior approval of the depository. Therefore, the depository should make adjustment entries in the records accordingly. The entry made by the depository is the evidence for hypothecation. According to the bye-laws of the depository, he should inform to the issuing company about the transfer of securities, the name of the beneficial owner at regular intervals. The issuer company should also provide the necessary information in respect of the securities held by it. The beneficial has the option out of a depository. Then he has to inform the message to the depository. The depository inturn passes the message to the issuer company within 30 days. If the beneficial owner/transferee fulfills the conditions and pays the fee as specified by SEBI, then the issuer issues the certificate of securities. The transactions recorded by the depository will be treated as evidence on par with Section 2 of the Banker's Book Evidence Act 1891. If any loss occurs due to the behaviour of the beneficial owner, it can be recovered by the depository from the D.P.

The SEBI monitors, directs and guides all the depository transactions. It is the most powerful organisation. It controls all the activities of the depositories. The SEBI conducts the **enquiry and inspection** of the depositories in the interest of the public. The SEBI is empowered to call for the information or make an enquiry into the affairs of the **Issuer Company/beneficial owner and D.P.** It has the power to give appropriate directions for the welfare of the investors or to prevent the affairs in detrimental to the future of the investor or market. Any person can appeal to the **Security Appellate Tribunal**, if he does not satisfy with the SEBI orders. Any person is liable for the punishment with imprisonment for a period of 5 years or with fine or with both if he violates the rules and regulations/bye-laws. The SEBI can collect the information and assess the situation from time to time.

The **SEBI** has the full powers to make the regulations regarding the maintainance of records. For the commecement of business, it can issue a licence to the depository. It can also make regulations in the following situations:

- **(a)** For proper maintainance of records.
- **(b)** Prescribes the process for surrendering a security certificate.
- **(c)** Rights of depository.
- **(d)** Obligations of the depository.
- **(e)** The process of creating pledge.
- **(f)** The manner of hypothecation by the beneficial owners.
- **(g)** Fee payable for the issue of certificate of securities.
- **(h)** Rights and obligations of the issuer company, a participants.
- **(i)** The entry norms for the admission of scrips to the demat.

Bye-laws

The SEBI is empowered by the act to regulate the working affairs of the Depository, D.P. and Issuer Company. The bye-laws are made by the depository in accordance with the provisions of the act. The SEBI should approve the bye-laws prepared by the depository. The contents of the bye-laws are presented below:

1. The entry level norms for the admission of securities in the depositories.
2. The procedure for the removal of a security in the depository.
3. The conditions for dealing the securities.
4. The appointment procedure for the D.P.
5. The process of dematerialisation of securities.
6. The procedure of affairs of the transactions in a depository.
7. The system for protecting the interests of the participants.
8. The manner for protecting the interest of a beneficial owner.
9. The process of pledge in respect of the securities held with a depository.
10. The process of furnishing the information to the issuer company.
11. The process of furnishing information to the SEBI.
12. The auditing process-reviewing and monitoring.
13. The manner of internal control standards.
14. The procedure for the settlement of any disputes between the parties.
15. The rights and obligations of the depository.
16. The rights and obligations of the D.P.
17. The procedure for the distribution of dividends to the beneficial owner.
18. The manner for the distribution of interest to the beneficial owners.
19. The procedure for transmitting the information which is received from the issuing company to the beneficial owners regarding the dividend declaration, share-holders meetings and other matters.

The SEBI has the authority to direct a depository to make any bye-laws or to amend or revoke any bye-laws in writing. If any depository neglects or fails to comply with the orders/directions, it may make modifications or revoke the bye-laws for the welfare of the investors.

The Depository Act can be implemented by making some amendments to the **Securities Contract Act, Income Tax Act, The SEBI Act, Indian Stamp Act, Companies Act, and Benami Transactions Act.**

2. SEBI and Regulations

The SEBI has the authority to make regulations and control the affairs of the depository. The regulations of the SEBI are presented below:

- **(a) Registration**
- **(b) Certificate of commencement of business**
- **(c) Depository Participant (DP)**
- **(d) Rights of the Depository**
- **(e) Rights of D.P./Issuing company**
- **(f) Inspection**
- **(g) Default.**

(a) Registration

Every depository must register with the SEBI. It grants the registration for the depositories. For that purpose, the interested firm should apply to the SEBI in a prescribed manner along with an application fee of **Rs. 50,000**. The application form should be accompanied by the draft and bye-laws of the proposed depository. The proposed depository may be established by an individual institution or combination of other institutions. Generally the following institutions may think about the set up of depository services:

- **(a) Commercial Banks.**
- **(b) Recognised Stock Exchanges**
- **(c) Development Financial Institutions**
- **(d) Foreign Banks**
- **(e) Body Corporate (Financial Services Organisation)**
- **(f) A body corporate recognised by a foreign country for providing the custodial services.**
- **(g) A recognised financial institution which engages in the financial services outside India.**

Every proposed depository company should satisfy the following conditions:

1. Able to pay an annual fee of **Rs. 10,00,000** to the SEBI.
2. Payment of registration fee of **Rs. 25,00,000** within 15 days.
3. Compliance with the regulation of the SEBI, bye-laws and Act.
4. False information should not be furnished by the proposed depository.
5. Amendments can be made to the bye-laws from time to time as directed by the SEBI.
6. Only depository services are allowed as per the law.
7. Other than the depository services are prohibited.
8. The sponsor of the proposed depository should have atleast 51 per cent of the equity capital and the rest by the participants.
9. The depository participants are allowed to invest upto 5 per cent of the equity.
10. No foreign entity will be allowed for more than 51 per cent of the equity.
11. The depository should redressal the grievances within 30 days from the complaint given by the participants/beneficial owners, and should inform to the SEBI regarding the number of complaints registered and resolved.
12. The Depository should apply for the certificate of commencement of business within one year of registration.

(b) Certificate of Commencement of Business

The proposed depository will submit the application form for the registration along with other required documents and fee. The SEBI gives 1 year time to the depository for getting the certificate of commencement of business. The SEBI scrutinises all the contents relevant to the efficiency and better functioning of the depository, before granting the certificate. It may consider the following factors for granting the certificate of commencement of business:

1. The depository should be financially sound. It must have the networth of more than **Rs. 100 crores**.
2. The bye-laws of the depository must be in compliance with the provisions and it should be approved by the SEBI.
3. The depository services will depend on the technical capability of the depository. It should take care of the automatic data processing systems.

4. The data processing must be protected against the unauthorised access, dissemination of records, alteration, destruction etc.
5. The network of the depository system must be secured against any unauthorised access.
6. The depository should provide a continuous electronic means of communication among the four parties *i.e.* **Depository, Depository Participant, Issuer Company and Issuer's agent**.
7. The depository should provide a better quality of network services on par with the world standards.
8. The electronic access to the data storage sites and to the premises is controlled, monitored and recorded.
9. The depository should establish adequate procedures and provide arrangements for maintaining the back-up facilities.
10. The depository should provide the insurance arrangements for indemnifying the beneficial owners for any loss due to the negligence or default by him.
11. The SEBI should make a physical verification of the infrastructure facilities and systems provided by the depository.
12. The certificate of the commencement of business should be in the interest of the investors.

(c) Depository Participant

According to the SEBI regulation and Depository Act, every depository participant should apply to the SEBI for the grant of registration. Through the depository, the D.P. should pay a registration fee of **Rs. 5,000** along with the application form. Within **30 days**, the depository should certify and recommend the same by forwarding the form to the SEBI. Then the SEBI considers the requirements of the D.P. The D.P. must satisfy anyone of the following categories:

1. A public financial institution **(IDBI, IFCI, ICICI)**.
2. A foreign bank.
3. A bank.
4. A state government sponsored financial corporation.
5. A NBFC with some conditions.
6. A financial consortium led by (1) to (4) organisations.

7. A recognised stock exchange.
8. A registered custodian.
9. A clearing corporation.
10. A registered stock broker **(The minimum networth of Rs. 50 lakhs)**.

On verification of the eligibility, the SEBI grants the certificate. It may be intimated through the depository. The D.P. should satisfy the SEBI that he has adequate infrastructure and systems. Only in the interest of investors and market, the registration will be made. The SEBI permits the D.P. only under the following conditions:

1. The D.P. should pay the registration fee of **Rs. 1.00 lakh** within 15 days.
2. The D.P. should be in compliance with the provisions of the Depository Act.
3. The D.P. must comply with the bye-laws, agruments of the depository.
4. The Depository should hold a certificate of the business commencement before permitting the D.P.
5. The D.P. should inform if any wrong information is found in any manner or if there is any change in such information.
6. The D.P. has to pay an annual fee of **Rs. 1,000** to the SEBI.
7. The grievances of the beneficial owner should be settled within **30 days**.
8. The depository should inform about the nature and the number of grievances redressed.
9. The validity period of the DP's registration is **5 years**.
10. 5 years on payment of **Rs. 10.00 lakhs.**

(d) Rights of the Depository

The Depository should comply with the SEBI regulations, bye-laws and the Depository Act. The rights and obligations of the depository are mentioned in the Depository Act. The depository should state in the bye-laws and is eligible for the dematerialisation on the following elements (instruments):

(a) Scrips, bonds, shares, debentures or other marketable securities of any company.

(b) Units of mutual funds, commercial paper, certificate of deposits, venture capital funds, right issues, securitised debt, unlisted securities and money market instruments.

To dematerialise its securities, the issuing company may make an agreement with the depository. The agreement should be made among the three parties, if the issuer company appoints a Registrar to the Issue. The parties are: **the Depository, the D.P. and the Registrar to the Issue**. The Depository should be in a position to coordinate and reconcile the records of securities ownership with the issues and the D.P. on daily basis. He should have an excellent means of electronic data transfer with all the ingredients. The SEBI should satisfy regarding the efficient service of the transfer of securities of the depository. He should allow the participant to withdraw or transfer his accounts in compliance with the law. To protect the interest of the beneficial owners, the depository has an obligation to arrange the insurance facility. He has the obligation to maintain the integrity of the electronic which he holds. He should have the obligations to take all the precautionary approaches to secure the data safely. The depository should maintain the undermentioned records:

1. The particulars of the securities that are **materialised and dematerialised**.
2. The particulars about the date of the transfer of securities.
3. The details regarding the transferors and transferees.
4. A register and an index of the beneficial owners, the full details about their holdings at the end of every month.
5. The correspondence made with the D.P., Issuer's company and beneficial owners.
6. Other records as specified by the SEBI from time to time.
7. All the records must be maintained for atleast 5 years.
8. The depository inform the place where the documents are maintained by it to the SEBI.
9. In dematerialisation process, the depository should extend cooperation to the involved parties for the prompt and accurate clearance settlement of securities transactions and conduct of business affair.
10. Without the knowledge of the SEBI, the depository should not assign any work/task to any other person.

(e) Rights of the Depository Participants

The Depository bye-laws specify that every D.P. should make an agreement with the beneficial owner of the asset. For each beneficial owner, he should open and maintain separate accounts. The D.P. should register the transfer of securities by taking the instructions from the beneficial owner. The process should be implemented in a specified manner by the bye-laws of the depository. The D.P. should record the instructions of the beneficial owner and make entries in his account accordingly. The following obligations should be fulfilled by the D.P.:

1. The D.P. should maintain the statement of accounts with the beneficial owner and provide the statements to him.
2. The beneficial owner will be allowed to withdraw/transfer from his account as per the agreement.
3. The D.P. should provide continuous means of electronic communication to the beneficial owners.
4. The D.P. should have the capabilities to review, evaluate, control the systems and monitor the internal accounting.
5. The D.P. should maintain the integrity of the data processing system.
6. The D.P. should ensure that the records are to be kept safely.
7. He should maintain his records and reconcile with every depository daily.
8. He should submit periodical returns to the SEBI and to the depository in a specified format.
9. The following records are to be maintained by the D.P.
   - **(i)** Record of transactions with the depositories and beneficial owners.
   - **(ii)** The full particulars of the dematerialised/rematerialised on behalf of the clients.
   - **(iii)** The register of instructions received and executed.
   - **(iv)** The records of notice, entry and approvals.
10. The records should be preserved for 5 years.
11. The D.P. should not assign any work to anyone without the approval of the SEBI.
12. All the records should be made available to the depository.

The issuing company should enter into an agreement with a depository for the issue of the government securities. The beneficial owners are required to submit the particulars of the security certificates for dematerialisation and surrender the certificates to the D.P. The D.P. in turn forwards the same to the depository along with the agreement copy of the beneficial owner. The D.P. should maintain the records which contain all the information with the correspondence made to the depository. After receiving the security certificate, the issuer company immediately cancels it and further entries will be made accordingly. The issuer company should also maintain a record of certificates which have been dematerialised. The issuing company should take the following steps:

(i) The issuing company should make a reconciliation of the records which are dematerialised by the depository on daily basis.
(ii) If the Government is the issuer, it should also reconcile the records of the dematerialised securities on daily basis.
(iii) The Issuer should make arrangements to continue the electronic means of communication with the depository.
(iv) The Issuer Company must provide the information to the depository about the dematerialised securities *i.e.* the details of book closure, record dates, annual general meetings, other meetings, dividends, interest, conversion methods, redemption of debentures, warrants, call money dates etc.
(v) The Issuer Company should provide any other information to the depository regarding the materialisation of securities.

(f) Inspection

The SEBI has the full authority to undertake the inspection of books, documents, records etc. of a depository/D.P./Issuing Company. The SEBI can enquire about the technical capabilities of the systems of the depository. The SEBI has the authority to investigate the affairs of the Depository, D.P., Beneficial owner and Issuing Company. The enquiry will be conducted by the SEBI for the following purposes:

1. To ensure the smooth functioning of the affairs as specified by the law.
2. To respond to the complaints from the investors.
3. To look after the compliance of all the provisions. **(SEBI Act, Bye-laws, Depository Act).**
4. To take the veto powers in the interest of the investors.

(g) Default

The Inspection Committee will submit its report to the SEBI after the completion of inspection. The SEBI may take an action in case of the default by suspending the registration or cancelling the depository or D.P. The SEBI may suspend the registration on the following grounds:

1. Any violation of the provisions of the SEBI, Bye-laws, Depository Act and Agreements.
2. Any failure to furnish the full information regarding the rules and regulations.
3. If any violation of the SEBI directions and fails to pay the annual fee.
4. During the inspection of the SEBI, any non-cooperation by the parties.
5. Furnishes false information or misleading information.

The SEBI has the authority to cancel the registration of the Depository/D.P./Issuing Company/Beneficial owner on the following grounds:

(i) repeated defaults
(ii) if any fraud or conviction of any offence by any party.

16. STATE FINANCIAL CORPORATIONS (SFCs)

The Industrial Commission had recommended for the establishment of the financial institutions in India. After the independence, a number of financial institutions have been established. The institutions also involve in regional levels for accelerating the growth of industries by pro-financial and other assistance.

The State Financial Corporation Act was passed by the Central Government in 1951 to provide small and medium industries at state level. The State Government is empowered to establish the finance corporation to operate within the state level. In India there are **18** such corporations functioning in the country. The development financial institutions provide financial assistance to the large industries. Therefore, the SFCs can render the assistance to all kinds of industries like private companies, partnership firms and sole trading concerns. They are expected to concentrate on small cottage and medium industries. The SFCS provide financial assistance up to **Rs. 30 lakhs** to a single firm or company.

Functions

The functions of the SFCs are presented below:

1. To provide loans to SSI, firms and companies.
2. To grant the loans to industries repayable with in **20 years**.
3. To subscribe the debentures to the industrial concerns.
4. To provide financial guarantees for the industrial enterprises.
5. To provide the underwriting facilities for stocks, shares and debentures.
6. To act as an agent of the IFCI or the Central Government in respect of loans sanctioned to the industries.

Resources

The capital of the corporation will be determined by the concerned state government. The capital structure may be in between **Rs. 50 lakhs to Rs. 5 crores**. The share capital can be subscribed by the state government, the RBI, insurance companies and other financial institutions. The public can subscribe upto 25 per cent of the capital. The SFC's main sources of finance are issues of bonds, borrowing from the RBI, loans from the state government, refinancing by the IDBI and deposits from the public.

17. SMALL INDUSTRIES AND DEVELOPMENT BANK OF INDIA (SIDBI)

The Small Industries and Development Bank of India was established for the purpose of providing loan assistance, promotion and development of industries. It was established under the SIDBI Act 1990 and got passed in the Parliament. It renders the financial assistance to the SSI sector. It also coordinates the functions of financial institutions. It is the coordinator among the SFCs, SSIDCs, scheduled banks and cooperative banks. All the institutions work for promoting, financing and developing the small scale industries.

Resources

The financial resources will be available from the IDBI. It will sanction the loans for the SIDBI; and it also purchases the share capital. The SIDBI also mobilises the resources from the financial markets. It raises the funds on short-term basis from the RBI. It can also borrow the funds from the Central Government. The authorised capital of **Rs. 250 crores** may be increased to the extent of **Rs. 1000 crores**. The issued capital of the SIDBI is wholly subscribed by the IDBI.

It commenced its operations on 2-4-1990. The portfolio of the small scale sector of the IDBI was taken over by this corporation. Thereafter, the SIDBI has been looking after the affairs of the small sectors on behalf of the IDBI. Now, it has been functioning for the welfare of the small sector industries.

18. MERCHANT BANKING

Introduction

Funds are tapped from the capital market to finance various mega industrial projects. In attracting the public savings, the Merchant bankers play a vital role as specialised agencies. The primary business of a merchant banker is the resource raising function. The primary market hold the key of rapid capital formation, growth in industrial production, and exports. There has to be accountability to the end use of the funds raised from the market. The trends in the primary market in India suggest that merchant bankers have been playing a very significant role in the corporate sector's drive for mobilising the funds from the public. If the number of issues and amount increases the number of the merchant brokers also increase. Therefore, the field becomes a highly competitive market where it requires a special skill in handling the situation. The financial assets that are sold to the public should represent the genuine claims on future cash flows and viable assets. The Merchant banks have a social responsibility in building the industrial structure in India.

Origin of the Merchant Bankers

In the 19th century, a British merchant used to send an agent out to little known parts of the world. The agent took with the manufactured goods that were produced in the home country to sell, and at the same time he would buy the products of that country and ship them home. For this trade, money had to be remitted from one country to another, the bill of exchange which was the instrument in usage throughout the Europe since a long time came to be used more and more. The bill of exchange of London became the means of financing the trade practically in the whole world. The well-established merchant agreed to do for commission; and gradually the practice of accepting the bills to finance the trade of others took the shape of accepting the bills to finance their own trade. These firms in London are styled as the Merchant Banks. The oldest merchant bankers in London were the Barring Brothers. It was very prominent in Europe in the 19th century. The Industrial revolution made England into a powerful trading nation. Rich merchant houses which made their fortunes in the colonial trade had diversified into Banking. They themselves involved in the acceptance of the Commercial bills pertaining to domestic as well as international trade.

They became as "Acceptance Houses, Discount Houses and Issue Houses". The Merchant banker was primarily a merchant than a banker. The merchant banker was entrusted with the funds by his customers. Merchant banks in Britain involved in:

(a) Issue Capital
(b) Foreign Loan Business
(c) Finance Foreign Trade
(d) Managing Individual Funds and Undertaking
(c) Foreign Security Business etc.

They also involve in financing the sovereign government in the form of long-term loans.

Several Merchant banks were set up in the U.S.A. to arrange the capital and enterprise to promote railways, industrial projects and trade and commerce. The Investment bankers replaced the brokers and promoters in the issue of securities. They actively involved in launching and organising the Industrial chits, mergers, acquisition and transformation of the private companies into public owned companies. The growth of the Investment bankers were facilitated by the enactment of Federal Act 1914, with the emergence of the U.S. Dollar as the leading global currency and expansion of the U.S. Banking System. The Investment Bankers involved in buying and selling of Corporate bonds, securities on commission basis, deal in municipal, state and federal securities, trading and investing in the securities, originating and distributing the new issues etc. After the great crash of 1929 and depression, their business faced heavy financial losses. Then the federal government enacted several laws to reform the Wallstreet practices to protect the interest of the investors. The increased regulation and control made the U.S. banks to undertake the merchant bank functions in global capital markets. Investment Bankers fully involved in financing the investors for "Initial Public Offering" (IPO) of securities sold in the New Issue Market. They bring the buyers and sellers together. They create market and make arrangements to the public issues. They also help as a finder for the private placement of securities.

Definition of the Merchant Banking

Merchant Banking services are mainly related to the Issue house activities. Webster Dictionary defines the Merchant banking as "a bank that specialises in banker's acceptances and underwriting or syndicating equity or bond issues."[3]

According to Rossenberg M.J.[4], Merchant banking means "an organisation that underwrites securities for corporations, advises such clients on mergers and involves in the ownership of commercial ventures." The meaning of the merchant bank is that, it is an organisation that underwrites the securities and advises such clients on issues. The Securities and Exchange Board of India (Merchant Bankers) Rules, 1992 defined a Merchant banker as "any person who is engaged in the business of the issue management either by making arrangements regarding selling, buying or subscribing to securities as manager, consultant, advisor, or rendering corporate advisory service in relation to such issue management."[5]

According to Cox. D. Merchant Banking—"Merchant banks are the financial institutions providing specialist services which generally include the acceptance of bills of exchange, corporate finance, portfolio management and other banking services."[6]

The notification of the Ministry of Finance defines a Merchant banker as "any person who is engaged in the business of the issue management either by making arrangements regarding selling, buying or subscribing to securities as manager, consultant, advisor, or rendering corporate advisory service in relation to such issue management."[7]

Merchant banks undertake the task of the new issue management, project counselling, preparation of feasibility reports, selection of underwriters/brokers and bankers to the issue. The merchant bankers are responsible for clearing of all the legal formalities from the SEBI for making the public issue. The merchant bankers have been handling a number of public and rights issues. The profession of the merchant banking is concerned with catering the needs of trade and industry by playing a role of intermediary, consultant, liason officer and as a banker. There is a strong need for the merchant banking agencies, because of a major chunk of public savings lying untapped. However, they have been playing a useful role in procuring the support of capital market for the corporate sector for financing their operations. They have been working for the long-term end of the markets that create a niche for a specialed bank.

Main Objectives of the Merchant Banking Company

The Merchant Bankers render their specialised assistance in achieving the main objectives. They are presented below:

1. To carry on the business of the merchant banking, assist in the capital formation, manage advice, underwrite, provide stand by assistance, securities and all kinds of investments issued, to be issued or guaranteed by any company corporation, society, firm, trust, person, government, municipality, civic of body, public authority established in India.
2. The main objective of the merchant banker is to create a secondary market for bills and discount or rediscount bills and acts as an acceptance house.
3. Merchant bankers involve in assistance and promotion of economic endeavour, identification of projects, promoters, preparation of project reports, project feasibility studies, market research, pre-investment studies and investigation of industries at micro and macro level.
4. They also provide services to the finance housing schemes for the construction of houses and buying of land.
5. They render the services like foreign exchange dealer, money exchanges, authorised dealer and to buy and sell foreign exchange in all lawful ways in compliance with the relevant laws in India.
6. They also involve in acquiring and holding one or more membership in stock exchange/National Stock Exchange, trade associations, commodity exchange, clearing houses, or associations in India or any part of the world.
7. They help to promote or procure in corporation formation or setting up to concerns and undertakings as a company, body corporate, partnership or any other association or person for engaging in any other association or persons in any industrial, commercial or business activities.
8. Their objective is to perform financial services including factoring and syndication of both the loans *i.e.* short-term and long-term with financial institutions, bank and others to manage mutual funds and to provide financial software programme.
9. The objective of the merchant banking is to carry on the business of financing the industrial enterprises.
10. They invest in buying and selling of transfers, hypothecate, and deal with the disposal of shares, stocks, debentures, securities and properties of any other company.

Obligations and Responsibilities

Merchant bankers has the following obligations and responsibilities:

1. Merchant banker should maintain proper books of accounts, records and submit half yearly/annual financial statements to the SEBI within the stipulated period of time.
2. No Merchant banker should associate with another merchant banker who does not register with the SEBI.
3. Merchant bankers should not enter into any transactions on the basis of unpublished information available to them in course of their professional assignment.
4. Every Merchant banker must submit himself to the inspection by the SEBI when required for and submit all the records.
5. Every Merchant banker must disclose information to the SEBI when it requires any information from him.
6. All Merchant bankers must abide by the code of conduct prescribed for them.
7. Every Merchant banker who acts as the lead manager must enter into an agreement with the issuer settling out mutual rights, liabilities, obligations relating to such issues with particular references to disclosers, allotment, refund etc.

Code of Conduct

According to the 13 Regulation of the SEBI Regulations 1992 (Merchant bankers), every merchant banker should comply with the following code of conduct. They are:

(a) The Merchant banker must observe high standard of integrity and fairness in all his dealings.
(b) He should render at all times high standard of services, exercise due deligence and independent professional judgement.
(c) If necessary, he must disclose to his clients the possible sources of conflict of duties and interests.
(d) He should not indulge in unfair practice or competition with other merchant bankers.
(e) He should not make any exaggerated statement about his capacity or achievement.
(f) He should always endeavour to give the best possible advice and prompt, effective and cost effective service.

(g) He should maintain the secrecy of all confidential information received during the course of service to his clients.

(h) He should not engage in the creation of a false market or price rigging or manipulation.

Merchant Banking in India

After the termination of the managing agency system in India, there was a strong need of legal and financial services to the corporate sector which required an alternative agency. On such situation, Merchant banking emerged. The Merchant Banking system in India was introduced by Grindlays Bank in 1967. It was the first bank which received licence from the RBI. It started with the management of capital issues rendering the services according to the needs of the emerging new class entrepreneurs for diverse financial services ranging from production to marketing research. It also provided services to the large and medium range companies. The CITI bank established its Merchant banking wing in 1970. Later on the Banking Commission which was established in 1972 fell the need for the establishment of the merchant bank institutions to offer services like syndication or financing, promotion of projects, investment management, advisory services to the corporate sector. The SBI was the first commercial bank of India to launch its merchant banking division in 1972 on the recommendation of the banking commission in 1972. Later other commercial banks and financial institutions like Indian Bank, Punjab National Bank, Indian Overseas Bank, Bank of Baroda, Syndicate Bank, Chartered Bank, LIC, GIC, UTI etc. also started the merchant banking divisions. Some brokerage houses were diversified into this area like J.M. Financial and Investment Consultancy Services Pvt. Ltd., Tata Consultancy Services Ltd., etc. Among the development banks, the ICICI started the merchant banking activities in 1973. It was followed by the IFCI in 1986 and the IDBI in 1991.

Activities/Services Rendered by the Merchant Banks

Merchant banks have been rendering diverse services and functions as organising and extending finance for the investments in projects, raising of EURO dollar loans, equipment leasing, mergers and acquisitions, valuation of assets, investment management, and promotion of investment trusts. All these services are not offered by all the merchant bankers. But different merchant bankers are specialised in different services. The Merchant bank is a multi-service oriented agency. Merchant banking is a creative activity. In India, the merchant banks have been engaging in the following activities:

(a) Corporate Finance Services (management of public issues, credit syndication).
(b) Advisory Services (project counselling, financing, capital restructuring).
(c) Services to the NRIs. (evaluation of investment portfolio, promotion of industries).
(d) Leasing (equipment, machinery etc.)

Merchant banking activities are regulated in India by:

1. Guidelines of the SEBI.
2. Guidelines of the Ministry of Finance.
3. Companies Act, 1956.
4. Securities Contract (Regulation) Act, 1956.
5. Listing guidelines of the Stock Exchange.

1. Guidelines of the SEBI

After the abolition of the CCI, its place was occupied by a legal organ called **'Securities and Exchange Board of India'**. The issue of capital and the pricing of issues by the companies has become free from prior approval. The SEBI has issued guidelines for the issue of capital by the companies. The guidelines broadly cover the requirement of the first issue by a new company or the first issue of a new company set up by the existing company. The SEBI is the most powerful organisation to control and lead the primary and secondary markets. According to the SEBI guidelines, if any company approaches the public, by the issue of share capital through the public issues, must be kept open for three working days and it should be mentioned in the prospectus. In the case of right issue, the subscription time should not be kept more than 60 days. The gap between the rights and public issues should not exceed 30 days. The issued capital must be fully paid up within 12 months of the date of issue. The minimum amount of subscription by the investors in the public issue either at par or premium has been fixed at Rs. 5000. The amount of the issue should not exceed the amount specified in the prospectus.

Over subscription amount retention by the company is not permitted under any circumstances.

The SEBI has announced the new guidelines for the disclosures by the companies leading to the investor protection. They are presented below:

(a) If any company's other income exceeds 10 per cent of the total income the details should be disclosed.

(b) The company should disclose any adverse situation that affects the operations of the company and that occurs within one year prior to the date of filling the offer document with the registrar of the companies of the stock exchange.

(c) The company should disclose the information regarding the utilisation of the plant for the last 3 years.

(d) The promoters of the company must maintain their holding atleast at 20 per cent of the expanded capital.

(e) The minimum application money payable should not be less than 25 per cent of the issue price.

(f) The company should disclose the time taken for the disposal of various types of investor's grievances.

(g) The company can make firm allotments in the public issues as follows:

1. Indian Mutual Funds **(20%)**.
2. FIIs **(24%)**.
3. Regular employees of the company **(10%)**.
4. Financial Institutions **(20%)**.

(h) The company should disclose the safety net scheme or buy back arrangements of the shares proposed in the public issue. This scheme is applicable to a limited number of 500 shares per allottee and the offer should be valid for a period of at least 6 months from the date of despatch of the securities.

(i) According to the guidelines, in case of the public issues at least 30 mandatory collection centres should be established.

(j) According to the SEBI guidelines, regarding the rights issue, the company should give advertisements atleast in 2 newspapers about the despatch of letters of offer. No preferential allotment may be made along with any rights issue.

(k) The company should disclose about the fee agreed between the lead managers and the company in the memorandum of understanding.

The guidelines will apply to all the issues to be made after the promulgation of the ordinance by which the Capital Issues Act has been repealed. Further the SEBI issued guidelines for the **"disclosure and investor protection"** as presented below (issued by the SEBI vide GL/IP No. 1/SEBI/PMD 92-93, dated 11-6-92).

(a) First Issue of the New Companies.
(b) First Issue of the existing private/closely held companies.
(c) Public Issue by the Existing Listed Companies.
(d) Underwriting.
(e) Issue of PCD/FCD/NCD.
(f) New Financial Instruments.
(g) Reservation in Issues.
(h) Deployment of Issue Proceeds.
(i) Employee Stock Option Scheme.
(j) Promoter's Contribution and lock-in period.
(k) Bonus issues.
(l) Guidelines for the protection of the interest of the debenture holders.
(m) General.

(a) First Issue of New Companies

According to the guidelines, a new company is defined as: "one which has not completed 12 months of commercial operations and its audited operative results are not available, where it is set up by the entrepreneurs without a track record." They will be permitted to issue the capital to the public only at par. If a new company is being set up by the existing companies with a 5 years track record of consistent profitability. It will be free to price its issue provided the participation of the promoting companies would not be less than 50 per cent of the equity of the new company. The issue price is made applicable to all the investors uniformly provided that the prospectus or offer documents would contain the justification for the issue price.

A draft prospectus that contains the disclosures will be vetted by the SEBI, before a public issue is made. No private placement of the promoter's share should be made by the solicitation of the share contribution from unrelated investors through any kind of market intermediaries. The shares of the above companies can be listed on either the O.T.Ç. or any other stock exchange.

(b) First Issue by the Existing Private/Closely held Companies

According to the guidelines, the first issue by the existing private companies with 3 years track record of consistent profitability should be permitted to freely price the issue and list their securities on the stock exchanges. The pricing would be determined by the issuer and the lead managers to the issue and would be on justification for the issue price.

(c) Public Issue by the Existing Limited Companies

The SEBI permitted these companies to raise the fresh capital by freely pricing their further issues. The Issue price will be determined by the issuer in consultation with the lead managers. The draft prospectus will be vetted by the SEBI to ensure the adequacy of disclosures. The prospectus should contain the net asset value of the company and a justification for the price of the issue. It should also disclose high and low of the shares for the last 2 years.

(d) Underwriting

According to the SEBI guidelines underwriting is mandatory for the full issue and a minimum requirement of 90 per cent subscription is also mandatory for each issue of capital to the public. The number of underwriters would be decided by the issuing company. If the company does not receive 90 per cent of the issued amount from the public subscription plus accepted development from the underwriters, within 120 days from the date of opening of the issue, then the company should refund the amount of subscription. The lead managers must satisfy themselves about the networth of the underwriters and the outstanding commitments should disclose the same to the SEBI. The underwriting agreements may be filed with the stock exchanges.

(e) Issue of FCD/PCD/NCD

The SEBI issued guidelines on the convertible and non-convertible debentures are as follows:

In case of the issue of fully convertible debentures, the debentures may be converted after 36 months and the conversion is made optional with the put and call option. The crediting should be made if the conversion period is after 18 months. In the prospectus, the premium time of conversion stages should be indicated. The interest rate for the debentures will be freely determined by the issuing company.

In case of the issue of debentures with the maturity of 18 months or less are exempted from the requirement of appointment of the Debenture Trustee. The trust deed should be executed within 6 months of the closure of the issues. The debenture holders are free in case of conversion, if it takes place at or after 18 months from the date of allotment, but before 36 months. The rating is compulsory in case of NCD/PCD if maturity period exceeds 18 months. The prospectus should inform all the information regarding premium amount, conversion period, rate of interest and all other particulars. The SEBI may prescribe additional disclosure requirement from time to time after the due notice.

(f) New Financial Instruments

The Issue of Capital should made adequate disclosures regarding the terms and conditions, redemption, security conversion, and any other relevant features of the instruments such as deep discount bonds, debentures with warrants, secured premium notes etc. Therefore, the investor can be made reasonable determination of the risks, returns, safety and liquidity of the instruments. The disclosures should be vetted by the SEBI in this regard.

(g) Reservation in Issues

The reservation can be made by the company with the consent of the SEBI in the following manner.

In case of the issue of capital by the new companies, reservations to the employees, promoting companies, associate companies, working directors on a suitable percentage is permitted to the share-holders of the group companies. In case of the existing companies, it can be offered on a preferential basis. The share-holders of the promoters companies should also be eligible for the preferential allotment. Reservations to the NRIs should be made according to the schemes prescribed by the RBI from time to time.

(h) Deployment of the Issue Proceeds

After closing the issue, the company should report to the SEBI regarding the collection of money. If the application money and the allotment amount together exceed Rs. 250 crores, the company would voluntarily disclose and make arrangements for the use of the proceedings of the issue as per the disclosure to be monitored by one of the financial institutions. In issue of the above size and beyond, the amount to be called upon the application allotment and on various calls should not exceed 35 per cent of the total quantum of issue.

(i) Employee Stock Option Scheme

The employee stock option is a voluntary scheme to motivate the employees to have a higher participation in the company. A suitable percentage of reservation can be made by the issue company for its employees. However the reservation amount should not exceed 5 per cent of the issue. Equal distribution of shares among the employees will contribute to the smooth working of the scheme. The company may like to have the non-transferability of shares at its discretion in the new issues. The allotted shares to employees cannot be transferable for a period of 3 years.

(j) Promoter's Contribution

The promoter has the choice to contribute the share capital which is offered to the public. The promoters, directors, his friends, his relatives and associates can contribute upto 25 per cent of the total issue of the equity capital and upto Rs. 100 crores and 20 per cent for issuing the above 100 crores. In case of the fully convertible, 1/3rd of the issue amount should be contributed by the promoters, directors, friends and associates in the form of equity before the issue is made. In case of the PCDs, 1/3rd of the convertible portion should be brought in as the contribution of promoter before the issue is made. The minimum subscription by each of his friends/relatives and associates, should not be less than Rs. 1.00 lakh. The promoter must bring his full subscription to the issue in advance before the public issue. The promoter's contribution should not be diluted for a lock in period of 5 years from the date of commencement of the production or date of allotment.

Further, all the firm allotments, preferential allotments to collaborators, share-holders of the promoters companies whether corporate or individual should not be transferable for 3 years from the date of commencement of production or date of allotment. The share certificates issued to the promoter and his associates should carry the inspection **"not transferable"** for a period of 3-5 years as may be applicable from the date of commencement of production or date of allotment.

(k) Bonus Issue

The SEBI issued guidelines in case of the bonus issue. The company should ensure the following while issuing the bonus shares:

1. The bonus issue is made out of free reserves or share premium collected in cash.
2. The reserves created by the revaluation of the fixed asset should not be capitalised.
3. The investment allowance reserve is considered as free reserve for the calculation of the residual reserves.
4. All contingent liabilities would be taken into account in the calculation of the residual reserves.
5. The residual reserves after the proposed capitalisation should be atleast 40 per cent of the increased paid capital.
6. The declaration of the bonus issue in lieu of the dividend is not made.
7. The bonus issue should be made only after the full payment of the share capital.
8. There should be a provision in the articles of association for capitalising the reserves.
9. The company should get a resolution passed in its general body meeting for the bonus issue.
10. Before the bonus issue, the company should not default in the payment of interest and the dues to employees.
11. The Company should implement the bonus issue within 6 months after the approval of the board.

(l) Protection of the Debenture Holders

The SEBI issued guidelines to protect the interest of the debenture holders in two aspects. They are:

1. Servicing of the Debentures

As per the SEBI guidelines, a debenture redemption reserve should be created by all the companies raising debentures on the following basis:

- **(i)** The company may redeem the debentures in greater number of instalments.
- **(ii)** The company may distribute dividends out of general resources in certain years.
- **(iii)** A moratorium upto the date of the commercial production can be provided for the creation of the DRR **(Debenture Redemption Reserve).**
- **(iv)** The Company should create the DRR equivalent to 50 per cent of the amount of the debenture issue before the redemption commences.
- **(v)** Drawal from the DRR is permissible only after 10 per cent of the debenture liabilities has been actually redeemed by the companies.
- **(vi)** The DRR may be created either in equal instalments or higher amounts if profit permits.
- **(vii)** In case of the PCDs, the DRR should be created.
- **(viii)** In case of the convertible issues by the new companies, the creation of the DRR should earn profits from the year for the remaining life of debentures.

2. Protection of the Debenture Holders Interest

- **(i)** The debentures are issued by the companies for the purpose of avoiding the shares acquisition in other countries.
- **(ii)** The debenture-holders have the right to appoint a nominee director on the board.
- **(iii)** The lead bank of the company will monitor the debentures raised for working the capital funds.
- **(iv)** Institutional debenture holders should obtain a certificate from the Company's auditor.

(m) General

1. The subscription list should be kept open for at least 3 days to the public issues and upto 60 days to rights issue.

2. The quantum of the issue should not exceed the amount specified in the prospectus.
3. No retention of over-subscription is permitted under any circumstances.
4. After closing the issue, the company should submit a compliance report from the Chartered Accountant and forward it to the SEBI by the lead managers to the issue within 45 days.
5. The SEBI will have the full rights to prescribe further guidelines to bring transparency in the primary market.
6. Any violation of the guidelines by the issuers/intermediaries will be punishable through the prosecution by the SEBI under the Act.
7. The provisions of the Companies Act, 1956 and other applicable laws should be compiled in connection with issue of shares and debentures.
8. The SEBI should have the right to issue necessary clarifications to these guidelines to remove any difficulty in its implementation.
9. According to the RBI guidelines, the stock invest would now be restricted to the individual investors and the Mutual funds only. (RBI, Press release, Dated 6-9-94).

The Merchant bankers, irrespective of the form in which they are organised are governed by the Merchant Bank rules issued by the SEBI and the Ministry of Finance.

2. Guidelines of the Ministry of Finance

The Ministry of Finance, Department of Economic Affairs has issued guidelines in April 1990. According to the guidelines, any person or body proposing to engage in the business of merchant banking would need authorisation from SEBI. The guidelines indicated the following activities to be performed by the merchant bankers:

(a) Issue management
(b) Corporate advisory services
(c) Underwriting
(d) Portfolio management
(e) Managers to the issue

(f) Consultants to the issue
(g) Advisers to the issue.

The guidelines also provided relating to authorisation criteria, terms of authorisation etc. The authorised merchant bankers are required to observe the guidelines, follow the code of conduct and work as per the requirements of SEBI. The certificate of registration has been made to be valid for the period of 3 years from the date of issue of the certificate. If merchant bankers were already carrying on activities as registrars, share transfer agents, bankers to the issue, debenture trustees. They were required separate application to be submitted for each of such activity. The government issued orders to the Registrar of Companies for verification of prospectus, whether the prospectus has been drafted by the authorised merchant bankers or not. Hence the merchant bankers in India should follow the guidelines issued by the SEBI.

3. Companies Act, 1956

Companies raising funds from the market shall fulfill the regulatory compliances as per the rules and regulations. The merchant banker should select the suitable form of organisation like sole proprietorship or partnership firm or Hindu Undivided family or a corporate enterprise. The corporate form of enterprise is preferred by professionals who have the managerial expertise and skills. The scale of operations, borrowing facilities, better resources position are the best advantages of the corporate sector. Hence such enterprise may be incorporated under the Companies Act, 1956. A company can be a private limited, public limited or a government company. It can appropriately render category I merchant banking services. A detailed project report should be prepared before establishing the company. For forming a public company at least 07 persons and for forming a private company at least 02 persons are required as promoters. Sec. 12 of the Companies Act deals with the registration formalities of the form of company. The members should subscribe their names to the memorandum of association and comply with the Companies Act. The promoters should take a approval from the Registrar of Companies. The Memorandum of association, Articles of association and prospectus should submit to the ROC to get the approval. A certificate of incorporation will be issued by the Registrar, after fulfillment of all legal formalities. The Registrar will issue a commencement of business certificate for public companies. A private company is prohibited from inviting public to subscribe to its share capital.

4. Securities Contract (Regulation) Act, 1956

Merchant bankers play a vital role in the capital market. They work as sponsors of the capital issues. They render valuable services to the issuing company. They involve in determining the composition of the capital structure of the issuing company. They involve in public issues right from drafting of prospectus and application forms, compliance with legal formalities, appointment of registrars, underwriters, bankers to issue, listing of securities, selection of brokers, publicity and advertising agents and printers. Hence the merchant banker is a guiding force behind the company for making success of a public issue. He has to work under many regulations of the various Acts. The Securities Contract Act provides the broad framework of the functioning of stock exchanges in India. The objectives of the Act is to prevent malpractice insecurities transactions by regulating the business. Hence the merchant banker should fulfill all the conditions of the Securities Contract Act, 1956.

5. Listing Guidelines of the Stock Exchange

The Secs. 21-22A of Security Contract Regulation Act deal with the process of listing a share with recognised stock exchange. Listing means, an admission of a scrip to trade on stock exchange officially. Sec. 73 of the Companies Act reveals that listing of security is compulsory, if a company makes public issue. The legal provisions stipulate various conditions for the listing of a security with a recognised stock exchange. The merchant banker shall fulfil the conditions on behalf of the issuing company. He should provide the following services to issuing company.

- **(a)** The prospectus shall contain only the facts.
- **(b)** The prospectus should be advertised in the media 10 days before the issue.
- **(c)** Publicity material should be filed with stock exchange.
- **(d)** The company should abide by the advertisement code.
- **(e)** The prospectus shall indicate about the mode of payment.
- **(f)** The merchant bankers should take all precautions in printing of forms.
- **(g)** The application must provide space for "PAN".
- **(h)** The MB shall make arrangements for the acceptance of forms through the bankers.

(i) The MB shall also made arrangements for sending allotment letters.
(j) The MB shall send the share certificates within 2 months or 10 weeks of closing of issue.
(k) The MB shall produce a certificate from the auditor regarding allotment of shares.
(l) The merchant banker shall inform to the stock exchange about the date of completion, posting of refund orders, allotment letters, certificate of shares.

Companies Act, 2000

The Companies can issue the equity shares with differential voting rights'. The government has announced various amendments to the Companies Act, 1956 through the Companies Act, 2000. It covers the corporate governance, issuance of shares with differential rights, postal ballot. Shares with differential right means the equity shares that have differential rights in respect to dividend, voting or otherwise. Section 86 of the Act has been amended to allow the public companies to issue the shares with differential voting rights. The Central Government has also notified the relevant rules in March 2001. The substantive conditions prescribed are: "Three year profitability track record, shares with differential voting rights can be issued upto 25 per cent of the total share capital issued (*i.e.* effectively 33 per cent of the share capital before such issue) ban on conversion of "plain-vanilla" equity capital into equity shares with differential rights and *vice versa* and no default in meeting the investor's grievances. The other conditions include the approval of the shareholders by the postal ballot authorisation by the articles of association, non-conviction of any offence under the SEBI, the FEMA and the Securities Contract Act, no default in filing the annual accounts and returns, no default in the repayment of deposits, debentures and dividend repayment among others. The rules on the investor's grievances disqualification are vague. The rules specify that the Company should not be defaulted in meeting the investor's grievances. This is a very wide term and has not been defined. This could be a non-receipt of an annual report by a share-holder or related receipt of a dividend cheque amount to an investor grievance. The need is to distinguish between one off case and defaulters. Section 86 of the Act empowers a company to issue the shares with differential voting rights as to the dividend voting. Section 87(1)(a) of the Act provides that every member should have a right to vote. The rules notified for the postal ballot, the scrutinises is required to maintain the details of the shares, irrespective of whether they have voting, differential voting or non-voting rights.

Registration of Merchant Bankers and Regulation

The Ministry of Finance and the Department of Economic Affairs have issued guidelines for the merchant bankers. According to the guidelines, any person or body proposing to engage the business of merchant banking would need the authorisation of the SEBI. The authorised activities cover the issue management, corporate advisory services relating to the issue, underwriting, portfolio management and managers, consultants or advisers to the issue. The SEBI categorises the merchant bankers into 4 kinds. They are:

(a) **Category-I**—to carry on any activity of the issue management and also to act as an adviser, consultant, co-manager, underwriter, portfolio manager.
(b) **Category-II**—to act as an adviser, consultant, co-manager, underwriter, portfolio manager.
(c) **Category-III**—to act as an adviser, consultant, underwriter to an issue.
(d) **Category-IV**—to act only as adviser or consultant to an issue.

The minimum networth prescribed for the categories are Rs. 1 crore, Rs. 50,00,000, Rs. 20,00,000 and nil for categories I, II, III and IV respectively. The general obligations and responsibilities according to the regulations relate to their code of conduct, maintainance of books of accounts, records, submission of the half-yearly results, their appointment, restriction on appointment, responsibilities as the lead manager and submission of deligence certificate documents to the board.

Authorised Activities

The Merchant bankers will be permitted to involve in the activities as per the guidelines issued by the SEBI. Every activity performed by the merchant banker should be allowed by the SEBI. Without its permission no merchant banker will act in the public issues and other activities. The authorised activities of the merchant banker include the issue management, other activities like portfolio management services. The criteria for the authorisation of different activities are based on several factors such as:

(a) Professional qualification in finance or business management.
(b) Infrastructure like adequate office space, man-power and equipment.
(c) Experienced members in one merchant banking business as employee status.
(d) Capital adequacy.
(e) Past-track record, experience, general reputation and fairness in all transactions.

The Merchant bankers should get the permission from the SEBI within 3 months.

Terms of Authorisation

The following are the terms of the authorisation issued by the SEBI:

(a) All the merchant bankers must have the minimum networth as prescribed.
(b) The authorisation will be for an initial period of 3 years.
(c) Every merchant banker should pay the initial authorisation fee, the annual fee and the renewal fee.
(d) All the issues should be managed by atleast one authorised merchant banker in the issues of over 100 crores, the number could go upto a maximum of four.
(e) The responsibilities of each lead manager must be submitted to the SEBI before the public issue.
(f) The Merchant bankers should verify the prospectus contents and they should submit a certificate to the SEBI.
(g) The Merchant bankers should submit all the information to the SEBI from time to time such as documents, returns and reports as prescribed.
(h) The authorisation of the merchant bankers may be suspended or cancelled in case of the violation of the guidelines.
(i) The involvement of the merchant bankers in an issue should continue at least till the completion of the essential follow up steps *i.e.* listing of the instruments and despatch of the certificates/refunds.

(j) The Merchant bankers have adhere to the code of conduct as prescribed by the SEBI.

(k) The guidelines should be followed by the company and its functionaries. No exemption should be given to it, if it fails in any responsibility.

Penalty System

The SEBI can inspect the books of accounts, records, documents etc. of the Merchant bankers with the interest of the investors. If anything goes wrong, the SEBI may give reasonable notice to the merchant banker. If the situation is severe, it may appoint a qualified auditor to investigate the books of accounts. Penalties will be imposed for the default made by the merchant bankers. The SEBI categorised the following defaults as penalty points:

(a) General defaults	Penalty points	01
(b) Minor defaults	,,	02
(c) Major defaults	,,	03
(d) Serious defaults	,,	04

(a) General Defaults

The following activities are categorised under general defaults which attract one penalty point:

1. Non-receipt of the draft prospectus from the lead manager by the SEBI before filing with the ROC.
2. Non-reciept of the inter-se allocation of responsibilities of the lead manager in a issue by the SEBI prior to the opening of the issue.
3. Non-receipt of the due diligence certificate in prescribed manner by the SEBI before the opening of the issue.
4. Failure to ensure the submission of the certificate of minimum 90 per cent subscription to the issue as required under the Government of India, Press Note No. F2/14/CCI/90 dated 6-4-1990.
5. Failure to ensure the publishing of the despatch of refund orders, shares/debenture certificates, filing of the listing application by the issuer as acquired under the Government of India, Press Notification No. 2/6/CCI/89 dated 10-1-1990.

(b) Minor Defaults

The following activities are categorised under minor defaults. It attracts two penalty points:

1. Advertisement, circular, brochure, press release and other issues related to materials that are not being in conformity with the contents of the prospectus.
2. Exaggerated information given by the issuer or the merchant banker in the prospectus in any manner.
3. Delay in refund/allotment securities.
4. Non-handling of the investor grievances promptly.
5. Failure to provide adequate and fair disclosure to the investors about the risk factors in the prospectus.
6. Failure to exercise the due deligence in verifying the contents of the prospectus.
7. Violation of the Government of India Lr. No. F1/23/SE/86 dated 24-3-86 and the Government of India Lr. No. F/23/SE/86 dated 24-7-1987 regarding the advertisements on the new capital issues.
8. Failure to substantiate the matters containing the highlights of the issue in the prospectus.

(c) Major Defaults

The following activities are categorised under major defaults and it attracts three penalty points:

(a) The mandatory underwriting is not taken up by the lead manager.
(b) The association of unauthorised merchant banker in an issue.
(c) The SEBI released a press note on 28-2-91 regarding the excess number of the lead managers who are involved more than the permitted.

(d) Serious Defaults

The following activities are categorised under serious defaults and it attracts four penalty points:

(a) Unethical practice followed by the merchant banker or violation of the code of conduct.
(b) Non-cooperation with the SEBI in furnishing the desired information, documents, evidence as may be called for.

A merchant banker who reaches the cumulative penalty points of 8 attracts the termination/suspension of the authorisation by the SEBI. The maximum penalty points awarded in a single issue managed by the merchant bankers are restricted to four to take the correct action.

Defaults in the Prospectus

If highlights are provided, the following deficiencies can be treated as negative points:

(a) absence of risk factors in highlights.
(b) absence of listing in highlights.
(c) extraneous contents in the prospectus.

The total points allotted to the prospectus is 10. A merchant banker who scores 8 or more than 8 will be assigned with A^+ grade. A merchant banker who scores 6 or less than 8 points with A and with 4 or less than 6 points with B. The banker with a score of less than 4 points will be assigned C category. A merchant banker on reaching the cumulative penalty points of 8 deserves the action from the SEBI. It may be added that the above list is not an exhaustive one and the action could be taken by the SEBI for other reasons like non-fulfillment of the authorisation criteria (networth), carrying out business detrimental with the interest of the public, conviction in any economic offence by the merchant banker or any of its directors or its principal officer, violation of any other guidelines/notification which has a bearing on the functioning of the merchant bankers.

Recently in the awake of the important documents, merchant banking and financial services have become more sophisticated unlike before and therefore there is a great demand for highly specialised skill in planning, decision-making and controlling these areas. To cope with the challenges in the areas of the merchant banking and financial services, the country now needs a large body of trained professionals. To provide the necessary institutional infrastructure for imparting a specialised training, the Institute of Chartered Financial Analyst of

India (ICFAI) has launched an innovative programme, Merchant Banking and Financial Services (MBFS). This programme needs the qualification of the Post Graduation. It is meant for those managers who are qualified in finance area. The objective of this programme is to improve the conceptual, managerial, and operational skills of the managers engaged in the merchant banking and financial services. They also help in rendering the best services to their clients. The programme seeks to impart the knowledge of basic concepts in Merchant Banking and to improve the ability to rationally evaluate the alternatives in the decision-making process. It is divided into 5 groups. The groups and their subjects as follows:

1. Foundation Group (Financial & Cost Accounting, Financial Management, and Quantitative Methods).
2. Group A (Financial Services, New Issue Management, Asset Based Financing).
3. Group B (Security Evaluation and Investment, Portfolio Management, Mutual Funds and Venture Capital).
4. Group C (Corporate Advisory Services, International Finance and Capital Market, Management of Financial Services).
5. Project work and Viva.

Project Preparation and Appraisal

Project counselling is one of the basic activities of the Merchant Banking. It's a part of the financial services. It renders to its clients for the preparation of the project report and pre-investment studies. Merchant Bankers are involved in feasibility studies and project reports. The appraisal of the project will be made by the merchant banker in analysing the financial soundness of an investment project. Before the preparation of the project report, the merchant banker has to satisfy himself that the project is viable and it meets the requirements of the term lending institutions. The following steps are involved in the project preparation and appraisal.

(a) Project Identification.
(b) Project Selection.
(c) Feasibility Study.
(d) Appraisal of the Project.
(e) Social Cost of Benefit Analysis.

(a) Project Identification

Project is a plan to do something. It is a proposal for the capital expenditure items to create facilities like providing goods and services. The investment proposal can be for setting up of a new unit, expansion or diversification. It is a creative activity. The idea generation is a desire of the entrepreneur. Projects can be identified on the basis of information about the environment and technical process evolved in the country or elsewhere. Project Identification is highly influenced by the factors such as agricultural raw materials, forest products, fishing product, mineral resources, human skills, the needs of the population, family budget, national income, GDP, NDP, per capita income, purchasing capacity, tastes and habits of the customers etc. Market surveys are to be conducted for assessing the demand and supply gap of a product. This can be done only through Project Identification. It must be remembered that if you want to select a project, the demand and supply gap should be more. Import substitution product of a project is well encouraged by the government.

(b) Project Selection

Project Selection is the most important task before an entrepreneur. It is followed by the Project Identification Process. The objective at this stage is to decide whether the project can be studied in details and what should be the scope of the further studies. The findings at this stage are embodied in the pre-feasibility study. The information and findings which are available in this stage must be screened and the priorities should be fixed. For the screening purpose, the project ideas are developed into pre-feasibility studies. They provide a wide variety of information about the plant size, availability of raw material, plant location, availability of technical manpower, proximity to near markets, transportation, abundant power supply, availability of financial facilities, tropical environment, soil suitability and other infrastructure facilities and the government policies about the industrial sector. The project selection exercise is the commitment of the entrepreneur.

(c) Feasibility Study

After the selection of the project, it is mostly desirable to implement the plan. A detailed and indepth analysis will be carried on by the expert namely 'feasibility study'. It is the final document in the formation of a project proposal. The amount of expenditure involved in the preparation of the feasibility study can be debited to project cost, it can be treated as the promoter's contribution. It contains all the technical and financial data which is essential for the evaluation of the project. It should examine the public policy in respect to the industry. The study should also think about the different alternative techniques of the production in terms of the process choice, ecology, friendliness, choice of raw material and choice of the plant size. Before the presentation of the financial data, market analysis has to be done to determine the economic levels of the production. The financial data is another important factor in the preparation of the feasibility report. It should cover the preliminary assessment of sales revenue, capital cost, operating cost, administrative cost, marketing cost, selling and distribution costs, levels of leverage and other elements. The study should also estimate about the fixed asset cost and working capital requirements at different levels of production.

(d) Appraisal of the Project

Appraisal of the project is the other step in confirmation of a desired project. The terms in the project evaluation, appraisal and assessment are used interchangeably. They will be used in the analysis of the financial soundness of an investment project. The analysis will be made on the basis of the projected cash flows. The appraisal will be carried out by the promoter. This will be helpful to the merchant banker. The merchant banker involves in the management of the public issue and underwriting, and ultimately the financial institutions will lend the money. Project evaluation will be made in comparison in respect of various alternatives to technology, raw material, production capacity, location and local production etc. It may involve the following steps:

1. **Technical Appraisal**
2. **Economic Appraisal**
3. **Financial Appraisal**

Technical Appraisal of a project is primarily concerned with the selection of the best available technology, design and other infrastructure facilities. The quality of a finished product will depend upon the technology adopted by the company. It will undertake the study about the project regarding the plant capacity, degree of integration, by-product recovery and flexibility of the plant. The capacity of the plant will be determined by several factors such as product mix, product specification and raw material composition. It depends on several situations. While appraising the project, the flexibility of the plant should be taken into consideration. Spare capacity should be made available in the plant to maintain the interrupted production in the event of unforeseen situations. Flexibility creates more strength to a given project. It should also consider the inputs, location and technology process. The delay in the implementation of the project leads to cost and time over runs implications. The planning control tools like PERT, CPM, CAD etc. should be used in the technical appraisal of the project.

Economic appraisal of a project reflects in two ways. The first aspect of impact is on employment and foreign exchange. The proposed project may generate direct employment and indirect employment. Direct employment means the new employment opportunities created by the project within the sphere of the unit. Indirect employment means providing employment opportunities created in projects relating to both input and output sides of the project under appraisal. A project may be export oriented or import substitution unit. Therefore, the project will show an impact on balance of payments. If the project is 100 per cent export oriented unit, then it may reflect an increase in the foreign exchange. If the unit is import substitution concern, the calculation of the foreign exchange savings should be alone. The analysis of the net foreign exchange may be done for the entire life years.

Financial appraisal is concerned with the analysis of profitability of resources invested in the project without considering their resources. It is concerned with the projects benefits after considering the market prices. It may be made with 3 popular methods. The three methods can be classified as:

1. **Simple rate of return method**
2. **Pay back period**
3. **Discounted cash flow method**

Simple rate of return is the method of calculation to arrive the ratio of the net profit for a year to the initial investment with a consideration of fixed and working capital. The capacity utilised is the barometer for expecting a return on the project. It is useful to the short-term projects. It helps in making a quick assessment of profitability.

Pay back period is another method for financing the appraisal of a project. It measures the number of years required to recover a project total investment from the cash flow generated by it. This method is easy to calculate; and in terms of liquidity, it is advisable for the financial appraisal of the project. The shorter the pay back period, the quicker the recovery of the initial investment.

Discounted cash flow method considers the magnitude and timing of the expected cash flows in each period of the projects life. The discounted cash flow techniques are further classified as "Internal rate of return" and "Net present value method". The internal rate of return is the discount rate that equates with the present value of the expected cash flows. According to this method, the project is selected if it exceeds the required rate of return. The Net present value method tells us about the selection of a project. If an investment proposal amount discounts the cash flows, it becomes zero or more. If it is not, the project will be rejected. When the NPV is zero, the project would cover all expenses and has no excess returns. If a project NPV is positive, it is acceptable and if the NPV is negative, the project should be rejected. The two DCF techniques lead to the acceptance or rejections of decisions.

Financial Analysis

Financial analysis is a part of the financial appraisal. It takes into account the financial features of the project with reference to the sources of financing. It helps to determine the smooth functioning of the profit for the entire life cycle. It contains two major aspects which are liquidity and capital structure analysis. For the two aspects of analysis, ratios are employed to know the financial status of a project in a given period. Liquidity ratio reveals the projects' ability to meet its short obligations. The two ratios are calculated to measure the position of liquidity, the current ratio and quick ratio. The current ratio can be calculated by the following formula. It reveals the relation between the current assets and current liabilities.

$$\text{Current ratio} = \frac{\text{Current assets}}{\text{Current liabilities}}$$

Current assets consists of cash, bank balance, investment in securities, accounts receivable and inventories. Current liabilities are payable within one accounting period like creditors, bank O.D. advances from customers, short term loans from banks etc. An ideal current ratio is 1.5 to 1.0. Therefore, the project should be always in mind to maintain the ideal current ratio. Another ratio is "quick ratio". This ratio reveals how far a firm can quickly collect the cash from the sources. The quick ratio can be calculated by the following formula:

$$\text{Quick ratio} = \frac{\text{Current assets} - \text{Stock}}{\text{Current liabilities}}$$

An ideal quick ratio is 1:1. The firm should always maintain this ratio.

Long-term solvency ratio measures the projects ability to meet the long-term commitments of the creditors. The creditors have the legal authority to fulfill the claims. The two long-term solvency ratios are:

(i) Debt utilisation ratio.
(ii) Debt equity ratio.

Debt utilisation ratio indicates the projects indebtedness. It is a relation between Total debt and Total assets of the company. It is the combination of debt and equity proportion in a project.

Debt equity ratio is also referred to as debt capitalisation ratio. It is the value of the total debt divided by the book value of the equity shares. It can be calculated by applying the following formula. The short-term obligation less than one year duration is to be excluded:

$$\text{Debt equity ratio} = \frac{\text{Long-term liabilities}}{\text{Share holder's equity}}$$

The other ratios relating to long-term stability are mostly used by the development banking institutions. They are fixed assets coverage ratio, debt coverage ratio, interest coverage ratio etc. Fixed assets coverage ratio shows the number of times. The fixed assets cover the loan proportion. The ratio can be calculated through the formula:

$$\text{Fixed assets coverage ratio} = \frac{\text{Net fixed assets}}{\text{Term loan}}$$

Debt coverage ratio measures the earnings to cover the payment of interest and principal amount. It measures the degree to which the fixed payments are covered by operating profits. It emphasises the ability of the project to generate adequate cash flow to service its financial liverage. An ideal debt coverage ratio is 2. Another ratio is Interest Coverage ratio. It measures the earnings to meet the interest cost. It can be computed by the following formula:

$$\text{Interest Coverage Ratio} = \frac{\text{Profit Before Tax + Interest}}{\text{Interest}}$$

The most important tools of the financial analysis is **"break even point"**. It is an essential point of the financial appraisal. Break even point means the level of production and the sales at which the total reserves are exactly equal to the operating costs. It indicates the volume necessary for the profitable operation of the project. The BEP analysis shows how much quantity of goods to be produced at desired levels of profit. If the BEP is too high, the price of the product may be increased and it needs revision. The viability of a project can be assured with the help of the break even analysis. For the break even analysis, the income statement should be prepared and analysed. The income statement contains all the financial data regarding the sales, fixed expenses, variable expenses and profit. Therefore, we cannot ignore the role of the BEP in the financial appraisal of a project.

(e) Social Cost Benefit Analysis

Earlier, the project appraisal aspect covered only the private costs and benefits. Social Cost Benefit is another dimension of the project appraisal. Cost Benefit Analysis is meant for the evaluation of public investment. Now-a-days the mega projects are well-established with the blessings of public. The public contribution in mega projects cannot be ignored. India is a vast populated country with a high potential investors to peace the industrial sector. Merchant banker's role is more important in this context to tap the savings of Indian community. Cost benefit analysis is concerned with the examination of a project for maximization of net social benefit. In this analysis, a careful observation will be made about the proposed projects in the society. The analysis will be made about the advantages and disadvantages in terms of a common monetary unit. A project which approaches this analysis has its objective function of the net benefits to the society. Social benefit will be reflected in the form of price of a commodity. The economist uses as a measure of preference. In many situations, the prices are not observable. The maximisation of the net benefit should be finally equivalent to the maximisation of social utility or social welfare. Social cost and benefit and Private cost and benefit are different from market imperfection, external environment and redistribution. Market imperfections means the industrial policy of the government. Since markets were regulated and prices were controlled by the government earlier in our nation, the resources used by the private sector had been under priced. The recent phenomenon of deregulation has freed several resources prices from the control of the government. For example The foreign exchange rate is now determined by the market forces. This situation will be more useful to a nation. Externalities is a measurement of the proposed project regarding the advantages and disadvantages. A proposed project which is established may create infrastructural facilities like roads, power, communication, transport, banking etc. These benefits are however not considered if the projects have harmful environmental effects. The environmental policy is the most important information of projects. The cure for the poverty is the development and it may cure some kinds of pollution. The promoter of a project do not bother about the project benefits to the society. But the government or society thinks about the possible benefits regarding the investment in various projects. Industrial projects are established by either private or public sector to remove the poverty and to improve the life style of a poor citizen. All the five year plans in India have poverty alleviation as their basic objective. But they failed. The opportunities which were provided by the industrial units cannot be availed by the poor. They are unskilled and illeterate. They do not have the skills that factory type of employment demands. The poor will be benefitted only by encouraging the cottage industries and rural-based industries like agro-based material processing, painting, fishing, dairy, animal husbandry, poultry etc. The projects promoted by the industrialists are not suitable for integrating the poor into the market oriented activity.

After the completion of the project appraisal and evaluation of different alternatives are being examined, ultimately the selection of the project lies in the hands of a promoter. The next step is to approach the capital market for the mobilisation of funds. The approach to the public by a company for the requirement of capital is called as "public issue". The public issue of securities is the main important task before a merchant banker. The main function of the merchant banker is to prepare a plan and to make arrangements for the public issues for the successful completion of the project construction. The availability of funds may reduce the time period of a commercial enterprises commencement. When the companies seek to raise the resources for the implementation of a new project, they retain the services of a merchant banker. Merchant bankers are identified as 'issue houses'. Merchant bankers are the issue managers to a public issue and they have to assist the company in all the stages connected with the issue. The functions of a merchant banker can be classified as:

1. Pre-Issue Management
2. Post-Issue Management

Public issue requires the fulfilment of many legal formalities and involvement of various agencies activities which have to be timely coordinated. It may be described as a social event like a 'marriage'.

PRE-ISSUE MANAGEMENT

Pre-Issue Management involves many steps before approaching the market. It is concerned with the issuing of share and pricing of shares. The pre-issue management can be categorised as follow:

1. Issue of shares.
2. Marketing Coordination and Underwriting of Issue.
3. Pricing of Issues.

1. Issue of Shares

Funds raised through the public is called as 'Primary Market'. Public issue of securities, shares or debentures are made in the primary market. There is no fixed place for the issue of new securities. The household savings constitute the primary sources of capital formation in the country. The net savings ratio will encourage the capital market. It is the job of the merchant banker to help the company in the mobilisation of the pooled savings. The shares and debentures have to compete with other financial instruments to attract the savings. The public issues are offered through a prospectus. The prospectus is a document which invites the public to contribute the share capital to attain better returns on their investments. Wide publicity about the offer is to be made through different media like newspapers, periodicals and television. The merchant bankers will put their entire efforts to make it successful. The issue of equity shares are further categorised as issue of shares at the first time, issue of shares made by the existing companies either by public issue or right issue. Right issue of share means the new issue of shares to the existing shareholders at a stated proportion and at a fixed price. Rights shares are issued at a premium which is freely determined by the company making issue. Issue of shares can be made as follow:

(a) Public issue through prospectus.
(b) Offers for sale.
(c) Private Placement.

(a) Public Issue through Prospectus

This is the most common and popular method of public issue through prospectus. Shares and debentures are issued in this method. For the public issue, every company has to fulfil the legal formalities with the SEBI. The SEBI has the full authority to permit the Companies to enter into the Capital market. A fixed number of shares at a stated price will be issued in the primary market. According to the SEBI guidelines, a company which has not completed 12 months of commercial operation can issue shares only at par or face value. If a new company is set up by an existing company with 5 years track record, the new company is free to determine the price of the share. The prospectus has to be vetted by the SEBI before the public issue. The merchant banker has to draft the prospectus and get clearance from the officials. Sections 55 to 68A of the Companies Act deals with the issue of prospectus. The prospectus contains all the information regarding the Company's activities. Section 2(36) of the Companies Act defines the prospectus as "any document described or issued as prospectus and includes any notice, circular, advertisement or other document inviting deposits from the public or inviting offers from the public for the subscription of purchase of any shares or debentures of a body corporate". It is a document which invites the public to subscribe the issued capital. This invitation can be made only by a public limited company. The Companies Act Section 55 indicates that the draft prospectus has to be signed by the directors of the Company and they would release that document at a fixed date. Section 60 tells us about the registration of a prospectus. The registration should be done before its publication. It has to be registered by submitting a copy to the Registrar. The copy of registration must be accompanied by the consent of experts. Copy of contract fixing compensation of a managing director, a copy of every material contract, consents of auditor, legal adviser, attorney, solicitor, bankers, brokers etc. After the registration of the prospectus, the Registrar must issue within 90 days. The prospectus should contain all the information about the Company as presented below:

1. The main objective of the Company.
2. Particulars about the signatories to the memorandum of association.
3. Qualification shares of directors.
4. Number and classes of shares.
5. Number of redeemable preference shares.
6. Particulars about the board of directors and managing directors.
7. Minimum subscription for the shares.
8. The time and opening of the subscription list.
9. The amount of application money, allotment money should be indicated.
10. Premium on shares issued.
11. Name of the underwriter and their commission.
12. Particulars of the preliminary expenses.
13. The benefits provided to promoters, if any.
14. Particulars about the contracts made by the Company.
15. Voting and dividend rights.
16. Capitalisation of profits and surplus from the revaluation of assets.

According to the Companies Act Section 62, there will be a civil liability on the part of the promoters, directors and experts, if they submit the false information in the prospectus. Damages for mis-statements in the prospectus may be claimed by any shareholder. The punishments in regard to various offences are presented below:

For any untrue statement in the prospectus—2 years imprisonment + with a fine of Rs. 5,000.

For issuing of application of shares without the prospectus—a fine of Rs. 5,000.

Application in fictitious names for the Registration of Shares—imprisonment of 5 years.

Encouragement to invest for false information company—imprisonment of 5 years or fine Rs. 10,000.

(b) Offer for Sale

The sale of shares through intermediary of issue-house or firm of a stock broker is called as "Offer for sale". The Company sells the shares or debentures to the issue-house at an agreed price. Then the issue-house resolds the shares to the public at a stated price. In this context, the company need not issue a prospectus. But a statement in lieu of prospectus should be filed with the Registrar of Companies 3 days before the allotment of shares or debentures. In this method, the company can get a substantial earnings because no flotation costs are involved.

(c) Private Placement

The issue of shares or debenture or preference shares by the Company to the individual investors is called as "private placement." The company will sell the securities directly to the genuine investors. There is no need of issue of prospectus in the private placement. In the private placement market, the individual investors means "UTI, LIC, GIC, SFCs, pension funds, Insurance fund owners". The issuers could be a public limited or private limited company. The financial intermediaries in this market are rating agencies, trustees, financial advisors, merchant bankers. In this market the investors have sufficient knowledge and well experience in evaluating the merits and demerits of the financial investment. The merchant banker will play an important role in deal of private placement. His role cannot be ignored. The private placement provides a time saving channel in mobilisation of required resources. It also saves the substantial amount of expenses in the form of floating expenses. It is possible to raise funds from this method within 2 or 3 months. But public issue will take at least 6 months to one year. In placement market, the investors are more perfect about the assessment of their buying financial asset. The private placement is equal to the primary market which combines equity and debentures. The SEBI has put a restriction on FIIs, regarding the investment in shares of a particular company in private placement process.

2. Marketing Coordination and Underwriting of Issue

The successful closure of public issue depends upon the efficiency of a merchant banker to that issue. The merchant banker will have to coordinate many activities relating to issue with different agencies. Appointment of brokers, Registrars, underwriters, Lead Managers Bankers, Shares transfer agents is to be done. The issue has to be groomed, publicity compaign and arrangements for printing and mailing to be made. In this situation the merchant banker should attend to the following functions of a public issue:

- **(a) Coordination**
- **(b) Marketing**
- **(c) Underwriting**

(a) Coordination

According to the Companies Act and SEBI guidelines the Merchant Banker has to submit the information on behalf of the client company. They should make arrangements for drafting the prospectus with the help of the experts legal advisers, attorney and solicitors. The acceptance of financial intermediaries should be obtained and should file with other statements to the Registrar of Companies. After the preparation of prospectus, it has to sent to the SEBI for vetting. Then, it can be filed to Registrar of Companies. The merchant banker has to coordinate with the **Brokers, Bankers and Registrars to the issue**.

(b) Marketing

After the completion of drafting of the prospectus, it has to be sent to the SEBI. The SEBI will scruitinise the prospectus and will take a decision in this regard. After despatch of prospectus to the SEBI, the merchant banker will make arrangement with company representatives and advertising agents to finalise the arrangements relating to the date of opening and closing, registration of prospectus launching, publicity compaign and fixing the date of board meeting. According to the SEBI guidelines, the issue should be open for a minimum period of 3 days. At the time of public issue, the state of the secondary market, number of other issues, tax payment time proximity to festival times etc.is the most important factors.

(c) Underwriting

The public issue is the process of mobilisation of required fund by the company. Usually the companies will approach the primary market to tap the savings of small investors. A well known company, a strong brand image concern, a high growth company, can easily mobilise the funds by the public issue. But sometimes they may not attract the investors and the issue may be a flap. In this juncture the third party will come into picture and gives assurance about the success of the issue. The third party is called as **"underwriter"**. The underwriter will ensure the company that if any unforeseen situation arises, the underwriter would accept the unsubscribed portion of the issue. For this purpose he is entitled to get a commission. The commission paid to the underwriter is known as underwriting commission Underwriting agreement is a contract between underwriter and issuing company. The underwriter may be a broker or a merchant banker or financial institution or a financial intermediary. The maximum liability of a underwriter is restricted to the amount underwritten by him. According to the SEBI, it is a mandatory, it is not an option. The minimum requirement of 90 per cent subscription is mandatory for each issue of capital to public. The number of underwriters can be decided by the issuing company. The outstanding underwriting commitment should not exceed 5 times the net worth of the underwriter.

The merchant banker will be held responsible for pre-issue and post-issue activities of the public issue. The success of the issue will depend upon the efficiency of a merchant banker

POST-ISSUE MANAGEMENT

Merchant bankers in post-issue management activities should move according to the guidelines issued by the SEBI. SEBI is the regulatory authority in the capital market. The company and the merchant bankers are required to take various steps in post-issue activities. SEBI has emphasized merchant bankers complying with post-issue activities with the following requirements:

- **(a)** Approval of SEBI should be obtained for any areas of joint responsibilities apart from advising on inter se allocation or responsibilities.

(b) Merchant bankers should prepare advertising material as per the SEBI norms.

(c) Merchant banker and issuing company should submit a certificate regarding 90 per cent of subscription received from the public.

(d) Merchant banker should ensure that the issuer company dispatches refund order/allotment certificates by the registered post only. He should also ensure that the refund are marked "account payee" and indicate the place where it is encashable.

(e) SEBI is required to be advised on completion of the following post-issue activities:

(i) date of closure of the issue

(ii) date of allotment

(iii) date of dispatch of certificate/refund by registered post

(iv) date of listing at the stock exchange concerned.

FINANCIAL INSTITUTIONS

Summary

Financial institutions are the active players in the capital market. They involve in the mobilisation of funds and in channelising the savings towards the productive way. These institutions provide credit to the commercial enterprises. The financial institutions are classified as Regulatory, **Intermediaries, non-intermediaries and others**. The functional institutions may be categorised as Banking and non-banking. The financial institutions are further classified as Intermediaries and Non-intermediaries. The intermediaries involve in the mobilisation of the deposits from the customers to dispose the funds at interest for various purposes. The Non-Intermediary institutions lend the money from their own resources. All the non-banking institutions act the NBF intermediaries.

The central bank plays an important role in the monetary and banking structure of a nation. It supervises, controls and regulates the activities of the banking sector. The central banks are not profit oriented enterprises. The central bank is the nucleus of the Indian Financial System. The RBI is the Central Bank of the country. The RBI functions are based on the mixed economy. The government objective is to stabilise the economy by framing the policy matters. The monetary policy is basically concerned with the regulation of money supply and interest rates.

The banks deal mainly with money and credit. Banks are the oldest, biggest and fastest growing financial mediators in India. They provide various types of financial services to the customers. The bankers accept deposits from the public and grants loans. The role of banks would be easily assessed from the progress and development of the globe. The industrial and economic evaluation would have occurred with the presence of banks. Banks are the financial nervous of the business community. There are different kinds of banks such as: Commercial banks, Industrial banks, agricultural banks, exchange banks, central banks, savings bank and miscellaneous banks. The miscellaneous banks are categorised as **Investment banks, acceptance banks, merchant banks and discount houses**. The commercial banks have been categorised into various categories of the banking system. They are classified as branch banking and unit banking. Another classification of banks are group banking and chain banking. They are also classified as Deposit banks and Investments banks. The nature and significance of emerging trends in Indian banking system can be studied since the early 1950s. The evolution of Indian banking system can be divided into three phrases (1951-1990). There are a number of financial institutions provide finance for the development of industries in the country.

REFERENCES

1. M.N. Mishra, *Money Banking and International Trade*, p. 246, S. Chand & Co. 1987.
2. *Ibid.*
3. Pramod Kumar Agarwal, *Merchant Banking in India, Financial Services*, Delta Publishing House, Delhi-97, p. 46.
4. *Ibid.*
5. A. Sudhakar *Merchant Banking—Capital Markets, Financial Services*, Delta Publishing House, Delhi, p. 65, 1999.
6. P.K. Agarwal, *Merchant Banking in India, Fin. Serv.*, Delta Publishing House, Delhi-1997, p. 46.
7. H.R. Mahajan, *Merchant Banking Rules and Regulations*, Himalaya Publishing House, Mumbai.

INDEX

Acceptance Houses 49, 231
Agricultural Credit Review Committee 205
Agricultural Refinance Corporation Ltd. 242
All India Rural Credit Review Committee 205
Amalgamation Scheme 164
Apex Financial Institutions 200
Appellate Tribunal 151
Arbitrage 120, 122
Assets Management Companies 33

Bad Deliveries 176, 278
Badla 116
Bailout Takeover 166
Bank of Baroda 297
Bank of Netherlands 198
Bank of Norway 198
Banker's Bank 202
Banker's Book Evidence Act 280
Banking
  Institutions 214
  Future of 30
  History of 13, 28
  Kinds of 224
Banking Companies Act 29
Banking Regulation Act, Enactment of 13
Bear 117
Bearish Market 117
Benami Transactions Act 282
Bennet, R.L. 11
Bill Market 49
Bill of Exchange 292
Bills Re-Discounting Scheme 255
Board of Financial Supervision 203
Bombay Money Market 48
Bombay Stock Exchange (BSE) 110, 137
  Index 138
Book Building Process 158
Break Even Point 321
Brokers 121, 124, 327
Budiwalas 122
Bulk Buyers 277
Bull 117
Bullion Market 49
Bullish Market 117

Call Money Market 54
Capital Adequacy Norms 130
Capital Control Act 19
Capital Formation 4
Capital Issues Control Act 19, 141–42
Capital Market 40, 57, 190
  Components of 59
  Growth of 58
Carry-Forward Facility 112
Cash Credit 218
Cash Reserve Ratio (CRR) 209
Central Bank 13, 47, 51
Central Bank Act 47
Central Banking 198
  Enquiry Committee 236
  Policy 49
Central Co-operative Banks 229
Certificate of Registration 126
Chartered Bank 297
China 5
Chore Committee 247
CITI Bank 297
Cleared Securities 113

Clearing Corporation of India Ltd. (CCIL) 52
Commercial Banks 15, 26, 40, 49, 196, 232, 237
Commercial Bills 292
Companies 48, 162, 324
Companies Act 16, 40, 52, 80, 110, 112, 141–42, 164, 181, 183–84, 189, 191, 200, 307, 309, 325
Company Law Amendment 188
Company Law Board 181, 182
Company Law Reforms 24
Comptroller and Auditor General of India (CAGI) 148
Constructive Speculation 119
Consumer Disputes Redressal Forum 184
Consumer Education Research Centre (CERC) 180
Controller of Capital Issues (CCI) 16, 19, 142
Cooperative Banks 49, 196, 227
Cooperative Societies 48
Corporate Advisory Services 34
Corporate Management 21
Corporate Sector 34
Credit Authorisation Scheme 211–42
Credit Guarantee Corporation 13
Credit Guarantee Scheme 240
Credit Rating 188, 247
Credit Rating Agency 148
Credit Syndication 34
Crowther, A. 47
Current Account 216
Custodians 273

Datta, Arun K. 57
Debenture of Land Development Banks 206
Debenture Redemption Reserve 305
Debt
  Management 208
  Recovery Tribunals 26
Dehejia, V.T. 246
Department of Economic Affairs 182
Deposit Banking 235
Deposit Insurance Corporation 206
Depositories Act 278, 284–85, 288
Depository Participant (DP) 279
Depository System 277
Destructive Speculation 119
Development Assistance Fund 255
Digital Economy 109, 247
Direct Market 46
Discount Houses 49, 231, 330
Discounted Cash Flow Method 319
Discounting of Bills 219
Disinvestment 24, 66
Dutt Committee 22, 243

Economic Development 4
Enron Project 264
Escrow Account 155–60
Export and Import Bank of India (EXIM) 208, 247, 262
Export Credit and Guarantee Corporation 242
Export Risk Insurance Corporation 241

Federal Act 293
Finance Ratio 6
Financial Development 4
Financial Institutions, Importance of 257
Financial Markets 45
Financial Reforms 3
Financial Regulatory Framework 142
Financial Sector Reforms 24
Financial System 5, 141
  Evaluation of 11
Five Year Plan 238
Fixed Deposit Schemes 30, 216
Foreign Currency Accounts 209
Foreign Exchange Management Act (FEMA) 21, 40, 110, 205
Foreign Exchange Regulation Act (FERA) 16, 21, 28, 205

Foreign Exchange Regulation Authority 204
Forward Delivery Contract 114

G.S. Patel Committee 111
Gadgil, D.R. 246
Gilt-Edged Market 34
Grindlays Bank 297

Hazari Committee 243
HDFC Bank 28, 30

IDBI 208
Idle Funds 223
Imperial Bank of India 13
Income Tax Act 110, 191, 282
Indian Bank 297
Indian Financial System 4
Indigenous Bankers 38
Industrial Credit and Investment Corporation 256
Industrial Development Bank 247, 251
Industrial Finance Corporation of India 247, 248
Industrial Investment Bank of India 267
Industrial Licensing Act, 1969 5
Industrial Policy 9, 22–23
Industrial Reconstruction Bank of India (IRBI) 267
Initial Public Offering (IPO) 3, 7, 293
Inspector Raj 24
Institute of Chartered Financial Analyst of India 314
Insurance Regulation Authority 268
Insurance Regulatory and Development Authority Act (IRDA) 25, 29
Interest Rates 210
International Money Market 48
International Organisation of Securities Commission 143
Investment 330
Investment Banking 236

J.M. Financial and Investment Consultancy Services 297
Jobbers 121
Joint Parliament Committee (JPC) 179
Joint Stock Companies 34
Jumbo Transfer Deeds 153

Kent, R.P. 198
Kerb Deal 120, 124
Khan Committee 29
Khan, S.H. 29
Khanna Committee 32
Kothari Pioneer 32

L.C. Gupta Committee 111
Land Development Bank 229
Laspeyres Index 137
Lead Bank Schemes 206
Liberalisation, Privatisation and Globalisation (LPG) 26
License Quota 24
Life Insurance Corporation (LIC) 13, 15, 21
Liquidation 115
Livingston, F. 57
Loans 218
  Refinance of 254
Lock in Period 7
London Money Market 48

Mahalanobis Committee 243
Mandiwala 117
Manipulation 119
Maratha Committee 247
Mega Issues 61
Merchant Banking and Financial Services (MBFS) 315
Merchant Banking 34, 247, 292, 297
  Definition of the 293
  Origin of the 292
  Objectives of the 294
Merchant Banks 161, 231, 310, 330
Mixed Banking 236
Mobile Baking 31
Monetary Control, Techniques of the 207
Monetary Policy 3

Money Market 34, 47–48
  Characteristics of the 48
  Definition of the 47
  Developments in the 51
  Investor, Goals of the 50
  Need for a 49
Money Multiplier Account 217
Moneylenders 10, 38
Monopolies Inquiry Commission 243
Monopoly Restrictive Trade Practice 21
Monopoly Restrictive Trade Practice Act (MRTP) 5, 22–23
Moratorium 254
Mutual Funds 32, 40, 48

N. Vaghul Committee 271
Narasimham Committee 28, 203, 247
National Agricultural Credit Fund 206
National Agriculture Stabilisation Fund 206
National Bank for Agriculture and Rural Development (NABARD) 208, 263
National Bank of Austria 198
National Clearing System 270
National Credit Council 245
National Depository System 270
National Trading Report System 270
Native and Stock Brokers Association of Bombay 109, 137
Negotiable Dealing System (NDS) 52
New Industrial Policy (NIM) 25
  Functions of 61
New Issue Management 34
New Issue Market 46, 60, 191, 293
New Issue Ratio 7
New Power Policy, 1991 10
New Private Banks, Emergence of 28
New York Money Market 48
Non-Banking Financial Companies (NBFC) 31, 40
Non-Cleared Securities 113
Non-Government Securities 53
Non-Intermediary Institutions 196
Non-Profit Assets (NPAs) 26

Odd Lot Dealers 122
Oil and Natural Gas Corporation (ONGC) 264
On-Line System Trading 191
Organised Markets 47
Oriental Bank of Commerce 29
Overdraft 219
Overseas Bank 297

Paasche Index 137
Pay Back Period 319
Payment Mechanism 46
Permitted Securities 113
Pherwani Committee 111
Pooling of Interest 163
Portfolio Management Services 34
Post Offices 231
Pre/Post-issue Activities 66
Preference Shares 154
Price Weighted Index 137
Primary Dealer 271
Primary Market 34, 323
Primary Market Advisory Committee 147
Private Placement 64
Privatisation 24
Project Counselling 34
Public Financial Institutions Laws (Amendments) Act 251
Public Issue 64
Punjab National Bank 297
Pyle, J.F. 123

R.N. Malhotra Committee 25
Ready Delivery Contract 113
Reduction in Subsidies 24
Refinance Corporation of Industry Ltd. 239
Refinancing Institutions 30
Regional Rural Banks 13, 263
Registration of
  Stock-Broker 172

Sub-brokers 133
Transfer 185
Reichs Bank of Germany 198
Relation Ratio 7
Reserve Bank of India (RBI) 10, 13, 26, 29, 35, 47, 48, 51, 58, 146, 185, 190, 200–01, 220, 240
Monetary Policy of the 206
Rigging 120
Risk Capital and Technology Finance Corporation (RCTFC) 266

Satellite Dealers (SDs) 52–53, 271
Savings Bank Account 217, 49
Secondary Market 34, 46, 60, 108
Secondary Market Advisory Committee 147
Securities and Exchange Board of India (SEBI) 19, 141
SEBI 8, 10, 25, 34, 40, 65, 80, 124–25, 129, 133, 135, 158, 188, 191, 327
Act 10, 145, 166, 288
Constitution of 146
Insider Trading regulations 162
Objectives of 144
Powers of 144
Regulations 165, 296
Securities Appellate Tribunal 130, 151, 280
Securities Contract (Regulation) Act 16, 19, 36, 40, 111–12, 119, 123, 182, 185, 200, 308
Securities Contract Act 109, 120, 124, 142, 178, 282
Securities Exchange Commission 143
Securities Market 34
Securities Regulation 129
Seed Capital Assistance Scheme 255
Selective Credit Control 211
Share Transfer Agents 148
Shipping Credit and Investment Corporation of India 264
Shroff Committee 236, 239
Sick Industrial Companies (Special Provisions) Act 166–67
Simple Rate of Return 318
Sleeping Lion 109
Small Industries and Development Bank of India (SIDBI) 291
Small Scale Industries 229
Specified Sector Loans 254
Specified Securities 113
Spot Delivery Contract 114
Stag 117
Stamp Act 282
State Bank of India 48
Nationalisation of 13
State Cooperative Banks 228, 263
State Financial Corporations (SFCs) 290
Statutory Liquidity Ratio (SLR) 209
Stock Exchange in India 123
Functions of the 123
Stock Holding Corporation 34, 247
Stock-Broker 128
Sub-brokers 133
Syndicate Bank 13, 297

Tandon Committee 247
Tarawaniwalas 122
Tata Consultancy Services 297
Tax Reforms 24
Technical Advisory Committee 53
Technical Development Fund Scheme 254
Technology Courses 109
Technology Development and Information Company 272
Tejwala 117
Term Deposit 216
Times Bank 30
Torrent Project 264
Tourism Finance Corporation of India 247, 265
Track Record 65
Traders 10
Transfer of Securities 184
Treasury Bills (TBs) 52
Trust Act 184

Underwriters 161, 328
Underwriting 63, 239, 301
Unit Trust of India (UTI) 15, 21, 32
United Commercial Banks 13
Universal Banking 29–30
Unorganised Markets 47
Unprofitable Branches 31
Unwanted Undertakings 163
US-64 Scheme 32
USA 233

Valley Project 264
Varma Committee 111
Vasudev Committee 32
Venture Capital Unit Scheme 272

Wash Sales 120
World Bank Funds 257